ETIOLOGY OF
CHRONIC ALCOHOLISM

ETIOLOGY

of

CHRONIC ALCOHOLISM

By **OSKAR DIETHELM, M.D.**

Professor of Psychiatry
Cornell University Medical College
Psychiatrist-in-Chief, The New York Hospital
(Payne Whitney Psychiatric Clinic)

CHARLES C THOMAS · PUBLISHER

Springfield · Illinois · U.S.A.

CHARLES C THOMAS • PUBLISHER
BANNERSTONE HOUSE
301–327 East Lawrence Avenue, Springfield, Illinois, U.S.A.

Published simultaneously in the British Commonwealth of Nations by
BLACKWELL SCIENTIFIC PUBLICATIONS LTD., OXFORD, ENGLAND

Published simultaneously in Canada by
THE RYERSON PRESS, TORONTO

Library of Congress Catalog Card Number: 54-12009

Printed in the United States of America

CONTRIBUTORS

1. DIETHELM, OSKAR, M.D.: *Professor of Psychiatry, Cornell University Medical College; Psychiatrist-in-Chief, The New York Hospital.*

2. SHERFEY, MARY J., M.D.: *Assistant Professor of Clinical Psychiatry, Cornell University Medical College; Psychiatrist to Out-Patients, The New York Hospital.*

3. FLEETWOOD, M. FREILE, M.D.: *Instructor in Psychiatry, Cornell University Medical College; Psychiatrist to Out-Patients, The New York Hospital.*

4. BLEULER, MANFRED, M.D.: *Professor of Psychiatry, University of Zurich (Switzerland); Director, Psychiatric Clinic Burghölzli, Zurich.*

5. BARNETT, MILTON L., PH.D.: *Assistant Professor of Anthropology, University of Wisconsin.*

PREFACE

This monograph represents the results of a five year program of investigations into the etiology of chronic alcoholism. The studies were supported liberally by the National Research Council (Committee on the Problems of Alcohol) and carried out by a team of investigators from various disciplines.

We wish to express our appreciation to the following journals for permission to quote material originally published by them: *The American Journal of Psychiatry* and *Bulletin of the New York Academy of Medicine*.

O. D.

CONTENTS

ETIOLOGY OF
CHRONIC ALCOHOLISM

RESEARCH IN CHRONIC ALCOHOLISM

O. Diethelm, M.D.

The toxic damage caused by alcohol can be fully comprehended only if one considers the individual health problem from a broad bio-social point of view. Individual susceptibility to toxic agents, including alcohol, as well as the individual's physiologic and psychologic expressions, vary greatly. The statements that a certain amount will not cause toxic effects must be taken with considerable reservation, and only within narrow limits can it include individual susceptibility. Studying the effect of alcohol biologically, including physiologic and pharmacologic investigations, psychologic and psychopathologic studies, and social and cultural research will offer pertinent information. The findings in any of these fields, however, must be considered in their interrelationships as they affect the biosocial individual, the person.

These were the basic considerations when our department started a five-year research program in 1947, supported by a grant from the National Research Council (Committee on the Problems of Alcohol). Research was carried out by a group of investigators from various disciplines, forming functional teams for specific investigations. As chronic alcoholism is primarily a psychiatric problem, the general direction of the research program was alloted to the psychiatrists, and the patients were studied in the Payne Whitney Psychiatric Clinic (New York Hospital) which is the teaching hospital of the Department of Psychiatry of Cornell University Medical College. Ample laboratory facilities were made available for physiologic, pharmacologic, psychologic and psychopathologic investigations. Whenever feasible, the same patient was studied by the various investigators over a period of several months. All types of patients in whom alcoholism presented a problem were selected and about an equal number of male and female patients were studied. The patients were in-patients and for at least four weeks under 24 hour observation. Afterwards they assumed their usual work obligations, leaving the hospital from 8:30 a.m. to 5:30 p.m. and for weekends. They were requested not to consume any kind of alcoholic beverages, and their urine was tested for alcohol after each return to the hospital. This type of procedure permitted a study of physiologic, psychologic, and interpersonal behavior and experimental manipulations.

1. DISCUSSION OF DIAGNOSTIC TERMS

In recent years there has been considerable vagueness concerning the diagnostic terms used in American literature. There was a better understanding in European publications, but with too rigid adherence to older concepts. To find suitable new terms which will be acceptable to the vast majority of investigators from different scientific fields is a most difficult task. Present limited knowledge is not sufficient to reformulate our conceptual thinking in the field of alcoholism. It was therefore decided to examine current terms critically and re-define them so that no misunderstanding would occur for readers. Disagreement with our concepts, together with increased knowledge, may lead to better understanding and more suitable terms.

In this monograph the following definitions are used: A patient suffers from *chronic alcoholism* if he uses alcohol to such an extent that it interferes with a successful life (including physical, person-ality, and social aspects), and he is either not able to recognize this effect, or is not able to control his alcohol consumption although he knows its disastrous results. An *excessive drinker* is an individual who uses alcohol frequently and in large quantities and may even behave pathologically when under the influence of alcohol. He is, however, capable of overcoming the habit when he becomes aware of the necessity for it.

This definition of chronic alcoholism is closely related to the original definition of A. Forel and E. Bleuler. It differs, however, because the psychopathologic symptoms and related histopathologic findings are not stressed. These findings occur only in a limited num-ber of the large group of patients which can be included in our defi-nition. Patients with psychopathologic symptoms of deterioration of the type found with cortical damage need to be singled out and in-vestigated as a special group. The same applies to patients who at death show definite histopathologic changes in the brain. There also seem to be special factors which lead to the physical changes which are included in chronic alcoholism, e.g., cardiovascular and liver damages. Psychopathologic, physical and histopathologic findings may occur, but not necessarily in the large group of chronic alcoholics. In the group studied these findings were rare. Psychopathologic changes, related to the psychopathic or psychoneurotic personality setting in which chronic alcoholism occurred, were frequent. For various reasons, prolonged dietary deficiencies have not been important in our group which may explain the infrequent occurrence of some of the physical signs.

Our definition of chronic alcoholism includes the simple dependence on alcohol (drunkard, Einfache Trunksucht), and the chronic alcoholism of E. and M. Bleuler.[1] In M. Bleuler's comparative study of Swiss alcoholics, our definition was applied. It seems that in the American group studied behavior difficulties were less obvious than in the Swiss group, and the alcoholism was more frequently hidden by the family.

Addiction to alcohol would be synonymous with our definition if the concept of addiction is broadened to mean dependence and without necessary tolerance and withdrawal symptoms (despite claims in literature, e.g., Russian publications, there are no clear-cut withdrawal symptoms to alcohol cessation if one evaluates physiologic symptoms which are related to other factors, e.g., loss of blood, disturbance of water and chloride, and head injuries). The concept of addiction to drugs is at present under critical review by many workers in this field, and its application to the problem of alcoholism might be postponed until further clarification has been reached.

The term of compulsive drinker is an undesirable term because "compulsive" has a well defined meaning in psychopathology. The use of this term has led to the assumption that alcoholics suffer from compulsion neurosis or a condition allied to it. Dr. Sherfey's findings do not agree with this assumption.

The definition which the Alcoholism Subcommittee of the World Health Organization proposed is practical but does not differentiate the types sufficiently to offer a satisfactory basis for a far-reaching investigation of etiological factors. The three stages in the development of alcoholism which are accepted by this committee cannot be supported in its rigid form by scientific evidence.[2] Other definitions and groupings have been used in sociologic and medical studies but have not exerted wide or lasting influence.

2. PSYCHOPATHOLOGIC INVESTIGATIONS

There have been few psychopathologic investigations in chronic alcoholism during the last 30 years. The findings of the Kraepelinian period are requoted in literature. Following American and German interests in pre-illness personalities, descriptions of well-defined types of personalities of the alcoholic have been offered. There is not sufficient evidence to support the claim that specific personality types predispose to alcoholism. A hasty assumption by Ferenczi, which was refuted by E. Bleuler, that homosexual factors were essential is still quoted but not investigated. The significance of oral factors has been stressed but it has not been possible to clarify their role.

The development of psychodynamic psychopathology has offered possibilities for a better understanding which have been used insufficiently. It was therefore important that our patients be studied and reviewed psychopathologically. Dr. Sherfey's chapter gives the findings which were determined by a group of psychiatrists who carried out the dynamic psychotherapy and investigators who were interested in special psychopathologic studies. The resulting clarification of the significance of various psychoneurotic reactions, of psychopathic personalities, and of psychodynamic factors is offered in a form which does not force conclusions and can be extended along the line of differing theories.

E. Oberholzer confirmed these groupings by means of the Rorschach test which he administered to the patients who were unknown to him. His results and those of Sherfey's analysis were compared by me and discussed separately with the two investigators. It was of interest to note that only 4 patients corresponded to the classical picture of chronic alcoholics of Rorschach's original study. These findings with the Rorschach experiment support the previously discussed need for clarification of terms used in literature.

The Thematic Apperception Test of Murray[3] did not prove to be of value in this study because the patients were investigated so thoroughly during their psychotherapy that whatever was revealed in this test was obtained during the first four weeks of therapy.

The observation in the hospital permitted a detailed description of the patient's behavior and especially his relationship to others in this social setting and to the nurses and physicians. The Payne Whitney Clinic social behavior chart[4] which contains items such as grooming, socializing, promptness of attention to routine, emotional display, sarcasm, argumentativeness, was kept on a 24 hour basis by a large staff of nurses, well trained in this type of psychopathologic observations and charting.

Among studies which have been started recently and the results of which are not ready for publication are the study of individual thinking patterns and of living-out and acting-out in the alcoholic intoxication of these patients. In a state of alcoholic intoxication some persons show a lack of their usual restraint and display suppressed emotions and tendencies. This living-out is more frequent in alcoholic intoxication than acting-out in the psychoanalytic sense. When acting-out occurs the intoxicated person displays emotions and actions which were repressed and therefore not known to the person in his conscious life.

3. PHYSIOLOGIC STUDIES

In any physiologic investigation the role of emotions present must be evaluated. Their influence may be negligible and their determination may therefore be unimportant in many investigations. Whenever physiologic research is carried out in the field of personality disorders, the role of emotions is of greatest significance.

The relationship between emotions and physiologic functions is now well established. Our own interest has been for 20 years to establish the relationship of specific emotions of different intensity to physiologic functions. The method which has proved to us most fruitful is a biologic assay by means of the reaction of the duodenum of the rabbit. Dr. A. T. Milhorat modified Cannon's original method and under his direction Dr. M. F. Fleetwood applied it to the investigation of alcoholic patients. As is discussed in detail in the corresponding chapter of this book, Dr. Fleetwood has succeeded in establishing the presence of biochemical substances of varying intensity in the blood in the presence of the emotions of anxiety, tension and resentment.

The definition of these three emotions and their characteristics are outlined in Table 1. Anxiety is characterized by apprehension, usually without an adequately known cause as distinguished from fear. Dependent on its intensity, the span of attention and retention is decreased, sleep disturbed and often accompanied by anxiety dreams. The physiologic symptoms are well known. In the blood a norepinephrine-like substance is found which corresponds in its amounts to the varying intensity of anxiety (page 54). Tension is experienced as inner tautness with irritability, muscle tension, dependent on intensity, concentration difficulty and thinking disorders, and difficulties in falling asleep. An acetylcholine-like substance in the blood is related to the varying degrees of psychological tension (page 54). Resentment is conceived to be a reaction of bitterness and desire for revenge, with hostile and sarcastic attitudes and, in intense degrees, suspiciousness and even paranoid misinterpretations. After atropinization of the rabbit intestine a substance can be demonstrated in the blood which amounts vary according to the degree of resentment (page 54).

Other investigators in the field of psychology and psychopathology may not agree with our formulation. However, the definitions offered make it possible for them to understand the terms used and phenomena observed. There seems to be little difficulty for well trained psychopathologists and clinical psychiatrists to recognize signs present in a patient. Its application to animal experimentation is more difficult. The use of Milhorat's method by H. Liddell and his associates in their conditioned reflex experiments on sheep has demonstrated the validity of separating the emotions of anxiety and tension.

Psychologic and psychopathologic studies of emotions have progressed along different lines in various places. Through the contribution of psychoanalysis and dynamically oriented psychopathology in general the emotion of anxiety has become of leading interest in this country. In European, especially German psychiatry, the emotion of tension was recognized in the last century and its psychopathologic significance demonstrated, among others, in catatonia. Experimental psychologic differentiation of these two emotions was then demonstrated by Jones and Diethelm.[5] The study of resentment has been furthered most by French and German psychologists and psychiatrists. These brief references to literature seem indicated for orientation to many readers. The important fact is that there exists a close correlation between what we call the emotions of anxiety, tension, and resentment and the findings in the blood.

A corroboration of the relationship of these three emotions and corresponding biochemical findings was found by E. Oberholzer in the Rorschach protocols of the patients studied. He administered the test and interpreted the results without having obtained knowledge of the patient's emotional reactions. The results of the biochemical and psychological investigation were compared with the Rorschach studies. There was a strong agreement (about 90%) of all these findings in the presence of anxiety or resentment while a lesser agreement (75%) existed with the emotion of tension. It was unfortunately not possible for Dr. Oberholzer to get the material ready for this publication.

In our study of alcoholic patients drinking was related to the presence of special emotions. Consumption of alcohol made the corresponding biochemical findings in the blood disappear within a few minutes. The same result does not occur in everybody. There were some non-alcoholic patients in whom tension and resentment were affected little by alcohol. The significance of this observation is not conclusive but might indicate a physiologic difference or a dependence on special psychopathologic influences.

The nature of these substances in the blood needs to be determined by future chemical analysis. There are strong indications that the substance occurring in the presence of anxiety is related to noradrenaline and that of tension to acetylcholine. The substance which is found with resentment is unclear.

Many other possible physiologic investigations could not be pursued, e.g., the significance of ACTH and cortisone. The studies of R. J. Williams[6] on rats are most stimulating but could not be carried out without a strictly controlled diet. Recently a metabolism unit of seven beds has been established in the Payne Whitney Clinic and investigations along the lines suggested by Williams might be feasible. The significance of liver changes in alcoholism deserves attention. A current survey by Sherfey seems to indicate that liver cirrhosis occurs especially in excessive drinkers and less frequently in the above defined chronic alcoholic.

4. CONSTITUTIONAL FACTORS

There was justified doubt, supported by Sherfey's studies, that chronic alcoholism was caused by major genes and that Mendel's laws could easily be applied. It seemed necessary to use methods which did justice to the many clinical groups which had been noted and in which the interpersonal relations in the families could be evaluated. In addition, it seemed important to take physical, especially endocrinologic factors into consideration.

Our group was most fortunate in obtaining Professor M. Bleuler's participation for a year. As one of the recognized leaders of psychiatric genetic research, he had applied the above principles to the study of the group of schizophrenic illnesses.

It was possible for Bleuler to interview a considerable number of our alcoholic patients as well as their relatives, so that he did not have to depend on information in case records obtained by somebody else. The careful physical studies carried out in the hospital on each patient and his own examination permitted him to include physical characteristics. The control study which he carried out later on a group of patients in Switzerland is the first study of this type and gave valuable results.

Among his findings which are of great interest are the lack of evidence of a higher incidence of epilepsy or oligophrenia among the offspring of alcoholic parents. These findings disproved claims which have been perpetuated in scientific and lay literature for over half a century. Endocrinologic pathology of a varied nature was found in a majority of these patients. It remained unclear whether endocrinologic factors cause a disposition to alcoholism or to significant emotional reactions or personality disorders. A justified conclusion seems to be that the genetics of alcoholism are related to those of other psychopathologic disorders. Bleuler's studies emphasize that alcoholism is a symptom of a psychopathologic development and not a disease entity. These findings support the clinical-psychopathologic result of Sherfey. Another important outcome of these genetic investigations is that in alcoholism environment and inherited constitution cannot be separated. Both, interdependently, may be important etiologically, and support our thesis that alcoholism must be considered a bio-social problem.

These studies throw some light on chronic alcoholism but do not explain why some children of alcoholics become alcoholics while others can drink considerably and remain in good health. Neither genetic studies or animal experimentation have offered leads for the exploration of disposition to alcoholism. Following the path of the investigation on rats by C. Richter, one of our co-workers (Tobach) is investigating what type of rat does not choose alcohol in the experimental situation.

5. CULTURAL ANTHROPOLOGY

There are frequent statements in literature that cultural as well as racial factors are important in the development of alcoholism. The infrequency of alcoholism among the Chinese and Jews is often explained on a racial basis. Our group of patients studied included one Jew which demonstrates the rare request of Jewish patients for admission to the Payne Whitney Psychiatric Clinic for treatment of alcoholism. This is in contrast to the high number of Jewish patients who seek admission for other pychopathologic disorders.

The well segregated 6000 *Chinese* in New York's Chinatown offered an opportunity to investigate possible social differences in alcoholism. The Department of Sociology and Anthropology of Cornell University, which has studied Chinese culture, assigned Milton L. Barnett to our group to carry out these investigations. A preliminary survey of city and private hospitals carried out by Dr. Richard P. Wang, and of police records had revealed that incidence of alcoholism was relatively low among this Chinese group. A study of broad cultural context was necessary for an understanding of the sociologic factors. Dr. Barnett's team included therefore sociologists, cultural anthropologists, psychiatrists and sociologically trained field workers.

The results of this broad study are presented in the last chapter of this book. Space does not permit the inclusion of the large sociologic material on Chinatown and the detailed cultural description, based upon which an evaluation of drinking habits and an understanding of alcoholism among these Chinese became possible.

It seems important that among the Chinese there is an attitude of ridicule toward the intoxicated person and of ostracism to repeated intoxications. The behavior of the individual reflects on the whole family. Children, growing up in this disapproving attitude to intoxication, will be affected by it. It may be assumed that disapproval of drunkenness in public can act as a deterrent to the development of alcoholism, especially as their social disapproval is strengthened by the strong moral obligation of the drinker to protect his family name. The strong disapproval of drinking by women may explain the rarity of habitual excessive drinking by women. (This conclusion seems to be supported by the increased excessive drinking and of alcoholism among women in America and European groups when alcoholic beverages became more readily available to women and their drinking in public places accepted. This observation refers, however, to only one among several other factors leading to this increase.) Another factor which Barnett stresses is that drinking, except for reasons of conviviality is deplored, and that it should accompany meals. It seems obvious that it will be easier in such a society to acquire the reputation of being a drunkard than in our own social and cultural setting. A larger number of chronic alcoholics is found among Chinese who are no longer attached to the closely knit society of Chinatown. The incidence of alcoholism among these Chinese seems to be, however, considerably less than the average of the population of New York. In this study, it was not possible to evaluate the significance of the heavy eating which is combined with drinking. Whether this food intake is merely a deterrent to acute intoxication or also, on a physiologic or phychologic basis, to the development of chronic alcoholism, needs to be studied.

The inverse relationship of drug addiction to alcoholism is frequently mentioned. The frequency of drug addiction among these Chinese is unknown. Our studies of a few non-Chinese drug addicts who have previously been excessive drinkers have not explained whether alcohol and drugs took care of the same needs. (This statement does not refer to barbiturates which decrease emotional tension and therefore can replace alcohol in persons who use alcohol to alleviate this emotion.) Further studies are at present directed to a clarification of drug addiction and alcoholism.

An interesting observation is the important role which gambling plays among these Chinese. In our patients, a gambler's psychology was frequent although gambling in the usual form had not seemed important in their daily lives. It is interesting to speculate that inhibition of the actual satisfaction of gambling may have a relationship to alcoholism.

The *American Indian* is alleged to be susceptible to alcohol, to show uncontrolled and dangerous behavior when intoxicated and to develop readily a craving for alcohol and chronic alcoholism. Scientific literature does not seem to offer any proof for this assumption which has led to far reaching bias and stringent laws. A several weeks' study was carried out by myself on an isolated Apache reservation and the results compared with brief visits to other reservations. The generous help of the physicians and federal employees on these reservations permitted me access to patients in the hospitals and to examine the police records of the last three years as well as those Indians who were arrested for drunkenness during my stay on the reservation. Through the aid of Indian leaders who stressed my position as a physician from an Eastern University, I became accepted and was able to obtain an understanding of drinking customs. For financial reasons these Indians primarily used a highly intoxicating home brew although they preferred beer. A small number liked whiskey. The situation on a reservation resembles localities during prohibition where an insufficient police force tried to enforce regulation, and where punishment was severe for those who were found guilty. From such a point of view, the current drinking customs become intelligible. There was no indication from this direct observation that the American Indian is more susceptible to alcohol than the other inhabitants of the United States. The behavior when intoxicated is an accepted uncontrolled behavior and essentially the same as found in other groups of our population, especially the late adolescents. There is no indication that it relates to special constitutional factors. Differences between the reactions of American Indians and other inhabitants of this country seem to depend on sociologic and not racial factors. This conclusion is supported by a study of 30 veterans who as members of our armed forces had the same access to acoholic beverages as the other soldiers. A review of their service records did not reveal a high percentage of disciplinary difficulties or any other indication of drunkenness. In my interviews a careful review of their army and pre-army careers was carried out with special attention to their use of and reaction to alcoholic beverages. This anamnesis as well as the record of these Indians since discharge from the armed forces support the above statement that there is no indication of a racial disposition to susceptibility to alcoholic intoxication and chronic alcoholism.

6. CONCLUDING REMARKS

The studies in the etiology of alcoholism, which are presented by the various investigators, offer important findings and promising leads for further investigations. Far reaching conclusions and generalizations are carefully avoided. Such a statement is unnecessary in a scientific presentation except in a field where biased attitudes have led to dogmatic statements. There is great need for research in the etiological and therapeutic aspects of individual alcoholism. Scientifically controlled studies in the broad social field are of utmost importance if society wishes to understand the significance of alcoholism in the life of the community, in work and in leisure time, in traffic, in youth and later life, in social and physiological readjustments.

There is a tendency to exaggerate or to minimize the problem, turning to so-called statistical information, obtained on an inadequate basis. Acute intoxications, especially if accompanied by socially objectionable behavior, are found distressing while the more serious but less obvious chronic alcoholism is tolerated or even defended.

These studies demonstrate the value of a joint attack by physicians, physiologists, chemists, psychologists, social scientists, and anthropologists, as well as psychiatrists and other psychopathologically trained investigators. The concept of such an investigation was in the mind of the Chicago physiologist, Anton J. Carlson, whose vision and humanitarian attitude has been the great force in a scientific study of alcoholism in this country.

Treatment of alcoholism must cover many aspects. Therapy must be directed intensively at the individual by psychodynamic and physical procedures. In many patients support from other persons who have overcome similar difficulties or who have a practical understanding may permit a patient to lead a successful life with abstinence from alcohol. Alcoholics Anonymous has been helpful to many. In European countries the Blue Cross organization has exerted a valuable influence since its origin in 1896 by aid to alcoholic patients and by bringing about evolutionary changes in social abuses. Educational programs have, however, often lagged behind the progress of scientific knowledge. The Quarterly Journal of Studies on Alcohol and various educational organizations in this country and abroad are trying to disseminate factual knowledge to scientific workers and to lay people.

Alcoholism has become accepted as an important individual and public health problem. Public understanding has increased but it is still difficult to exercise the right not to drink without being questioned. This fact, which makes it difficult for former patients to find social security, illustrates the need for better education. Further progress will depend to a large extent on broadly conceived investigations of etiologic factors.

BIBLIOGRAPHY

1. BLEULER, E.: *Lehrbuch der Psychiatry.* 8th Edition, revised by Bleuler, M. Berlin, Springer, 1949.
2. Report of first session of W H O, Subcommittee on alcoholism. *Quart. J. Stud. Alcohol, 13:*175, 1952.
3. KNEHR, C. A., VICKERY, A. and GUY, M.: Problem-action responses and emotions in thematic apperception test stories recounted by alcoholic patients. *J. Psychol., 35:*201–226, 1953.
4. KOHL, RICHARD N.: Administrative aspects of a teaching hospital. *Am. J. Psychiat., 107:*481–487, 1951.
5. DIETHELM, O. and JONES, M. R.: Influence of anxiety on attention, learning, retention and thinking. *Arch. Neurol. & Psychiat., 58:*325, 1947.
6. WILLIAMS, R. J.: Individual metabolic patterns and human disease: An exploratory study utilizing predominantly paper chromatographic methods. *Biochem. Inst. Studies, 4:*no. 5109, 7–21 (The University of Texas Publication) 1951.

PSYCHOPATHOLOGY AND CHARACTER STRUCTURE IN CHRONIC ALCOHOLISM

MARY JANE SHERFEY, M.D.

This paper reports the results of a study of the underlying psychopathology and character structure in patients with chronic alcoholism.

Because of man's intimate familiarity with chronic alcoholism throughout his recorded history, the illness has had numerous definitions, none of which is adequate. In this study, chronic alcoholism is defined as that condition in which an individual harms himself or his family through the use of alcohol and either cannot be made to realize it, or realizing it, no longer has the ability to overcome the habit.

The various degrees of alcoholic intake must also be defined, ranging from total abstaining to alcoholism. Five types of drinking habits are distinguished with the understanding that no sharp line of demarcation exists between them:

1. *Total abstaining*—the use of no alcohol under any conditions. (The term "tee-totaler" is avoided because of the moralistic connotation it may carry.)

2. *Moderate or social drinking*—occurs in the individual who drinks only on social occasions, conducts himself well when intoxicated, and only occasionally, if at all, drinks to the point of obvious muscle incoordination.

3. *Heavy social drinking*—occurs in the individual who drinks heavily on social occasions, and usually with frequent or regular intoxications to the point of obvious muscle incoordination and intoxicated behavior. The drinking does not seriously handicap the individual in his life adjustment.

4. *Excessive drinking*—the condition in which alcohol is used frequently and in large quantities in a pathological manner; but the

drinking does not produce serious harm to the individual, or if it does, he is capable of overcoming the habit.

5. *Chronic alcoholism*—as defined above.

While it is true that many chronic alcoholics go through the first four defined conditions to the fifth one of alcoholism, it is not accurate to consider them as "stages" in the development of chronic alcoholism. These drinking habits exist in everyone and the majority of people maintain their specific drinking patterns throughout life. There are alcoholics who were never social drinkers, passing from total abstaining almost directly into chronic alcoholism.

By popular usage, the term, chronic alcoholism, has come to designate the condition in which any uncontrollable drinking is the outstanding symptom. This has led to a tendency in many investigators and laymen to consider all cases of chronic alcoholism essentially similar, and any treatment that is found successful in one case is automatically advised for all. However, other observers have been impressed by the differences in the symptomatology and the personalities of alcoholics and have attempted to classify them in various groups having more or less scientific validity.

These groups are either broad categories, distinguishing between the "primary," "essential," or "true" alcoholic and the "secondary," or "symptomatic" alcoholic and the many specific groupings that seize upon some psychopathological feature or theoretical approach.

In the broader categories, "primary" alcoholism comprises all cases in which drinking is considered to be the only apparent deviation from the normal. The fact that many alcoholics can go for long periods functioning well without drinking has led to the conclusion that they are normal *except* when, and because of, drinking. (Hence, such contradictory terms as "asymptomatic drinker" or "normal alcoholic.") The theory that the chronic alcoholic has some metabolic idiosyncracy to alcohol is based partially on this observation. "Secondary" alcoholism includes those cases in which other evidences of psychopathology are quite apparent. Few attempts have been made to study these other evidences.

The more specific categories are many and stem from whatever approach, theories, or discipline is adhered to by their authors. Thus, in the literature one finds alcoholics described, defined, or conceived of according to the following categories:

1. Superficial descriptive approach, producing such terms as the "reckless drinker," "decadent drinker," or "criminal alcoholic."

2. Categories utilizing the classical, text-book psychiatric nosology; i.e., neurotic, psychotic, schizophrenic, or paranoid alcoholics.

3. Categories drawing on the old Kretschmerian concepts, such as the pyknic, cyclothymic, or aesthenic body builds and personality types.

4. The somatic approach which denies psychodynamic causality and considers only hereditary, metabolic, hormonal, or allergic possibilities.

5. Psychoanalytical theory which considers all alcoholism to be dynamically determined and tends to emphasize, almost exclusively, the importance of infantile orality and regressive features.

6. Sociological and anthropological approach which tends to emphasize the causal importance of social pressures.

7. And throughout the literature there remains the old, unproven theories of alcoholism as addiction in the sense of morphine addiction, homosexuality as the sole cause, dipsomania, and the supposed relationship between alcoholism and epilepsy.

It is not surprising that an illness which transforms the ancient custom of drinking into pathology should arouse such confusion; yet it is essential that the basic nature of chronic alcoholism be accurately defined before research into causality can be scientifically conducted.

METHOD

As a part of a broad research program, this is a study of psychiatric case history material. The method consisted of analyzing all case records of alcoholics admitted to the Payne Whitney Clinic since 1932 and an intensive study of all patients under treatment in the clinic since 1946. A total of 161 cases was selected for study, including 27 patients treated by the writer for periods of three months to three years, and 49 patients treated by colleagues during the intensive research period.

Because of the well-known handicaps of case record studies, considerable care was exercised in the selection of cases. Of 455 charts chosen at random from the record room, only 85 gave sufficient data to allow reasonably valid conclusions. Numerous follow-up letters were posted, with only 45 informative replies in cases discharged from treatment before 1949. Follow-up interviews were obtained in 16 of these cases.

In all records used, the criteria of adequate data had to include:

a. A good description of the drinking history and patterns.

b. A good description of the life history.

c. A good description of the outstanding personality features.

d. A good description of the psychopathology.

Almost all records rejected were inadequate because brief hospitalizations made it impossible to obtain sufficient data.

In evaluating the patients' reports as to recovery, only factual data were considered, and the following criteria were established:

a. Complete recovery—total abstaining with reasonable life success, particularly as compared to success prior to hospitalization.

b. Good improvement—occasional drinking, socially or pathologically, but with reasonable life success.

c. Moderate improvement—continued pathological drinking but capable of holding a job and maintaining self independently.

d. Unimproved—continued alcoholism with symptoms as severe and handicapping as were present before hospitalization.

The records which were considered adequate for the present study did not permit an analysis of the early developmental dynamics; however, certain trends in the family histories of these cases were observed and are reported. The incidence of mental illness and alcoholism reported was arrived at by comparing the various groups with each other and the findings are to be considered initial observations.

There are no alcoholics in this group with criminal records nor of low intellectual endowment.

PSYCHOPATHOLOGIC GROUPINGS

On the basis of the underlying psychopathology and character structure, the cases fall into two general sections:

I. Cases belonging to specifically recognized diagnostic entities; i.e., cases in which excessive drinking is another symptom in well-defined, easily-recognized psychopathologic or physical illnesses.

II. Cases which do not belong to any usual diagnostic entity and in which excessive drinking is unquestionably the outstanding clinical feature. These cases fall into at least five different diagnostic groups based on the psychopathology and character structure.

I. Cases With Well-Defined Diagnostic Categories. (69 cases, 42.8%)

A. Paranoid Schizophrenia (14 cases, 8.7%). Without belaboring the complexities of psychiatric nosology, this group can be further classified as:

> 12 cases of paranoid schizophrenia
> 1 case of hebephrenia with chronic deterioration
> 1 case of a paranoid reaction without disorganization

Probably all psychiatrists in practice have had some experience with the schizophrenic who is a heavy drinker and is often considered a chronic alcoholic until the schizophrenic symptoms become obvious.

In these 14 cases, the typical picture is that of early pathologic drinking. (Average age of onset is 22.) During this early period, paranoid and other schizophrenic features appeared during heavy intoxication and disappeared during sobriety. Many of these patients were literally excused for the most ominous psychopathologic behavior because of being intoxicated.

Since these early symptoms are diagnostic and should be used in advising early therapeutic interference, the following is a list of the symptoms appearing in these cases. They are symptoms that were present only during intoxication, and not one of them occurred alone, or in itself can be considered diagnostic:

> Violent emotional outbursts, temper tantrums and vicious irritability; erratic, inappropriate affect with rapid mood swings; ideas of reference and paranoid misinterpretations; delusions, i.e., transient unfounded beliefs, usually paranoid, and consistent with the personality conflicts; hallucinations, usually transient and often associated with mystical and ecstatic experiences; chaotic sexual behavior, including promiscuity, intoxicated incestuous relations, and homosexual affairs; dramatic acting-out of frank overt sadistic and masochistic reactions with violent assaultiveness, bizarre self-inflicted injuries, and suicidal attempts; confabulation; increased obsessive cleanliness to the point of absurdity; psychomotor overactivity and uncontrolled behavior which usually involves the authorities.

As the drinking bouts become more frequent and prolonged, the behavior becomes increasingly paranoid and disorganized at all times.

Nonetheless, this early drinking period is longer than might be expected, ranging from 7–10 years. It is possible that the alcohol, by permitting acting-out and allowing the release of pathological emotions, staves off the onset of full-blown disorganization. The schizophrenic symptomatology, once developed, is unusually florid.

Bleuler first pointed out the frequency of alcoholism in schizophrenia, and considered alcoholic hallucinosis a schizophrenic phenomenon. He noted that the delirium tremens in schizophrenics were unusual in that auditory hallucinations were common and that the entire syndrome had dynamically determined content.

The relationship between alcoholism, paranoid features, and latent homosexuality deserves comment. Bleuler also pointed out the frequency of paranoid reactions in alcoholism and considered his "alcoholic paranoia" to be a schizophrenic manifestation.

None of these 14 patients was an overt homosexual, although at least two had transient homosexual contacts when intoxicated. Latent homosexual features, and the homosexual content of delusions and hallucinations were more evident than in any other group of alcoholics, and probably, for schizophrenics in general. This may be explained by the fact that the continual drinking provokes such emotional lability and lack of control that all underlying conflicts come to the fore more forcefully than in many schizophrenics without alcoholism. The use that the schizophrenic makes of alcohol in the pre-illness stage, especially as related to latent homosexuality, needs further investigation.

The 10 follow-up reports obtained suggest that the prognosis is neither better nor worse than for paranoid schizophrenia without alcoholism. One patient reported full recovery five years after hospitalization; one has remained anxious, suspicious, and poorly adjusted socially with continued heavy drinking three years later; one is a severely crippled, chronic paranoid patient; six are deteriorated state hospital cases; and one suicided in a hospital while actively delusional and hallucinatory.

Of interest is the fact that this group displayed the usual high incidence of mental illness, especially schizophrenia, in the family histories, but gave a relatively low incidence of alcoholism.

B. Manic-Depressive Reactions (11 cases, 6.8%). The excessive use of alcohol by manic-depressives, particularly during the manic phases, is well known and the study adds little new information to the subject.

The alcoholic problem is considered important in these patients because its use was unquestionably excessive and contributed significantly to the clinical picture, making the affective reactions more intense and increasing the incidence of serious toxic states.

In contrast to the schizophrenics, the onset of illness and the onset of excessive drinking coincided in all. Manic phases with marked excitements are outstanding. Depressions were not of the usual deep depression traditionally associated with the manic-depressive illness, but were rather brief periods of agitated depression complicated by the intoxications. Pre-menstrual and post-partum depressive swings of brief duration were frequent in the women.

A high incidence of mental illness, especially manic-depressive reactions, is reported in the family histories as well as a high incidence of chronic alcoholism.

Of five follow-up reports, two claimed recovery after two or more years.

C. Poorly Organized, Asocial Psychopathic Personalities (11 cases, 6.8%). All of these cases were males showing the psychopathology of the classical, text-book type. Psychopathic traits include poorly-defined goals with contradictory strivings; poorly-developed conscience with asocial and criminal behavior; dishonesty, irresponsibility, and rebellion against authority; bland emotional reactions and little anxiety; inability to profit from experience; inordinate need for narcissistic gratification with impulsiveness and temper tantrums; and a maladjusted sexual life with an inability to form mature and lasting relationships and frequently with strong homosexual features. The criminal behavior in these cases is petty and almost entirely related to a direct rebellion against family figures (i.e., illegal gambling, check-forging, and bad debts which parents invariably repay) and to immediate ego needs (i.e., stealing to obtain cash for drugs and alcohol, intoxicated driving, and disturbing the peace.) These are the psychopaths who show a life-long behavior abnormality and an early onset of psychopathy and chronic alcoholism.

Descriptions of the drinking habits were more inadequate in this group of records than any others. All were listed as chronic alcoholics and had been so since adolescence or the early twenties. Evidently the alcoholism was simply taken for granted by the attending psychiatrists, probably reflecting the prevalent nihilistic attitude towards psychopaths and alcoholism.

However, several facts were apparent. The serious psychopathic behavior usually appears in adolescence, and excessive drinking occurs at the same time. Alcoholism is so intimately related to the psychopathy that the drinking is often blamed for the life failure; not infrequently these individuals are held up as examples of the harmfulness of drink. Actually from a study of these 11 cases, there is no apparent fundamental difference between the psychopaths with alcoholism and those without. Rather, the difference is due to varying degrees of severity of certain underlying personality features and to a greater incidence of alcoholism in the significant family figures. (The meaning of the family history data is discussed later.)

Several leads point to these conclusions. These patients exhibited psychopathic behavior both when sober and when intoxicated; however, it was most obvious and flagrant during intoxication. Then, aggression and narcissistic demands were released leading to rowdy, argumentative, and self-assertive behavior; expansive grandiose plans and claims; sexual behavior rarely attempted when sober; and a kind of out-going ability to establish relationships with people not present when sober.

When sober, they are more bland, inadequate, and passive than the psychopaths without alcoholism; and it is not surprising that an inability to form satisfying sexual relationships with women, promiscuity, impotence, and latent and overt homosexuality are prominent. Alcohol seems essential to allow the acting-out of the asocial drives. Several cases reported that a very mild intoxication was all that was necessary to allow psychopathic behavior—all they needed was an excuse; and certainly these patients did not consistently drink to stupor, nor to relieve anxiety, but endeavored to maintain consciousness as long as possible. Often, if it were expedient, they would be able to "sober up" quickly.

The follow-up reports show that two cases were making adequate life adjustments three or more years after hospitalization, and six were unchanged.

D. Poorly Organized, Psychoneurotic Psychopathic Personalities (15 cases, 9.3%). This diagnostic category comprises only women, although the essential pychopathology may be similar to the inadequate psychoneurotic males to be discussed later. However, the major disorders in sexuality resulting from vicissitudes in the complex feminine development in our culture so color the personality that the clinical picture in the women appears quite different from that of the men.

These patients are called psychopathic because they display a life-long personality disorder consisting of poorly-organized personality features with contradictory strivings, traits, and attitudes. The total personality is immature with manifestations of every level of development appearing in adult life. Emotions are labile and poorly controlled with rapid mood swings, easy irritability, impulsiveness, temper outbursts, depressions and elations. Sexuality is chaotic with frigidity, masturbation, promiscuity, and all forms of perversions possible although none fixed nor satisfying. Anxiety is always present with strong physiological components. Body and sexual insecurity are marked so that anxiety and tension produce numerous short-lived psychosomatic symptoms. The conscience is strong, but there is an almost complete inability to live up to its standards; hence, guilt feelings are ever present, reinforcing masochistic trends. Latent and overt sadistic and masochistic features may be prominent with strong resentment reactions and vague paranoid defenses. Neurotic symptoms of all types occur, but are transitory and shifting. Eating problems are frequent with neurotic over-eating, food idiosyncrasies, dieting, nausea and vomiting. With such immaturity, a strong sense of the self is absent; and disturbances in the awareness of self and reality may occur. The abnormal E.E.G.'s indicate an unstable cerebral physiology of undetermined origin which may contribute etiologically to such symptoms. These individuals characteristically attempt to cope with their immaturity by one of the most immature of reactions: that of identifying themselves with others. They form passive relationships to one person after another. This leads to the easy suggestibility, overt compliance, unpredictable behavior, and sexual seductions with all the ensuing complexities and guilt reactions. The moods of depression, masochistic needs, and everpresent guilt feelings make these patients serious suicide threats. (Of the 15 cases, seven made serious suicidal attempts or threats, and at least three are known suicides.)

It is clear that with such personality structures, alcohol, drugs, or anything that might relieve, even temporarily, the pressure of the emotions and guilt would soon become a habit. The more precise role of alcohol is unclear, probably because it has many roles; that is, it is used to relieve different underlying emotions in the same and in different cases. (See discussion.) The patients usually start drinking excessively during adolescence or the early twenties and are alcoholics within a few years. This points to a more serious degree of illness than the neurotic psychopath without alcoholism who would have a greater ability to tolerate unpleasant emotions.

Often when sober, they give the impression of bland, rather sweet, quiet, and compliant women; when intoxicated, the underlying psychopathology is exhibited in a dramatic manner. Alcohol may be taken to relieve the tension, anxiety, physical discomforts, and guilt feelings; at the same time, it will intensify or alter whatever mood is present. Hence, when intoxicated they can be alternately depressed and withdrawn, or elated with psychomotor overactivity and over-talkativeness; they can change rapidly from resentful, hostile, overtly sadistic, assaultive behavior to depressed, self-accusatory, masochistic acts and fantasies. The more severe "binges"* lead to toxic states with a complete lapse of personal responsibility, or may carry a serious suicidal intent. These patients tend to have vivid, rich, immature imaginations; when intoxicated they may try to impress or please others by fabrications based on fantasy material. They seem at times to believe their own fabrications and are often accused of lying. Characteristically, periods of heavy drinking produce the upsurge of chaotic psychopathic reactions and are then followed by rapid, steady drinking to stupor; any other drugs available will be utilized to aid in the process. "Hang-overs"† are severe, and toxic deliria with brief

---

* The author knows of no scientific, precise term for the word "binge." The layman uses "bout," "binge," "bender," and "spree" synonomously to denote episodic heavy drinking of any magnitude in the alcoholic or non-alcoholic. Here "binge" is used to designate episodic heavy drinking in the alcoholic. It is useful to distinguish between the steady drinker and the true "binge-drinker." The latter drinks only episodically and between drinking bouts totally abstains. Frequently such a drinking pattern, which occurs some time in the course of most cases, indicates that the individual is making a strong, and partially successful, effort to overcome his illness.

† There does not seem to exist a scientific counterpart to the very expressive term "hang-over." This slang term is well fixed in the spoken language and has come to mean the physical and mental discomforts following any kind of overindulgence. The physical and psychological reactions in the alcoholic "hang-over" have been little stud-

parnoid features are not infrequent. In six of these cases, homosexual conflicts were obvious (although only one had had overt experiences), and in these six, paranoid features were marked.

The high incidence of unstable E.E.G.'s, together with the high incidence of mental illness and chronic alcoholism in the family histories, indicate the strength of the constitutional elements as well as the role of identifying with unstable, alcoholic relatives.

The 10 follow-up reports indicate that three patients made an adequate adjustment after three years, four were unchanged, and three had suicided.

E. Epilepsy and Epileptoid Reactions (7 cases, 4.3%). Of these seven cases, only two had epiplepsy, one with grand-mal and one with atypical petit-mal seizures; two cases were diagnosed as epileptic equivalents; the remainder showed epileptoid psychopathology with abnormal E.E.G.'s. The whole group needs further careful study, particularly because some alcoholic patients will have convulsions during toxic states which makes it difficult at times to determine whether or not a true epileptic illness exists.

The differential diagnosis between epileptoid states and other illnesses is likewise difficult at times. Most significant in the diagnosis of epileptoid states is the lack of dynamic determination of symptoms, the lack of easily recognized neurotic symptomatology, the episodic nature of the symptoms, and the fact that the most disturbing symptoms can be related to episodic disturbances in consciousness and reality.

In all these cases, alcoholism occurred either at the same time that the neural disorder appeared or later; and in all, alcohol seriously aggravated and complicated the picture. A brief description of these cases follows:

Case 1

Grand mal epilepsy with alcoholism in an immature, poorly organized personality with psychopathic features. Died at age 24, unimproved. Immediate cause of death unknown.

---

ied and are poorly understood. For instance, the difference between convulsions during acute intoxication and during the "hang-over" is not understood. Psychological reactions, such as presented by the patient with impotence who was potent only during "hang-overs," and the patient who described a strong feeling of elation during "hang-overs," need investigation.

Case 2

Atypical petit mal seizures and unprovoked rage reactions.

Case 3

Epileptic equivalents consisting of dizzy spells, amnesic episodes, fugue states, and wild excitements accompanied with convulsions and disorganization.

Case 4

Epileptic equivalents consisting of attacks of dizziness with ataxia and a grossly abnormal E.E.G.

Cases 5, 6, 7

Epileptoid psychopathology, including déjà-vu experiences, unreality feelings, unprovoked rages, amnesias, toxic delirious states, and convulsions. In one case, the convulsions occurred during intoxications, and in another during non-alcoholic febrile states. Personality features include asocial psychopathic behavior, attacks of unmotivated mood swings with irritability, hositility, and suspiciousness. Serious thinking difficultes, especially when under the influence of strong emotions, occurred and may have led to episodic confusional states.

Three follow-up reports all show no improvement with death occurring in one.

The family history studies indicate that three of the seven cases had histories of mental illnesses in the families; and four of the seven had alcoholism in the immediate forbears.

F. Brain Damage (5 cases, 3%). This group of alcoholic patients has received little attention in recent literature and deserves intensive study. In all these patients, alcoholism is associated in some way with the personality changes or mentation defects produced by the brain pathology; the nature of that association is unclear. It may be that they begin excessive drinking when the psychological and neurological handicaps associated with the structural changes threaten their life success in any way. At any rate, alcohol soon aggravates their difficulties by allowing the release of pathological emotions in a way that is characteristic of the group. When intoxicated, the emotional reactions in these five cases are very poorly controlled with intense rage reaction, cruelties with homicidal threats, assaultiveness, and self-mutilation. Convulsions, while intoxicated or during hang-overs, are frequent.

The five cases in this study are briefly described:

Case 1

Post-encephalitic behavior disorder following influenza at age 16 and considered a chronic alcoholic since that age.

Case 2

Head injury at age 12 with rapid development of psychopathic traits. Became alcoholic at age 38 with intoxications characterized by violent, explosive rages with assaultiveness. Died at 48 following long periods of drinking in a toxic delirium with convulsions. Autopsy showed a severe arachnoiditis, cerebral arteriosclerosis, and cerebral atrophy.

Case 3

Excessive drinker until age 40; then became a severe alcoholic following head injury. When drinking, developed exhibitionistic sexual behavior, incontinence of urine, and episodic confusional periods. Lost consciousness rapidly; had convulsions during hangovers; and had frequent delirium tremens.

Case 4

Personality changes following head injury at age 33. "Black-outs", rage reactions, and repeated drunkenness during which he re-enacted terrifying fantasied experiences with hallucinations. Pseudologia fantastica. Reports recovery three years after hospitalization.

Case 5

Probable history of epilepsy during childhood. Was treated for neurosyphilis at 21, and was an alcoholic by 22. Drunken behavior characterized by uncontrolled assaultiveness. At 28, developed diabetes mellitus followed by frequent insulin reactions and stupors with convulsions. Drinking provoked wide mood swings with suicidal attempts, rages, and self-mutilation.

Of three follow-up reports obtained, one has died, one is unimproved after two years, and one reports a three year recovered period.

The family histories give scanty data. Two of the five cases give definite histories of alcoholism in the immediate forbears.

II. Cases Which Do Not Belong to Any Usual Diagnostic Category (92 cases, 59.6%)

In these cases, chronic alcoholism is the outstanding psychopathological feature; however, a careful study of the cases reveals serious personality defects, and on the basis of these, the cases can be divided into five separate groups. These disorders have been described before and have been usually termed "character disorders."

The term "character disorder" is used to designate those cases in which abnormal attitudes, reactions, and defenses are fixed in the personality structure so that symptom-formation does not occur. Unfortunately, the term is so loosely applied to so many different personality types and illnesses that it has little value. Alcoholism cannot be considered in the category of "character disorders" since the drinking is symptom-formation of major proportions.

These patients rarely develop any of the usual neurotic illnesses; in a sense they need not do so because their neurotic needs and pathological emotions find gratification and expression through the use of alcohol.

The difference between the cases with alcoholism and similiar personality disorders without alcoholism seems to be a combination of the degree of the disorder, identification with alcoholic parental figures, the specific ability of alcohol to strengthen temporarily personality defenses and to allow the acting-out of otherwise suppressed emotional reactions.

The following groups are described in some detail. That there are other types of patients who become alcoholics is unquestionably true. This is particularly so of women, because our changing cultural patterns are encouraging more women to drink with social impunity. Certainly the five groups described below must comprise the majority of the alcoholic illnesses of this category.

In four of the groups, a distinction based on the psychopathology between males and females is made. If this distinction is valid, it is probably a cultural phenomenon based on the fact that intoxication is still so socially taboo in women that the social pressures block it from becoming habitual. In general, the female alcoholics have a higher incidence of seriously disturbing psychopathology than the males.

A. Rigidly Organized, "Obsessive-Compulsive" Personalities (Males. 22 cases, 13.6%). This group consists of intelligent relatively successful men in the middle-life period. (Age range on admission was 41–60.) Characteristic psychopathological features existing before the development of the alcoholism are:

1. Driving ambitions for intellectual and professional success. This is often achieved at the expense of family life and recreation. These

patients feel in constant competition with others, especially other men, and have few close male friends, partly for this reason.

2. Rigid, proud perfectionism of an obsessive-compulsive quality. This is expressed chiefly in perfectionistic work habits and meticulous, orderly personal habits as well as a strong sense of conscientiousness, honesty, and self-righteousness. The patients tend to be overcritical and fault-finding in details with themselves and others. Only two cases had clear obsessive-compulsive symptoms.

3. Rigidly controlled emotional reactions. They look upon any emotional expression as a sign of weakness and are often unaware of their own emotions. Outwardly, they range in appearance from pedantic coldness to an apparent placidity. The dominant underlying emotions are resentment and hostility. Tension states, migraine, and hypertension may be present.

4. Hypochondriacal trends. These range from narcissistic body overconcern to excessive bowel concern and hypochondriacal delusions during disorganized periods.

5. Poor heterosexual adjustment. Promiscuity when sober is rare but would occur when intoxicated. One case was an overt homosexual and two gave histories of having had no sexual relations at all. Most important was the high number of cases with close attachments to mothers and sisters with strong neurotic family ties which seriously interfered with their relationships to their wives. Premature ejaculations, impotence, and fear of impotence occur. Latent homosexuality features are usually not too apparent; but when they occur, especially in the middle-life period, paranoid projections are readily utilized.

These men are frequently heavy social drinkers during their early adult lives but would rarely become drunk or have hang-overs. Often they do their best work on a few drinks, alcohol relieving tension. They pride themselves on their ability to hold their liquor. Illness sets in during the middle-life period when the following factors begin to operate:

1. Marital and family life is patently unsuccessful beyond the hope of retrieving. Children may be disappointments and the relationships with their wives is not satisfying enough to withstand separation from the children.

2. Recognition of inability to progress further professionally with fear of demotion and competition with younger men.

3. Lessening of sexual powers with an upsurge of promiscuity drives and latent homosexual desires.

4. Early aging with fear of aging and dying.

These middle-life problems face every man in one form or another; yet with the rigid, proud, perfectionistic person who has actually made only a neurotic life-adjustment and has long used alcohol in a pathological manner, it is understandable that they would turn to it with increasing frequency.

With intensified fears, threats and frustrations, they tend to react with increased resentment and an intensification of all neurotic personality features. The gradual upsurge of emotions in the presence of increased drinking makes emotional control impossible and once they begin the process of expressing these emotions, they seem unable to stop. When intoxicated, they now lose their usual neurotic defenses, become unkempt, pour out vitriolic hostility, are sadistic, promiscuous, fanatically concerned with their health, are suspicious, jealous, and paranoid. They make public scenes, are often combative, assaultive, and belligerent. Hang-overs in which they express self-pity and self-justification begin. Sobriety is marked by increased perfectionistic rigidity, but quick relapses. Because of their professional prestige, they are often maintained in their jobs for long periods, which only increases their intolerable sense of inadequacy.

After prolonged drinking with avitaminosis, during febrile illnesses, or in the presence of cerebral arteriosclerosis, disorganizations and delusional formation may occur early in the course of the illness.

As might be expected, the prognosis for the alcoholism in this group is better than in any other. Of 12 follow-up reports after a three-year period, nine cases reported recovery. They respond to treatment rapidly, even if on a superficial level, utilizing their many assets, perfectionistic needs, and ability to repress advantageously.

In their family histories, the incidence of mental illness and alcoholism is low.

B. Rigidly Organized Neurotic Personalities with Paranoid Features (Females. 17 cases, 10%). This is a group of female alcoholics whose personalities are rigidly organized with masculine identifications. The underlying psychosexual conflict permeates most of their activities and inter-personal relationships. This conflict arises from lack of early positive identifications so that they can neither accept a feminine role in society, nor succeed in a masculine one. (Psychopathologically they resemble the group just discussed in many respects; however, obsessive-compulsive features are not so prominent.)

They may be of superior intelligence with ambitions for careers and independence; however, these are usually vague and poorly directed. They are described as aggressive, rigid, proud, dependable, active, and unaffectionate; will frequently marry passive men and dominate them. Upon marriage (only one of the group was single), they quickly become frustrated in the responsibilities of child-bearing and housekeeping. They often transfer their own thwarted ambitions onto husbands and children. If the husband fails, he is nagged; if he succeeds, they are jealous and competitive. With many interests, they often become leaders in their social circles; yet at times they can be ruthless in achieving selfish ends. They may be opinionated, stubborn, unforgiving, and readily utilize projection.

Affective life is characterized by a need for stern emotional control. They can push unpleasant emotions aside or can fabricate ingenious rationalizations, can minimize or simply ignore obvious emotional states, symptoms, and problems. Resentment is the strongest underlying emotion.

Early psychosexual development frequently ranges from avoidance of all emotionally charged relationships to latent or overt homosexual ones. (Three of the group had known overt affairs before marriage.) Sexual histories are incomplete in such cases; however, the impression is that they are frequently frigid or have strong sexual tension which they are unable to satisfy.

Alcoholism usually begins with marriage or within a few years thereafter, or with any attempts at a heterosexual adjustment. The marital histories are of rapid and increasing discord. Tension and resentment gradually mount and lead to drinking. When intoxicated, the core of the problem becomes more and more verbalized or acted-out. They are caught in an intolerable situation; the marriage is frustrating, yet to leave it involves not only their strong sense of responsibility to children but also the anxiety and fear of attempting an independent existence. During early intoxications, they may ignore their husbands and be erotic with other men—or women. As the impossible environmental stresses persist, hostility, belligerency, combativeness, vulgarities, and overt cruelties may appear as well as depression, moodiness, sullenness, suspiciousness, ideas of reference, paranoid misinterpretations, promiscuity, and spite-confessions. Such loss of emotional control and revealing of self is traumatic to these patients; they will then drink to stupor, or have (or profess to have) amnesias. Hang-overs are severe, and secret drinking occurs when alcohol is denied them.

The periods of heavy drinking and abstinences usually vary with the situational factors. Marriage, child-birth, deaths of significant relatives, moves to unfamiliar surroundings, illnesses, and operations may precipitate months of alcoholism. Fortuitous changes which remove the patients from resentment-producing situations may lead to periods of total abstinence.

Actual deterioration may occur when the over-all intolerable situation is intensely frustrating and prolonged. Rage reactions, lapses in personal appearance and daily habits, and resorting to any form of alcohol or drugs occur. Deliria and disorganization with paranoid delusions and hallucinations may eventuate.

As with most of the female alcoholics, the incidence of alcoholism in the family histories is high as well as the incidence of mental illnesses. The prognosis for the group seems poor. Of nine follow-ups after three years, one reports recovery. Two continued pathological drinking; three have died of accidents and pneumonia; and three have had prolonged hospitalizations with paranoid delusional states.

C. Poorly Organized, Inadequate Psychoneurotic Personalities (Males. 30 cases, 18.6%). This group is the one most frequently singled out as constituting the typical alcoholic; from our data the highest number of cases fall in this category. (This group may correspond psychopathologically to the poorly organized, psychopathic women described earlier.)

These men have passive, neurotic character structures with strong dependency needs. These features are fundamental and so interfere with success in life that the general picture is that of serious inadequacy and often complete failure.

They may be of superior intelligence, but have vague goals and poorly directed ambitions; they fail early in life and are usually alcoholics in their twenties. Only five of the thirty cases made even fair job successes, and only two had achieved professional training.

They do not seem to be irresponsible, but are so fearful of responsibility that their desperate attempts to make good inevitably fail.

Basically passive, dependent, and immature they may give the outward appearance of compliance, cheerfulness, kindness, warmth, generosity and charm. Others are shy, over-polite, self-conscious, and averbal. They rarely express resentment. Oral traits extend into all aspects of their existence; neurotic oral symptoms occur (i.e., eating phobia, overeating with resulting obesity, and stuttering). Their childish need for affection and approval colors every relationship. They tend to marry aggressive, domineering, or motherly women. Body overconcern is prominent and seems to be related to an inability to tolerate pain and to bids for sympathy rather than to narcissistic pride.

Psychosexually, impotence and fear of impotence are most outstanding. Only one case gave a probable history of homosexuality; the rest were seriously concerned with genital inadequacy and often accepted impotence for years rather than risking failure.

Fantasy life tends to be of an adolescent nature with self-glorification as the central theme.

Drinking usually begins very early and almost immediately is used to relieve self-consciousness and tension when faced with any situation in which personal success is important. Every life situation which requires the appearance of maturity produces anxiety and tension; they are constantly "fortifying" themselves. Every failure must be forgotten by more drinking. Constant rationalization produces hostility which varies in individual cases; some show considerable resentment, but rarely of the intensity seen in other groups. In contrast to previously discussed cases, there is a lack of force behind the resentment in these patients. Even their rages have the appearance of overdramatized ferociousness. The anger turns readily into self-pity, and it is much more amenable to outside suggestion.

During intoxications, all the behavorial tendencies described become exaggerated with the passive features dominating. They are alternately boasting and shy, aggressive and helpless, sympathizing and seeking sympathy, all in a brief span of time. They indulge in glorious success fantasies and may attempt to act them out.

As time passes, they become more and more aware of their own inadequacy. Attempts to stop drinking are sincere but lead to periods of false security and devastating "binges." Even in these "binges," the lack of aggressive behavior may be marked; they will leave home rather than face relatives and acquaintances; isolate themselves in hotel rooms; seek the company of strangers; and rarely disturb the peace or get into legal difficulties. "Hang-overs" are severe and are feared. They are marked by depression, self-pity, self-castigation, and weeping. Although drinking bouts may last five or six weeks, these patients tend to be such hearty eaters between and during them that delirium tremens are not too frequent. Some patients report they purposely eat as well as possible during bouts in order to prolong them. The knowledge of another lost job and family recriminations are sufficient to deter sobering-up as long as possible.

The incidence of mental illnesses and of alcoholism in the family histories is high. The prognosis in this group is poor. Only two out of seventeen follow-ups reported recovery. In treatment, they tend to form dependent relationships on the therapists and will remain enthusiastically abstinent so long as that passive relationship with utter approval is not threatened. Another important factor in producing the poor recovery rate may lie in the age of admission to the hospital. Nineteen of the 30 cases were admitted after the age of 35, and after ten or more years of alcoholism with all its failures and complex, difficult inter-personal relationships. However, follow-ups are insufficient to ascertain whether or not early treatment would necessarily be more successful.

It is said that all alcoholics must "hit rock-bottom" or "be ready" before treatment of any kind is effective. This statement seems to apply to this group of cases more than any other. Nonetheless, commonsense argues that, as we learn more about the disorder, early treatment will be more beneficial than late. All too frequently, these cases are treated after years of drinking have so crippled and scarred the life adjustment and personality that even a bare marginal adjustment is called a "cure."

D. Dependent Psychoneurotic Personalities with Depression and Tension (Females. 12 cases, 7.4%). The outstanding personality features of this group are the dependent, passive needs and reactions of depression, tension, and anxiety to feelings of rejection and loneliness.

These women are described as basically feminine and immature with strong needs for love, protection, and companionship. Some are shy, timid, and socially self-conscious. They have high moral standards and usually live up to them. Strong family loyalties with close attachments to parents and stronger siblings occur. Intelligent, they have few real intellectual interests. They are capable of close, warm, dependent, and meaningful relationships with men; tend to marry early and often become absorbed in husband, home, and children to the exclusion of outside activities. Need for approval is strong; and the reactions of depression and tension to disapproval precipitate involved complexities in their family relationships. They cannot discipline their children maturely; feelings are easily hurt; they brood. They tend to be very devoted but over-anxious, over-protective, fearful mothers. Mood swings are almost entirely reactive to the situation at the moment. Thinking is not orderly so that planning is chaotic or impulsive. They cannot express resentment nor tolerate the idea of it.

Psychosexually, some are frigid; others have strong sexual needs in which complete surrender is possible. Not promiscuous, pre-marital or extra-marital affairs are rare and, when present, are long and meaningful.

These patients become ill when their life situation does not provide satisfaction of dependent needs. This occurred in these cases as the result of marrying irresponsible, inadequate, unaffectionate, or impotent men; after the loss of some protective, supportive person; loss of children; when caught between neurotic gratification and family responsibility; or when faced with added family responsibilities with which they cannot cope. Because of their passivity with its indecisiveness, they are unable to resolve such conflicts by action. They may persist in impossible marriages for years with increasing depression, tension and anxiety. Alcohol is used partly to relieve tension, but mainly to allow the acting-out and verbalization of their passivity demands.

The age of onset of the alcoholism, its degree, and its course vary in each case and depend on the vicissitudes of the life history and the depth of the personality disorder. In some, there is an early history of brief recurrences of excessive intake during threatening periods. Severe alcoholism occurs when dependency gratifications are withdrawn, either for prolonged times or with seeming irrevocability. Emotions then reach pathological strength with depression or tension dominating the clinical picture. Irritability, restlessness, insomnia, and clinging to familiar supports, however inadequate, occur.

When intoxicated, they may show considerable hostility towards those who are failing them; but it rarely reaches the point of real aggression or assaultiveness. Rather, they become depressed, feel hopeless, blame themselves, and are alternately affectionate and angry. Some drink quietly, sit alone for hours day-dreaming, and finally pass into stupor. They do not become unpleasantly drunk in public but drink at home, involving their children in their conflicts. They verbalize futility and say that they drink to "stop thinking." When most depressed, they will drink anything to achieve unconsciousness as quickly as possible. Hang-overs are severe with overwhelming remorse and guilt.

The incidence of alcoholism in the family histories is high; that of other mental illnesses is low.

Of only seven follow-up reports, three described recovery after three years and four were still alcoholics.

E. Middle and Late Life Depressions (5 males, 6 females; 11 cases, 6.8%). This group comprises individuals who were abstainers or average social drinkers and had made an apparently stable life adjustment until the middle or late life period. How well-adjusted their earlier lives had been in fact is open to question. As in most such cases, good early histories and personality studies reveal many significant gaps.

In the later life periods, these patients are faced with disturbing events or reactions which threaten or wipe out their security. In our cases, such events include physical illness with threat of death and loss of earning power, professional demotion due to age, business reverses, death of spouse, late first marriages, disappointment in children, impotency and the appearance of repressed unacceptable sexual drives.

These illnesses differ from the usual middle and late life depressions in the less intense degree of affective change and in the use of alcohol. A sweeping depression does not occur. Characteristically, intoxication produces unusually dramatic changes in mood and behavior; and the more rigid and restricted the earlier life, the greater the change. The course of the alcoholism is rapidly down-hill with admission six months to five years after onset of drinking.

These people tended to have personality structures and cultural milieus which would forbid drinking, certainly intoxication. When drinking starts, they lose all defenses and emotional control. They are dishevelled, obscene, overtalkative, elated, depressed, insistently self-accusatory, or hilarious. Public scenes, combativeness, sexual exposures and, rarely, perversions, paranoid misinterpretations and delusions occur. Others become deeply depressed when intoxicated and must be guarded constantly against suicide, but recover immediatly on sobering. Regaining the usual personality features on sobering is the rule, and most are amnesic for the intoxicated behavior. Between bouts, several were described as "quiet and puzzled."

Aging factors are very important with cardiac conditions and cerebral arteriosclerosis complicating the reaction to alcohol.

The family histories show a low incidence of mental illness. The women give a higher incidence of alcoholism than the men.

Of eight follow-ups obtained, three reported recovery two or more years later; one patient had suicided; one continued drinking and died of coronary thrombosis 10 months later; and three continued drinking, ending in senile, agitated, paranoid disorganizations.

DISCUSSION

The actual drinking in chronic alcoholism in the cases studied is a symptom of several different illnesses. In none of these cases did alcoholism exist without previous personality defects antedating the drinking. These defects could be causally related to the drinking except in the epileptic reactions, in the cases with brain damage, and the middle and late-life depressions with their high frequency of neurological changes due to arteriosclerosis.

This is not to say that there may not be alcoholics who have no demonstrable prior personality defects serious enough to be termed illness. In our experience, however, they must be rare. It may be that cases of alcoholism occurring in an apparently normal person may be more frequent outside hospital practice. One such case is known, not reported here, where alcoholism developed in the setting of a sudden, unusually frustrating life situation and the excessive drinking disappeared abruptly when that situation was altered. It seems clear that these groups described in this report are composed of individuals with personalities that could not be considered within normal limits.

The probability of some abnormal physical reaction to alcohol, whether on a constitutional or metabolic basis, in alcoholism is not strengthened. It is suggested that, if it exists, it must be secondarily contributory. For example, a patient with a rigidly organized "obsessive-compulsive" personality who is capable of drinking heavily over many years becomes an alcoholic in the middle-life period. This may indicate a changed physiological reaction to alcohol. On the other hand, the early ability to drink heavily without losing emotional control is quite consistent with the total picture of the individual—he rarely loses emotional control under any conditions. Later, the loss of control is consistent with the inability to control increasingly intolerable emotions under the pressure of increasingly frustrating life situations. The psychogenic factors are sufficient to explain the onset of alcoholism; if the alcohol were not available, it might be expected that some other psychopathological reaction would be forthcoming.

The family history data need elaboration. A patient's or relative's report of alcoholism in a parent or grandparent may mean severe alcoholism or merely occasional intoxication, depending upon the memory and bias of the reporter. Few of our family histories go beyond the grandparent and many do not go that far.

In practically all these cases, the alcoholism or psychiatric illnesses occurred in forbears who were close to the patients, and the alcoholism occurred during the patients' childhood; hence, no matter what the constitutional background, the effects of the direct psychological influences of the alcoholic relatives on the children assume significant proportions. This significance is strengthened by the reports of many of these patients on their vivid memories of their disturbed childhoods.

If the trends reported here prove valid, several conclusions can be drawn:

1. The incidence of psychiatric illness in these groups is in line with that reported for those specific illnesses without alcoholism by other investigators.

2. The incidence of alcoholism is higher than would be expected in the general population or in other illnesses.

3. Women with alcoholism are more apt to come from homes where alcoholism existed than are men. Of 161 cases, 72 were women; 89 were men. Sixty-eight per cent of the women gave a positive history of alcoholism in the family, and 44.9% of the men

gave such a history. The lower incidence in men becomes more significant in view of the fact that the highest incidence fell in the largest group of male alcoholics. (Group B with 18 cases or 45% of positive family histories in men.) If this group is excluded, the incidence of positive histories in the men is 32.8%. The incidence in women is evenly scattered.

Again, this difference between men and women may be explained on a cultural basis. Since the excessive use of alcohol is more socially forbidden to women, they tend to require more potent psychodynamic forces to provoke its use.*

4. The earlier the onset of alcoholism, the greater the incidence of it in the family history. This is more true of the men than of the women, who have a relatively high incidence of alcoholic relatives at any age.

Further studies are needed. However, from this study, the single symptom of pathological drinking would seem to originate partially from psychodynamic relationships with alcoholic relatives, rather than from a constitutional origin.

It is understood that the borderlines between the groups described are not clear-cut. The groupings simply outline the more frequently occurring patterns. At times, it was difficult to decide whether a patient showed more of the features of one group than of another; and unquestionably there will be cases which seem to show features equally characteristic of several groups, or fall into diagnostic categories yet to be delineated.

In general, these patients use alcohol in a neurotic way; that is, the behavior during intoxication is an attempt to escape from a recognition of inadequacies; to ward off the awareness of unpleasant emotions; to verbalize or act-out frustrated neurotic needs; or to express repressed or suppressed emotions. This is why the alcoholic so consistently behaves differently when intoxicated than the normal person when intoxicated. In the writer's experience, intoxicated behavior is almost invariably the lead to understanding the underlying problems,

---

* It is a common observation that women use alcohol less frequently than do men; more women are total abstainers, are milder social drinkers, and are much less frequently heavy social drinkers. Hence, simply from the standpoint of having developed an habitual familiarity with alcohol or having used it in stress situations, they would be less apt to develop alcoholism.

hence the importance of a good history of the drinking pattern in each case.

This acting-out during intoxication also explains the dictum in the therapy of total abstinence. Once neurotic, immature modes of achieving satisfactions are used, their use tends to be repeated until gratification appears. To enforce abstinence forces the patient to find new, and, it is hoped, more mature ways of solving his conflicts. Relapses mean that new ways have not been found or are not mastered.

The fact that many alcoholics can temporarily refrain from exhibiting psychopathological behavior, even for long periods, is in no wise different from the course of most psychiatric illnesses where there is a history of an ebb and flow of psychopathological behavior depending on situational factors and the temporary mobilizations of inner resources.

The influence of alcohol on the various emotional states of anxiety, resentment, tension, depression, and elation is not clarified. However, several trends are noteworthy. Unexpressed resentment would appear to be the most frequent underlying emotion which provokes drinking and is relieved by it. Depression tends to be intensified by drinking rather than relieved. The effect on pathological elation is that of increasing underlying anxiety. Physiological tension is relieved. True and intense feelings of guilt are relieved or temporarily drowned by intoxication (which may explain the elation experienced by some patients during hang-overs), but is often intensified on sobriety with the recall of the psychopathological intoxicated behavior. Once severe alcoholism has developed, the effect is almost universally to promote expression of pathological emotions in some way so that social drinking becomes impossible.

The earlier and longer an individual drinks in excessive quantities socially, or tends to express or act-out neurotic needs when intoxicated, the more apt he is to become alcoholic eventually. This conclusion is based on the observation that many of the cases either drank excessively early in life or had long histories of heavy social drinking. This may mean that the early learning of this method of handling conflicts will set the pattern for its later excessive use.

The importance of obtaining a thorough history of drinking in all psychiatric patients is emphasized. The data on the drinking behavior are used in diagnosis and treatment.

Whenever cerebral pathology exists before, or during, the course of the alcoholism, the reactions produced by alcohol are more intense, chaotic, and disorganizing.

CONCLUSION

The psychopathological patterns allow the delineation and description of eleven different diagnostic groups.

On the basis of this study of the underlying psychopathology and personalities of 161 cases of chronic alcoholism, the author concludes that alcoholism is not a single entity or disease, but a symptom associated with several illnesses or syndromes. An adequate differential diagnosis is necessary for the understanding of each case.

BIOCHEMICAL EXPERIMENTAL INVESTIGATIONS
OF EMOTIONS AND CHRONIC ALCOHOLISM

M. Freile Fleetwood, M.D.

The investigations which are presented in this chapter have been carried on intensively during the last six years. They are based on the studies of A. T. Milhorat and his co-workers[7,23,24] who used a modification of an experiment of Cannon (1911)[5] and applied it to the study of emotions. Their main results were the findings of different biochemical substances in the blood in the presence of anxiety, tension, and resentment as defined on pages 8, 54.

The significance of these emotions in chronic alcoholics was investigated during the last six years by studies on normal subjects, on patients suffering from various psychiatric disorders, and on patients diagnosed as chronic alcoholics. Some of these patients were chronic alcoholics (see definition, page 4) while others were excessive drinkers. In each subject, these emotions were studied psychologically, psychopathologically, and biochemically. The method of these investigations and the results are presented in the first part of this chapter. The second part of the chapter contains studies of the effects of alcohol, mephenesin, and sodium amytal on alcoholic and non-alcoholic patients.

Different types of emotions co-exist in the same person and influence each other. The concomitance of different emotions is a source of error, and special emphasis has been given to a systematic and clear definition of the emotions under study. As a reaction to intense emotions, others may develop. However, the intensity of the primary emotion must be distinguished in order to obtain a better understanding of the personality, and for a clue as to psychodynamics involved. The pattern of each individual is different, and similar emotional experiences have a different meaning to each subject. A thorough understanding of any human being necessitates repeated observations of his reactions to different situations. In this study, the significance of emotional reactions during each person's life development was scrutinized in long term psychotherapy.

In all these studies it has been considered important to investigate the constantly changing emotional reactions, changes which might pertain to the specific emotion as well as to the intensity. In some cases it was possible to witness the development of emotional reactions while the patient was under experimental observation.

The main interest of these investigations was to determine the emotions which predominate when desire for alcohol develops, and in what way there might be a difference between these emotions in alcoholic patients and in those who were not dependent upon alcohol.

Different drugs have been reported in literature to be effective in the relief of intense emotions. The effect of some of these drugs was studied to determine whether any of them act on a particular patient, and in what way they would affect the chemical substances in the blood and thus throw additional light on their nature.

METHOD

Each investigation involved the determination of the type and intensity of emotions by psychiatric methods and the quantitative determination of substances present in the blood by pharmacologic methods. In some patients there was a study of the effect produced by different drugs on the emotions and on the related chemical substances in the blood. The drugs studied were: alcohol, mephenesin,* dibenamine,† morphine, sodium amytal, and dexedrine.‡

Subjects

The study comprised normal subjects and emotionally disturbed patients; from the latter group are separated the alcoholic patients.

Normal Subjects. The normal subjects were 24 members of the professional staff and college students (13 females and 11 males). Of these people, 13 were single and 11 married. Their ages ranged from 20 to 57. The average age was 30.3. All of them were working,

---

* 3 ortho-toloxy-1,2-propanediol (Tolserol, Squibb).

† N,N-Dibenzyl-B-chlorethylamine Hydrochloride (Smith, Kline, and French).

‡ Dextro-amphetamine sulfate (Smith, Kline, and French).

and engaged in their activities at the moment of the test. No physical examination or other blood studies were taken in these subjects. However, physical examination and routine laboratory tests had been done no longer than 6 months before the time of the test and the results were within normal limits. Psychological and biochemical determinations were made. The emotions and the blood from the same subject were studied in different life situations. Repeated tests were done from one to 40 times in the same subject.

Psychiatric Patients. The psychiatric patients numbered 147 (75 females and 72 males). They were in-patients in the Payne Whitney Psychiatric Clinic. Their ages ranged from 19 to 66, and the average age was 38.1. A complete physical examination and routine laboratory examination was done in every one of the patients studied. The laboratory examination included blood count, urine and blood glucose. These patients had no access to alcoholic beverages. The distribution of diagnoses among this psychiatric group was:

	Male	Female	Total
Psychoneurosis..................	12	8	20
Depression.....................	9	19	28
Schizophrenia..................	9	12	21
Psychopathic personality........	7	3	10
Paranoid......................	4	2	6
Senile reaction.................	1	1	2
Manic excitement...............	1	2	3
Alcoholism....................	29	28	57

Repeated tests, including psychiatric evaluation and biochemical determination, were made from one to 25 times.

Alcoholic Patients. From the group of psychiatric patients 57 were alcoholics (29 males, 28 females), who were in-patients receiving psychotherapy. Ages ranged from 19 to 66, and the average age was 40.3. The duration of drinking had ranged from 10 months to 23 years. All these patients had a balanced diet and vitamin supply was given if any deficiency was detected. No patient was taken for investigation until this deficiency had been corrected. Strict abstinence from alcohol was maintained during the whole period of the study. Whenever a patient was permitted to leave the clinic, his urine was tested for alcohol as soon as he returned.

Psychiatric Determination of Emotions

The subjects were well known to the psychiatric investigator (Diethelm). Their psychiatric history, their pattern of reaction through life, and characteristic response to emotions were thoroughly studied before any experimental studies were undertaken. The psychiatric examination involved the determination of the type and intensity of the emotional state, determined by subjective description and by objective signs.

Subjective Description. Emotions are subjective in nature; therefore, the patient's description of his emotional situations is essential. However, the following factors need to be taken into consideration in order to evaluate his statement. The subjective description of emotions is influenced by the variable usage of words by different people, modifications of language, cultural pattern, the degree of freedom in expressing emotions, the proportion of awareness of emotions, as well as the individual pattern of reaction. Subjective description also involves dynamic factors which may be conscious or unconscious, and these may be clarified by further questioning into what is meant by the words used. When the emotional reaction is explored, the patient becomes more aware of his emotions and this awareness may produce a secondary emotional reaction.

There are some people who do not seem to be aware of their emotions and who do not seem to be able to learn to recognize them. Others hide their emotions consciously for various reasons. One subject may say, "I am worried about being restricted in the hospital." This could mean anxiety, or a feeling of tension to frustration, or the expression of hidden resentment. One must also remember that experiences in life affect one's attitude to re-experiencing emotions, to experiencing others, and to expressing them.

The attitude towards the experiment is dynamically determined and may provoke various emotional responses; e.g., fear of the needle, fear of being touched, fear of being tested, fear of being a subject for an experiment. Attitudes towards subsequent experiments may be the same or may change greatly.

The experiencing of emotion provokes a secondary emotional state; for example, a patient may develop guilt from having an emotional reaction. Intolerable resentment may also provoke fear; the patient is afraid of what would happen if his hostility became overt and got out of hand. In this study, the determination of secondary emotions was always considered.

Objective Signs. Factors taken into consideration were: expression of the face, posture, movement, speech (pressure of speech, change of pitch in the voice), content of speech, and disorders of thinking (vagueness, mild incoherence or confusion, suspiciousness, paranoid misinterpretations). Active attention was tested in the grasp of questions and digit span. Concentration, retention, and memory were tested in the routine mental examination.

Perspiration, rate of respiration, dryness of mouth, and tearing were observed. Feeling of tiredness, bodily sensations and any other somatic complaints were recorded. The patients were questioned as to the occurrence of dreams and their content.

The investigator knew before the interview about the patient's past and current problems and the way in which he usually solved them. During the interview the subjective description of the patient's own emotions was obtained; their display and their effect on speech and thinking processes and on the physiological response of the body were noted. All the factors above have been taken into consideration to establish the type of emotions experienced by the patient.

Determination of the Intensity of Emotion. The intensity of affective display is influenced by the pattern of reaction: insufficient control of emotions or unusually high degree of control. Corresponding to the outline offered in Table 1, the emotions were evaluated as "marked," "moderate," or "mild." The suddenness or gradualness of onset depends on the individual reaction and it is very difficult to predict beforehand the type of reaction for the particular subject.

Since the determination of the type of emotion, the intensity, and the rapidity of development are difficult to diagnose accurately, the first two blood studies were considered preliminary. The succeeding studies permitted a good evaluation of the emotions. Patients on whom one was not able to carry out a very careful study of their special emotional reactions give less accurate results.

Pharmacologic Method

Blood (10–15 ml.) was withdrawn from the cubital vein from one to five minutes after a psychiatric examination had been made by Dr.

Diethelm. (Pulse readings were taken before the blood was withdrawn.) Heparin was added in amounts of 10–15 units/ml. of blood. The blood was collected in two tubes, one of which was maintained at room temperature, and contained 1 mg. of physostigmine, in addition to heparin. This sample (5 ml.) was tested within two to four minutes after being drawn to determine the cholinergic substance. Blood from which the adrenergic substance was going to be determined was collected in a centrifuge tube immersed in ice, and precautions were taken not to lyse the cells. When experiments with whole blood were performed, an additional tube was used. The whole blood was utilized for testing the adrenergic substance and was centrifuged at 300 r.p.m. for five minutes, after which the plasma was drawn off with a capillary pipette. The red cells were lysed by shaking the centrifuge residue with an equal volume of distilled water.

Rabbits, rats, and frogs were used as test objects. Rabbits and rats were maintained on a uniform diet* from seven to fifteen days before use. Rabbits and rats were killed by a blow on the head. Frogs were killed by pithing the occipito-atlantoid membrane. The methods employed in treating the organs of the different species will be discussed in detail.

Rabbits. The isolated duodenum from adult female rabbits of the New Zealand White, Chinchilla, Flemish, Checker, Albino, Black and Gray Dutch strains was used. The majority of our rabbits weighed from 3 to 5 kilos. Younger rabbits had been used (2 kilos) but it was found that the preparations did not last as long as did those from the bigger rabbits. (The first four determinations gave good results.)

The organ was cut into strips 2 cm. long which were suspended in a muscle chamber containing 40 ml. Tyrode solution through which a mixture of 90% O_2 and 10% CO_2 was bubbled. The general set-up of the experimental procedure can be seen in Figure 1.

The muscle chambers were placed in a water bath which was maintained at a temperature of 37.5°C. An Erlenmeyer bottle containing 500 cc. of Tyrode solution was placed inside the water bath as a reservoir for replacement of solution after each determination. The pressure of oxygen forced the Tyrode solution into the muscle chamber and the flow was regulated by a two-way stopcock. A "T" tube

* Rockland Farm pellets (Rockland Farms, N. Y.). The rats were fed with Purena (Ralston Purina Co., St. Louis, Mo.). Carrots were added to the diet.

permitted the oxygen to be used either for oxygenation of the muscle chamber or for transferring the Tyrode solution from the reservoir.

After the intestinal strip had been in the muscle chamber for five minutes, the contractions were registered on a kymograph by means of an isotonic lever with a magnification of about 10.

After each test the Tyrode was removed from the muscle chamber by suction through a glass tube, and the preparation was washed with

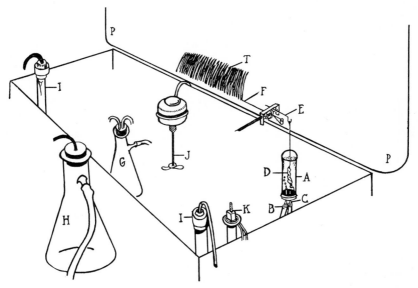

Figure 1. Constant Temperature Water Bath Containing One Muscle Chamber. The isolated duodenum of the rabbit, or the isolated colon and uterus of the rat are suspended in the muscle chamber containing 40 ml. of solution aerated with 6% CO_2 in O_2. The movements are recorded on a kymograph by means of an isotonic lever.

120 ml. of fresh Tyrode solution from the reservoir flask. Contractions of the intestine were recorded after the change of solution, but if the contractions were not uniform, we waited until this occurred before performing a new test. One ml. of whole blood, plasma, or of lysed red cells was added to the muscle chamber in which the test object was suspended.

Rats. Female adult rats of the Wistar strain were used. The uterus and ascending colon were treated by the method of Jalon,[21] in which the organs are brought to quiescence by decreasing the calcium con-

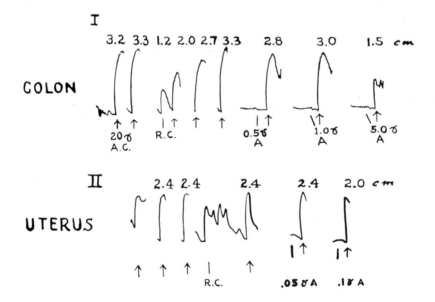

I

COLON

3.2 3.3 1.2 2.0 2.7 3.3 2.8 3.0 1.5 cm

↑ ↑ | ↑ ↑ ↑ | ↑ ↑ \↑
20γ R.C. 0.5γ 1.0γ 5.0γ
A.C. A A A

II

UTERUS

2.4 2.4 2.4 2.4 2.0 cm

↑ ↑ ↑ | ↑ |↑ |↑
R.C. .05γA .1γA

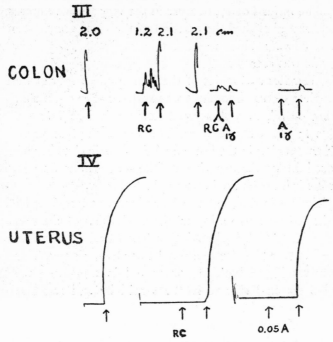

Figure 2. Quantitative Estimation of Adrenergic Substances in Blood of Patients with and without anxiety in the Rat Uterus and Colon.

I. Comparison of effect of epinephrine (A) and of red blood cells (R.C.) of very anxious patient on the rat colon. The effect of the R.C. on the contractions evoked by acetylcholine (A.C.) was equivalent to that of 3.6γ of epinephrine.

II. Effect of red blood cells (R.C.) of same patient (I) on rat uterus (insensitive to nor-epinephrine) was less than that of 0.1γ epinephrine. Note significant differences in amounts of "epinephrine" when determined by these two methods.

III. Absence of effect of red blood cells (R.C.) of a non-anxious subject on the rat colon. Addition of 1γ epinephrine completely abolished effect of acetylcholine (designated by unlettered arrows).

IV. Absence of effect of red blood cells (R.C.) of a mildly anxious patient compared with that of 0.05γ epinephrine.

tent of the Locke solution and by lowering the temperature of the water bath. The inhibitory effects of epinephrine are detected by first inducing a contraction of the uterus and colon by a standard dose of acetylcholine and then measuring the effect of the epinephrine in inhibiting the contractions induced by acetylcholine. In Figure 2, the effect of epinephrine on acetylcholine, on rat's colon, and on rat's uterus can be seen.

Applying a modification of the Jalon technique, using 20γ of acetylcholine instead of 1γ, because in the very sensitive uterus, 0.05γ of epinephrine abolished the reaction of the 1γ of acetylcholine completely, we were able to determine quantitatively how much epinephrine was present.

Frogs. Females and males of the Rana pipiens species were used. The complete rectus abdominus was suspended in a muscle chamber containing 40 ml. of well-aerated Locke solution. The experiment was done at room temperature. The Locke solution was changed through an opening in the bottom of the muscle chamber which was kept closed during the experiment. The contractions were registered by an isotonic lever on the kymograph.

Acetylcholine in different concentrations was tested and its effect was registered over two minutes' time. Washing of the preparation was done with 120 ml. Locke solution. Then 1 ml. of blood was added and its effect was likewise registered after two minutes. This experiment was conducted both in winter and in summer, since Welsh reported a seasonal change in the sensitivity and response of the frog's heart to acetylcholine.[27]

Drugs and Method of Administration. The effect of drugs* on the patients' emotions and on the chemical substance in the blood was studied in the following way: (1) a psychiatric examination and blood study were made; (2) the drugs were administered, and (3) a second psychiatric examination and blood study were made. The time lapse between the first and second examinations will be specified in the case of each drug.

Alcohol. The first test was done one-half hour before the patient started to drink. Alcohol in amounts of 6 or 8 ounces of whiskey was offered to the patient. The whiskey was taken, diluted or undiluted, at the rate of 2 ounces every 10 minutes. A second psychiatric examination and blood study were made 10 minutes after the last drink.

---

* The following drugs were used: Epinephrine hydrochloride (Lederle and others) diluted to 1:1000 with normal saline and kept in sterile ampules, using as preservative 0.5% chlorbutanol and 0.1% sodium bisulfate; Levoarterenol (Winthrop) as the bitartrate—each ml. contains 1088 mg. L-arterenol base; Gynergen (Sandoz)—1 ml. contains 0.5 mg. ergotamine tartrate; acetylcholine chloride (Merck); synthetic epinephrine (Winthrop-Stearns); mephensin (Tolserol—Squibb); sodium amytal (Lilly); dexedrine (Smith, Kline, and French); dibenamine (Smith, Kline, and French); adrenocorticothropic hormone (Armour); and whiskey (86.8 proof—43.4% alcohol by volume).

In some cases, more alcohol had been given to the patient, and a third determination was made. Another test was performed 22 hours later which will be explained later.

Mephenesin. The first test was made immediately, or within 10 minutes, after the oral administration of 0.5 to 1 gm. of mephenesin. The second determination was done after a period of 20 to 30 minutes. A third determination was made after a period of one to two hours following the administration of the drug.

Sodium amytal. A first determination was made 20 minutes before the administration of sodium amytal. The drug was injected intravenously slowly, in amounts equivalent to 0.5 to 0.7 gm. Blood was obtained immediately after the administration of the drug was stopped.

Dibenamine. A first test was done immediately before the administration of 0.240 gm. dibenamine. The effect of this drug was studied at ¾, 1½, and 2 hours after the drug had been given.

Epinephrine and nor-epinephrine. A blood test was done immediately after the administration of this drug, injected in doses of 16γ intravenously. Its effect was studied 10 minutes after injection.

Dexedrine. A first test was done 15 minutes before the oral administration of 0.015 gm. dexedrine. A second test was done 30 minutes after ingestion.

STUDY OF EMOTIONS

In order to present the material clearly, we shall discuss anxiety, tension, and resentment separately although they were studied simultaneously if any of the other two emotions existed.

Anxiety

Psychological Determination. Anxiety is felt as a danger. Subjectively, it is described as worry or a feeling of uneasiness or apprehension. Sometimes patients will give reasons for their anxiety, but generally it is a displacement of an unconscious motivation. In some people, anxiety may be hidden by aggressive, hostile behavior. The struggle against anxiety may develop tension.

Anxiety produces a decrease of the active attention, manifested in the digit span and in the slower learning of the maze test. It decreases retention ability (demonstrated on repetition of a maze test 24 hours

TABLE 1

PHARMACOLOGICALLY ACTIVE SUBSTANCES IN BLOOD AND THEIR ASSOCIATION WITH EMOTIONS

Anxiety (apprehension)	Nor-epinephrine-like substance* (gamma per ml.)	Tension (inner tautness)	Acetylcholine-like substance† (gamma per ml.)	Resentment (bitterness and desire for revenge)	Substance demonstrated after atropinization‡ (gamma per ml.)
Mild: Feeling uneasy Ill at ease Occasional palpitations	0.4 to 1.0	Mild: Feeling taut "Not relaxed" Muscle sensations	5 to 15	Mild: Mild bitterness Hostile	2 to 8
Moderate: Apprehension Occasional anxiety dreams Increased pulse rate Dry mouth Taut throat Moist palms Gastric distention Mild shortness of breath Occasional palpitations Decreased attention	1.0 to 2.0	Moderate: Feeling taut Mild irritability Muscle tensions Fatigue (localized or generalized) Mild difficulty in falling asleep (inability to relax) Mild concentration disorder	15 to 30	Moderate: Bitterness Hostile Irritable Sarcastic Critical of others Mild difficulty in falling asleep	10 to 20
Marked: Apprehension, anxiety (aggressive or hostile) Palpitations, dry mouth, taut throat, moist hands, etc. Gastric distention Urge to urinate Bowel movements Anxiety dreams Broken sleep Decreased retention Thinking disorders possible	2.0 to 3.0	Marked: Taut, irritable (emotional explosiveness) Intense muscular tension Fatigue Muscle aches Headaches Sleep difficulty Concentration difficulty Thinking difficulty	30 to 70	Marked: Strong feeling of bitterness and revenge Hostile attitude Irritable Angry Sarcastic Suspiciousness Paranoid misinterpretations Difficulty in falling asleep	15 to 30

* Activity expressed in amounts of nor-epinephrine producing equivalent effects.
† Activity expressed in amounts of acetylcholine producing equivalent effects. This substance is not identical with acetylcholine.
‡ For purposes of quantitative record, the activity of this substance is expressed in amounts of acetylcholine producing equivalent effects in the unatropinized intestine, although the substance obviously is not identical with acetylcholine.

after it was learned), and may produce difficulties in thinking, recognized by vagueness, and in some individuals may produce confusion when marked.[9]

In this study, anxiety has been classified as "mild," "moderate," or "marked." Mild anxiety is recognized clinically by the subject's feeling of mild uneasiness and occasional palpitations, mild shortness of breath, and decreased attention. Moderate anxiety produces palpitations, dry mouth, taut throat, gastric distention. Marked anxiety involves all the symptoms and signs present in moderate anxiety but in more intense form, plus the urge to urinate, increased bowel movements, anxiety dreams, broken sleep, decreased retention, and possible thinking disorders. The characteristics by which anxiety is recognized can be seen in Table 1.

Biochemical Findings in the Presence of Anxiety. *Quantitative determination.* The blood of patients and subjects who both showed, and did not show, clinically the signs and symptoms of anxiety described above were investigated. It has previously been reported that the blood from anxious patients presented an increase in adrenergic substances (Diethelm, Fleetwood, Milhorat[8,24]). The adrenergic substances were investigated by quantitative pharmacologic methods, using the rabbit's duodenum as the test object. The sensitivity of this test to epinephrine and nor-epinephrine varies from 0.05 to 0.1γ. An adrenergic substance was found in the whole blood of patients and normal subjects. Attempting to quantify our results, the rabbit intestine was tested first with epinephrine and nor-epinephrine in graded amounts of from 0.1 to 1γ. The intestinal strip was washed after each test with these drugs, and the effect of 1 ml. of blood was then determined. The effect of the blood was compared with the decrease in contractions produced by the epinephrine and nor-epinephrine. The amount of epinephrine or nor-epinephrine that produces the same effect as blood is called the epinephrine or nor-epinephrine "equivalent" of the solution. The effect of the blood, epinephrine, and nor-epinephrine as measured by changes in height of contraction was measured in centimeters, and can be seen in Figure 3. If the decrease produced by the blood was greater than that of the drugs tested, a larger amount of drug was used and the blood was tested again. This was done because it seemed that the addition of blood changed the sensitivity of the organ. With this method, in 284 experiments the minimal amount of adrenergic substance in the whole blood was 0 and the maximal amount was 1.5γ per ml. In some cases, after the relaxing effect produced by the adrenergic material, a contraction was elicited. It seems that two substances having different effects were present, and the increase obtained with the blood of one would

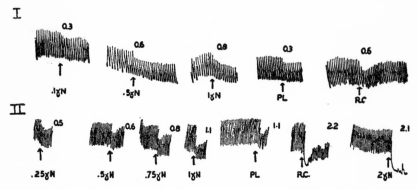

Figure 3. Quantitative Method of Measuring the Adrenergic Effect of Blood From Two Patients.

    Key: N—Nor-epinephrine
         Pl—Plasma
         R.C.—Red cells
         Numbers on top are measured in cm.

    I. Blood from a non-anxious patient. Plasma decreased the contraction 0.3 cm.; 0.1γ of nor-epinephrine decreased the contraction 0.3 cm. Plasma contained an amount of 0.1γ of nor-epinephrine equivalent. Lysed red cells decreased the contraction 0.6 cm.; 0.5γ of nor-epinephrine decreased the contraction 0.6 cm. The lysed red cells contained an amount of 0.5γ of nor-epinephrine equivalent.

    II. Blood from a very anxious patient. Plasma decreased the amplitude of the contraction 1.1 cm. One γ of nor-epinephrine produced the same decrease. Plasma had an effect equivalent to that of 1γ of nor-epinephrine. Lysed red cells produced a decrease of 2.2 cm. in the amplitude of the contraction, and 2γ of nor-epinephrine produced a decrease of 2.1 cm. The lysed red cells contained an amount of about 2γ of nor-epinephrine equivalent.

alter the quantitative results obtained by the other. This double effect has also been found by Gaddum.[17] The problem was then to find a way to suppress this interfering substance and to see if its effect was more marked in any of the different components of the blood. Blood was then separated into plasma and red cells and the red cells were lysed (see METHOD). In the red cells, the interfering substance which has cholinergic properties was absent in 208 experiments and present in six of them. In the six cases in which we found the interfering substance, incomplete separation of plasma and red cells could have been responsible for that effect. In the plasma, the cholinergic substance was present more often, although its activity disappeared rapidly. (Reference will be made to this later.) In general, one can conclude that this cholinergic material, when present, exists only in the plasma. Thus, the red cells, being free of the interfering material, were the best element on which to measure the adrenergic substance.

The concentration of the adrenergic substance was also greater in the red cells than in the plasma and whole blood, as stated earlier.[15]

Figure 3 shows the difference in amounts found in plasma and red cells. The plasma of the first blood (patient without anxiety) showed an amount of 0.100γ in comparison with 0.500γ contained in the red cells. The blood from the anxious patient showed an amount of 1γ in the plasma in comparison with 2γ in the red cells. The amounts in the whole blood and plasma were equal. On account of these results, experiments were continued in plasma and lysed red cells. In 103 experiments, the concentration of adrenergic substance in the plasma was only 34% of what it was in the red cells. It was earlier stated by this author[15] that the amount found in plasma was only 12% of what it was in the red cells. The data given here reflect a larger accumulation of experimental data, but essentially the same conclusion is reached; namely, that the amount is much greater in the red cells than in the plasma (Table 2).

TABLE 2
DETERMINATION OF ADRENERGIC SUBSTANCES IN THE
DIFFERENT COMPONENTS OF THE BLOOD

Test Objects	Red Cells		Plasma	
	Equivalents (mean)	No. of exper.	Equivalents (mean)	No. of exper.
Rabbit duodenum...............	1.14	103	0.39	103
Rat colon.....................	1.455	10	0.167	4
Rat uterus....................	0.063	19	0.022	7

Results in rabbit duodenum expressed as nor-adrenaline equivalent.
Results in rat uterus and ascending colon expressed as adrenaline equivalent.

Plasma also contains adrenergic substances but the amount is generally smaller, as the total results indicate, although in a few instances the plasma contained a greater amount than the red cells. Reliable determinations of adrenergic substance can be done, using plasma, under the following circumstances: (1) when plasma does not contain the cholinergic substance, and (2) if the plasma contains this interfering substance, tests should be repeated at different intervals until the interfering substance disappears. A specific lapse of time cannot be cited because it depends on the amount of the interfering substance found. The following example illustrates this point: ten minutes after withdrawal, one sample of plasma showed an amount of nor-epinephrine equivalent of 0.32γ, followed by an increase in tonus of 1.2 cm. Thirty minutes later, the nor-adrenergic substance was equivalent to 0.5γ and the increase in tonus diminished from 1.2 cm. to 0.2 cm.

A correlation between the amounts of adrenergic substance in red cells and plasma has not been established, and possibly a further knowledge of the metabolism of epinephrine and nor-epinephrine is required before such a correlation can be made. Experiments which clarify this point to some degree will be referred to later.

The reliability of our method was tested by using duplicate assays of whole blood, red cells, and plasma. The results were calculated as epinephrine and nor-epinephrine equivalents. No critical ratios were significant (Table 3).

Qualitative determination. The method employed proves the existence of an adrenergic substance, but does not clarify whether or not the adrenergic substance present is epinephrine. Cannon and Bacq[4] consider the substance increased during emotional states as Sympathin Excitatory. Euler[13] showed that Sympathin Excitatory is nor-epinephrine and that it showed not only excitatory properties but also inhibitory characteristics. Nor-epinephrine has been found in the adrenergic nerve[12] by biologic and colorimeter methods, in the suprarenal,[3] and in the extract of various organs.[10,11]

In order to investigate whether the substance increased was epinephrine or nor-epinephrine, a parallel quantitative test was used. The method consists of the simultaneous quantitative determination of the unknown substance, using two test objects that have different sensitivities to the known chemical substance investigated,

TABLE 3

ANALYSIS OF DIFFERENCE BETWEEN DUPLICATE SAMPLES

	Number of determinations	Range	Mean	Difference	Critical ratio	Experimental error
Nor-adrenergic sub-stance in the red cells						
Group I.......	40	0.5–3.0	1.09	0.01	0.07	±0.07
Group II......	40	0.4–3.0	1.08			
Tension substance in the whole blood						
Group I.......	48	0–49	28.50	0.21	0.24	±3.99
Group II......	48	0–51	28.71			
Resentment sub-stance in the whole blood						
Group I.......	40	0–18.3	6.18	0.86	1.4	±2.55
Group II......	40	0–16.0	5.32			

in this case, to epinephrine. Several authors have used two test objects to calculate the amounts of epinephrine and nor-epinephrine present in extracts, the one object being equally sensitive to the two drugs and the other being selectively sensitive to epinephrine. Of the test objects known to have different sensitivities to epinephrine and nor-epinephrine, we have chosen the rabbit duodenum, the rat uterus, and the rat colon. The rabbit duodenum has an equal sensitivity to epinephrine and nor-epinephrine;[3,20,28] the rat uterus is almost insensitive to nor-epinephrine, but it is the most sensitive and specific test for epinephrine.[17,28] The colon of the rat is extremely sensitive to nor-epinephrine but relatively insensitive to epinephrine.[17] As can be seen in Table 4, our results confirm the statements of the authors. It was found that the sensitivity of the rat uterus to epinephrine is 60 times what it is to nor-epinephrine (Gaddum's ratio is even larger than that of this author); that is 60γ of nor-epinephrine is needed to produce the effect of 1γ of epinephrine. The unknown substance present in the blood concomitant with anxiety was tested simultaneously in the rabbit duodenum and in the rat uterus, and then in the rat colon and in the rat uterus. (The rats' colon and uterus were treated by Jalon's method.)

TABLE 4

MINIMAL DOSES AND RATIO OF NOR-ADRENALINE TO ADRENALINE AS DETERMINED
BY DIFFERENT TEST OBJECTS, EXPRESSED IN GAMMAS OF
ADRENALINE (A) AND NOR-ADRENALINE (NA)

Test objects	Minimal dose to produce effect*		Ratio NA/A
	Gammas A	Gammas NA	
Rat colon.................	0.1γ	0.05γ	$\dfrac{0.2\text{–}0.8}{1}$
Rat uterus.................	0.003γ	0.012γ	$\dfrac{15\text{–}60}{1}$
Rabbit duodenum...........	0.05γ	0.08γ	$\dfrac{1.2}{1}$

* Sometimes the test objects are not sensitive to these doses, and larger amounts are necessary to produce an effect.

Comparison between the rabbit duodenum and rat uterus—The blood of patients separated previously into lysed red cells and plasma was tested simultaneously in these two test objects. The rat uterus tested almost exclusively epinephrine, and rabbit duodenum was equally sensitive to both drugs. If the substance present in the blood were epinephrine, the greater response should be present in the test object that is most sensitive; if the reverse were found, the substance investigated was not epinephrine, but more resembled nor-epinephrine. The results expressed as epinephrine equivalents are shown in Table 5 and Figure 2. The results of two parallel experiments showed a significant difference between the two substances. The epinephrine equivalent obtained in the rat uterus was 4% of that obtained in the rabbit duodenum. The significantly smaller response obtained in the rat uterus proves the substance increasing with anxiety is mainly *not* epinephrine.

Comparison between the rat colon and rat uterus—Next we compared the effect produced by the blood of patients with anxiety on the rat colon and rat uterus. Here again the effect produced on the colon (very sensitive to nor-epinephrine) was considerably greater than on the uterus (no sensitivity to nor-epinephrine). The difference in the amount found was significant. Amounts in the uterus were 4% of those obtained in the colon. Therefore, an adrenergic substance to which the rat uterus is not sensitive, but to which both the rat colon and the duodenum of the rabbit are very sensitive, is present in the blood of patients with anxiety.

TABLE 5

DETERMINATION OF ADRENERGIC SUBSTANCES IN LYSED RED CELLS

Parallel quantitative assay of rabbit duodenum and rat uterus

No. of experiments	Rabbit duodenum	Rat uterus	% Difference
41	1.081	0.044	4%

Parallel quantitative assay of rat colon and rat uterus

No. of experiments	Rat colon	Rat uterus	% Difference
10	1.455	0.062	4%

Results are expressed in gammas of adrenaline equivalent per/ml.

Differentiation with ergotamine—Euler and others[13] have found that ergotamine blocks the effect of epinephrine but does not modify the action of nor-epinephrine. These experiments were done in other biological tests. Experiments were performed to study the effect of ergotamine over epinephrine and nor-epinephrine in the rabbit intestine. It was found that ergotamine decreased by 73% the effect of epinephrine but did not modify the effect of nor-epinephrine (Table 6). The adrenergic substance found in the whole blood and in the red cells is also unmodified in its effect by ergotamine. A further similarity between nor-epinephrine and the adrenergic substance increased by anxiety was obtained by this method.

In order to study whether epinephrine and nor-epinephrine injected in patients could be found in red cells, and whether the injection of a known concentration of epinephrine or nor-epinephrine changed the amount detectable in the rabbit duodenum and rat uterus, the following experiment was devised: a first sample of blood was drawn and adrenergic substances were tested, then 16γ of epinephrine or nor-epinephrine were injected intravenously. Eight minutes afterwards a second blood sample was drawn from the cubital vein of the other arm and adrenergic substances were tested. The subjects were mildly to moderately anxious before the injection of the drugs. Subjectively, it was expressed as anxiety over the injection of an unknown drug; objectively, anxiety was observed by uneasiness,

TABLE 6

EFFECT OF ERGOTAMINE ON ADRENALINE AND NOR-ADRENALINE AND BLOOD ADREN-
ERGIC SUBSTANCES AS MEASURED ON THE DUODENUM OF THE RABBIT

Material	Effect	Decrease in effect*	No. of experiments
	cm. (mean)	%	
Adrenaline.....................	0.80		11
A + ergotamine...............	0.21	73	11
Nor-adrenaline.................	0.70		11
NA + ergotamine.............	0.71	0	11
Whole blood..................	0.35		9
Bl + ergotamine.............	0.35	0	9
Red cells......................	0.55		3
RC + ergotamine.............	0.56	0	3

* Decrease in effect due to ergotamine.

slurred speech produced by dry mouth, forced smile, etc. The blood obtained at that moment showed 1.2γ and 0.96γ of epinephrine equivalent in the rabbit duodenum. The results obtained before and after the injection of epinephrine and nor-epinephrine are shown in Table 7. The adrenergic material contained in the blood after the

TABLE 7

EFFECT OF INJECTION OF EPINEPHRINE AND NOR-EPINEPHRINE

	Rabbit duodeum			Rat uterus		
	I	II	Diff.	I	II	Diff.
Epinephrine (16γ).............	0.96γ	1.7γ	0.740γ	0.01γ	0.033γ	0.023γ
Nor-epinephrine (16γ)..........	1.2γ	2.0γ	0.80γ	0.00γ	0.015γ	0.015γ

injection of both drugs was found to be increased, as measured by both test objects. In the rat uterus the increase produced by the injection of epinephrine was greater than that of the effect of nor-epinephrine. The experiment suggests that epinephrine and nor-epinephrine injected could be found in the red cells, as demonstrated by the increase produced by the injection of epinephrine and nor-epinephrine. Since the rat's uterus is a better test for epinephrine, the increase produced by this drug was greater than that produced by the injection of nor-epinephrine. Furthermore, the adrenergic substance produced by anxiety was summate to the effect of the injection of epinephrine and nor-epinephrine. Sixteen γ of epinephrine were injected and an increase of 23γ was found. When nor-epinephrine was injected, an increase of 15γ was found. (This latter increase could possibly have been less since the rat uterus did not respond to the first blood. It could have been a minimal amount that was beyond the limit of the sensitivity of that particular rat.) However, in this result it is necessary to consider that the result obtained in the first determination could have been any amount less than 0.015γ to which doses that particular uterus was sensitive.

In the rabbit's intestine after an injection of epinephrine as well as nor-epinephrine, an increase was found which was considerably greater than the amount injected. There is no doubt that the increase found was related to the drug injected, since the injection of distilled water did not produce the increase. The fact that a greater amount was found than was injected could be explained by the fact that an injection of epinephrine produces the General-Adaptation-Syndrome, and the discharge of epinephrine is an integral part of the Alarm-Reaction and that during the General-Adaptation-Syndrome the adrenal medulla appears to discharge its adrenergic hormone.[26]

Amounts found in the different components of blood—The whole blood tested in the rabbit's intestine contained amounts varying from 0 to 1.5γ per ml. As mentioned previously, in the lysed red cells the amounts varied from 0.2γ to 3.500γ (Fleetwood); i.e., the red cells tested in the rabbit's intestine always contained a material that is not present in the whole blood. Gaddum has suggested that the lysed red cells contain adenine. The rabbit's duodenum is sensitive to adenine in contrast to the rat colon on which adenine has an effect different from that elicited by nor-epinephrine. Furthermore, the fact that with the whole blood no response was elicited in many circumstances probably was due to the fact that the red cells were not broken. In order to investigate the amount of adenine that the red cells contained, parallel tests between the rat's colon and rabbit's intestine were made. These tests showed that substances other than nor-epinephrine exist in the red cells that were tested by the rabbit's intestine and not by the rat's colon. This was especially evident in the subjects who did not have anxiety. No effect was found in the rat's colon, but in the rabbit's intestine amounts varying from 0.2γ to 0.4γ were found. In patients where anxiety was present both test objects showed a significant increase of adrenergic materials. The fact that the substance which increased with anxiety is not adenine is proved by the effect on the rat's colon (see Figure 2), and the significant difference found in patients with anxiety and patients with no anxiety when the blood was tested by the rabbit's intestine. As can be seen in Table 8, red cells tested in the rat's colon varied from no adrenergic substance to a maximum of 4.000γ. The amount of adrenergic substance contained in the red cells tested in the rat's uterus varied from a minimum of 0.007 to a maximum of 0.300γ.

TABLE 8

MAXIMAL AND MINIMAL AMOUNTS OF ADRENERGIC SUBSTANCES DETERMINED IN THE BLOOD OF SUBJECTS DURING DIFFERENT STATES OF ANXIETY AS MEASURED BY DIFFERENT TEST OBJECTS

Test object	Red cells			Plasma		
	Min.	Max.	No. of patients	Min.	Max.	No. of patients
Rat colon.............	−0.100*	4.000	10	−0.100*	0.500	4
Rabbit duodenum.......	0.200	3.500	58	−0.050*	1.000	58
Rat uterus.............	0.007*	0.300	18	0.007*	0.050	7

Results are expressed in gammas of adrenaline equivalent per/ml. of lysed red cells and plasma.
* The test is not sensitive below this amount.

In the plasma this adrenergic substance also has been found to increase in relation to states of anxiety in the three test objects. In the rat's colon and rabbit's duodenum amounts varying from 0 to 0.500γ and from 0 to 1.000 respectively have been found. (The test objects do not test amounts below 0.1 and 0.05 respectively.) The rat's uterus, which has an extreme sensitivity, always showed small amounts of epinephrine varying from 0.007γ to 0.050. (See Tables 2 and 8.)

In summary, this nor-adrenergic substance has been found to increase in the whole blood, plasma, and red cells. In the last two there were three different test objects: rabbit's duodenum, rat's uterus, and rat's colon.

Psychiatric and Biochemical Observation. The relationship between the intensity of anxiety and the amounts of adrenergic substance found in the blood in the three test objects is given in Table 9. In the rabbit's intestine, Figure 3 shows the effect of the blood of a very anxious patient and the blood of a patient in whom no anxiety was present. Figure 2 (Strips 1 and 3) shows the effect of blood, measured in the rat's colon, belonging to two subjects—one very anxious, and the other showing no adrenergic substance. Table 9 shows the amounts of adrenergic substance found when mild, moderate, and marked anxiety were present.

TABLE 9

AMOUNT OF NOR-ADRENERGIC SUBSTANCE CORRESPONDING TO DIFFERENT DEGREES OF ANXIETY

	Mild	Moderate	Marked
Rabbit intestine........	0.4–1γ	1–2γ	2–3.500γ
Rat colon.............	0.250–0.750γ	1–2γ	2–4γ
Rat uterus............	0.050–0.100γ	0.100–0.200γ	0.200–0.300γ

Normal subjects. Psychiatric evaluation of anxiety and determination of nor-adrenergic substance in the blood was performed in 24 normal subjects. In 17 of these subjects a parallel quantitative assay was done between (1) the rabbit's duodenum and the rat's uterus, and (2) between the rat's colon and rat's uterus.

In Table 10 a comparison of maximal and minimal amounts of adrenergic substance found in subjects and patients is shown. On the rat's colon, the blood of normal subjects with no anxiety produces no effect. The rat's uterus shows an amount of epinephrine equivalent of 0.008 to 0.020γ. The table shows that the maximum amount found in normal subjects with mild anxiety corresponds to the minimal amount found in patients (rat's colon). However, these data could be due to the fact that all the patients chosen for the experiment showed clinical anxiety from mild to marked degree.

The rabbit duodenum, on the other hand, showed that the same minimal amount of adrenergic substance was found in the blood of patients and subjects. As shown in the table, the maximum amount of nor-adrenergic substance found in the blood of subjects was 1.2γ of nor-epinephrine equivalent measured in the rabbit in-

TABLE 10

DETERMINATION OF ADRENERGIC SUBSTANCES IN THE BLOOD OF NORMAL PERSONS AND OF PSYCHIATRIC PATIENTS AS DETERMINED BY THE RABBIT DUODENUM, THE RAT COLON, AND THE RAT UTERUS

	No. of cases	Rat colon	Rat uterus
Normal subjects no anxiety............	6	0 (less than 0.1)	0.008–0.020γ
Normal subjects with anxiety..........	5	0.250–0.750γ	0.008–0.050γ
Patients with varying anxiety..........	30	0.750–4.000γ	0.012–0.500γ
		Rabbit duodenum	Rat uterus
Normal subjects mild-moderate anxiety..	6	0.4–1.2γ	0.018–0.050γ
Patients...........................	39	0.330–3.100γ	0.005–0.500γ (22 cases)

testine. This amount was found when subjects recognized subjectively the emotion of anxiety and objective signs of anxiety were manifest. However, no experimental procedure was delineated to produce anxiety in normal subjects. Our normal subjects with mild or moderate anxiety were obtained in the normal course of experimental procedure. For example, in testing the residents as a group, some of them recognized that their anxiety was due to a lecture that had to be delivered or to an interview with the director which would follow the experiments. Information about the reason for anxiety was occasionally given spontaneously, but only the description of the emotional state was requested. On some occasions we were spectators of the development of anxiety. The following case will illustrate the above: a member of the staff who had previously been tested when anxiety was not present and when the blood therefore showed minimal amounts of nor-adrenergic substances was told that he was going to be used as a subject to study the effect of a certain drug. At that moment he stated that he had a vascular anomaly which he feared might be adversely affected. He was told that the drug he was about to receive would not affect this condition. In spite of this reassurance, signs of anxiety were noticed, manifested by teasing, uneasy smiling, and slight pressure of speech. Blood was drawn before the intramuscular injection of distilled water. The blood, tested immediately before the injection of the distilled water, produced an effect of 1.2γ of nor-epinephrine equivalent (moderate anxiety). It seems clear that the reassurance received was not sufficient to stop his understandable anxiety about the effect of the drug on his vascular condition. It is interesting to note that the observed signs of anxiety were evident immediately after he was told of the injection; although the blood was drawn 10 minutes later, increasing amounts of adrenergic substance were found. Most of our normal subjects who volunteered for experiments showed mild to moderate anxiety when the injection of drugs was involved, especially if they knew the physiologic effects. The experiment shown in Table 7 illustrates the point: the subject who showed 1.2γ of nor-epinephrine equivalent knew the drug he was going to receive and told, after the experiment, that the fear of this drug was due to the fact that in one experimental class where it was injected, the animal used for the experiment died.

Control experiments in normal subjects were made to study the effect of the passage of time on the nor-adrenergic substance. Subjects were left alone in the room with newspapers and magazines to read. Blood was drawn four times at one-hour intervals. The results produced by the red cells were, respectively, 0.9γ, 0.7γ, and 1.0γ, of nor-epinephrine equivalent. There was no significant change in the amount of nor-epinephrine equivalent by the passage of time.

Marked anxiety and maximum amounts of nor-epinephrine equivalent were not found in the normal subjects. However, the type of this experiment does not permit us to discard the possibility that nor-adrenergic substances may be present in maximal amounts in normal subjects.

Psychiatric patients. In the psychiatric subjects, a wider variation in the concentration of nor-epinephrine in the blood was found as compared to that in normal subjects. Unlike normal subjects, the amounts of nor-epinephrine substances are considerable. This statement is valid for the three test objects used: rabbit duodenum, rat colon, and rat uterus. Maximal amounts of 3.500γ, 4.000γ and 0.500γ respectively have been found. Minimal amounts are equal to those of normal subjects in the rabbit duodenum and the rat uterus. In the rat colon the minimal amount in patients was 0.750γ, and in normal subjects without anxiety was zero.

Of the 150 examinations done in the red cells and tested in the rabbit intestine, only 21 patients have demonstrated marked anxiety clinically and the amount of nor-adrenergic substance has been greater than 2γ of nor-epinephrine equivalent. A great variability in the amounts of nor-adrenergic substance has been found. Figure 4 shows ten determinations performed on one patient who claimed a great deal of anxiety, and four determinations on another patient in whom anxiety was never a major complaint. These results show that

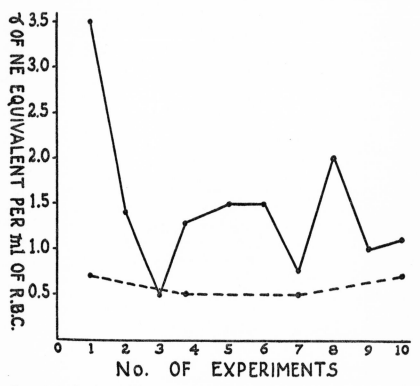

Figure 4. Comparison of Amounts of Nor-adrenergic Substance Found in Two Different Patients in Several Determinations. Dotted line indicates the results obtained in a patient who was never found anxious. Solid line indicates the results obtained in a patient who was very anxious. (The diagnosis was anxiety neurosis.)

not only is there a significant difference between patients, but also in the same individual. The patient to whom we refer had a maximum amount of 3.5γ compared with 0.5γ on another occasion.

The tendency to develop anxiety under circumstances that do not normally produce this reaction was observed clearly in one of our patients on the first administration of a drug (dibenamine) for experimental purposes (Figure 5). This 32 year old married woman had a severe anxiety neurosis of four years' duration. On the day of the experiment she was moderately anxious and had 1γ of nor-adrenergic substance in the blood. It was explained to her that the

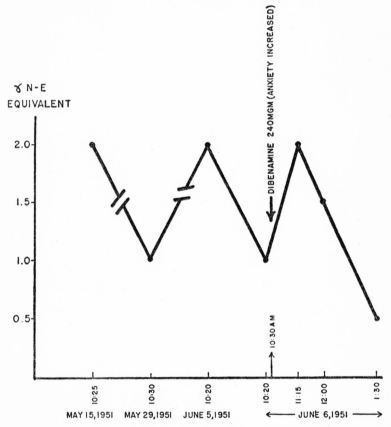

Figure 5. Effect of Dibenamine on a Patient With an Anxiety Neurosis. Key: N.E.—Nor-epinephrine.

drug was going to be given to study its effect on her emotions. Clinically she showed a marked increase in anxiety. She expressed it, "If you give me an aspirin, I will be just as anxious as I am now. It is the experiment that frightens me." A second sample of blood was taken 45 minutes after the administration of dibenamine and there was a considerable increase of the amount of nor-adrenergic substance (2γ). In another 45 minutes 1.5γ of nor-adrenergic substance was found.

The effect of extracting blood on patients who are frightened by injections was studied in the following case. This patient was a 25 year old woman who suffered from an anxiety neurosis and excessive drinking for three years. She was told that a vena puncture would be performed. Ten minutes elapsed before the test was done. The patient said that the time that she had had to wait had made her very anxious. Her blood contained 1.2γ of nor-adrenergic substance in the red cells, and 0.50γ in the plasma. It was decided to perform another test on another occasion when no warning would be given of the vena puncture that was going to take place. This was done. The results obtained when she was not aware that blood would be taken were: red cells 1.0γ of nor-adrenergic substance, plasma, 0.25γ of nor-adrenergic substance. The effect produced by the fear of vena puncture in this case was an increase of nor-adrenergic substance in the red cells as well as in the plasma.

In a few cases the amount of nor-adrenergic substance was found to be greater in the plasma than in the red cells, as opposed to the majority of results, where the amount present in the red cells was larger than the amount found in the plasma. These results occurred when anxiety was building up at the moment of extraction of blood. The two following examples will clarify the point. In one case, the patient was being made late for an important business appointment, and he was very anxious because of the delay produced by the test, and begged us to hurry. The blood showed: red cells, 0.25γ, and plasma, 0.5γ. The other subject, a physician, was told just prior to the test that he was going to have his first amytal interview. Knowing the effect of the drug, he was afraid of what he would learn about himself. The results obtained in the blood were: red cells, 0.75γ and plasma, 1.00γ.

Observations related here reflect only preliminary results, since the number of experiments is still too small to establish definite conclusions. However, they correlate with the experiments of Bain[2] and others, who state that epinephrine injected in the blood is taken up by the corpuscles and cannot be recovered from the plasma after five minutes.

Summary. A nor-adrenergic substance has been found to increase in three different test objects in relation to anxiety. It has been found to increase in the plasma as well as the red cells. It varies significantly between patients, and also in the same patient. It has been found that the amounts vary in relation to the intensity of the anxiety. Situations that produce anxiety increase the amounts found. This nor-adrenergic substance is found in normal subjects as well as in patients; however, maximum amounts have only been found in patients.

Tension

Psychological Determination. Emotional tension is produced when the dynamic factors, conscious or unconscious, involve a conflict which the person tries unsuccessfully to solve. The conflict may be within the self, between external pressure and internal desire, or where a situation is felt to be beyond the control of the self. Subjectively, it is described as a feeling of tautness, with tiredness and muscle sensations. Objectively, an effort at muscular control is observed in the patient's sitting on the edge of his chair, holding his hands tightly together, twining his feet and legs in a stiff or unnatural position. Tension, especially if it is of moderate or marked degree and, has lasted over a prolonged period of time, is usually accompanied by anxiety.

The psychologic processes are affected by emotional tension. Marked tension produces an alteration in prolonged attention (concentration). Mistakes are made in the serial subtraction of 7 from 100. Grasp, immediate memory and recall, as tested in the "Cowboy Story" of a psychiatric examination, may be affected adversely. The following signs and symptoms have been taken into consideration in determining mild, moderate, and marked tension by means of psychiatric examination. Mild tension is diagnosed when one feels taut and not relaxed. When moderate tension is present, the feeling of fatigue, localized or generalized, mild irritability, and more muscle tension are consciously present. When tension reaches a marked degree, it is accompanied by intense muscle tension, fatigue, muscular aches, irritability, short and harsh answers, headaches, and concentration or thinking difficulties (see Table 1).

Biochemical Findings in the Presence of Tension. The blood of subjects and patients who both showed and did not show the signs and symptoms described above was investigated. It had been reported before (Diethelm, Fleetwood, and Milhorat[8]) that the blood of a person suffering from emotional tension produced an increase in the tonus of the contraction of the rabbit intestine. To avoid confusion, this substance, which has an acetylcholine-like effect, will be called the "tension substance."

Comparison with Acetylcholine

Destruction of the substance—The first difference found between acetylcholine and this "tension substance" is that the latter is found in blood. It is well known that the activity of acetylcholine ceases almost immediately if it is mixed with blood because of the large amount of cholinesterase present in that element. If an acetylcholine solution is added to blood which does not demonstrate this "tension substance," this blood, tested immediately, is ineffective in causing the intestine to contract. However, Gaddum[6] showed that acetylcholine prepared from mammalian extracts had a rate of destruction in the presence of blood slower than that of pure acetylcholine. The "tension substance" is present in blood but it is not stable in this element. Its effect decreased or disappeared with the passage of time. First, experiments were done with the whole blood. Repeated tests with the same sample of blood were done after different intervals of time (5, 10, 20, and 30 minutes after the blood reached the laboratory). Diminution of the effect could be observed after five minutes. After 30 minutes it was found that its activity was reduced to ¼ of what it was previously. The decrease or complete disappearance of the activity depends on the strength originally present. Second, blood was separated into red cells and plasma. The plasma contains this "tension substance," and its effect disappeared very quickly, as in the whole blood. The lysed red cells do not contain this contracting material (see page 56). The "tension substance" exists only in the plasma when the blood is not protected by physostigmine. True cholinesterase has been found only in the erythrocytes and in the brain.[30]

Effect of physostigmine—Since the passage of minutes could alter our results so much, it was necessary to find a way to stabilize this cholinergic substance. Although this substance is not identical with free acetylcholine, the resemblance in pharmocologic effect suggested that physostigmine, which protected acetylcholine and inhibited the action of cholinesterase, might also protect this acetylcholine-like substance. The action of physostigmine over acetylcholine is a good test to distinguish acetylcholine from other substances like choline. Some writers consider the test sufficiently specific to conclude that if the effect is prolonged and increased, the substance actually is acetylcholine (Gaddum[6]). However, in studying the effect of physostigmine on the "tension substance," the following difficulties were found: Feldberg[14] states that physostigmine stimulates both the longitudinal and circular musculature. Chang and Gaddum[6] had reported that physostigmine produces an acetylcholine-like effect on the rabbit intestine. They suggest that this effect is due to a potentiation of the choline esters in the intestine, rather than to a direct action of physostigmine on the smooth muscle. In order to elucidate this point, the following experiment was performed: when 1 ml. of solution containing 200γ physostigmine was added to the muscle chamber (in 40 ml. of Tyrode solution) a cholingeric-like effect was obtained, thus corroborating the effect found by other authors. The piece of rabbit intestine was left in contact with the physostigmine solution for a period of 30 minutes at a temperature of 37.5°C. After this, the liquid was drawn off and tested on the rectus abdominis muscle of the frog. (Physostigmine is ineffective in the frog rectus.) No contraction was produced in the rectus abdominis. This experiment seems to indicate that the effect of physostigmine on the rabbit intestine is not due to a potentiation of a choline ester, since the frog rectus is sensitive to choline and choline esters; or else, that the amount used (1 mg.) was not able to potentiate the choline esters in that time. It also seems to indicate that the effect obtained with eserine is not due to a potentiation of choline esters present in the rabbit intestine, but, in corroboration with Felberg's opinion, to a stimulation of the smooth muscle fibers.

Experiments to overcome this difficulty were devised. The contracting effect of a given dose of physostigmine was studied on the isolated rabbit intestine and its effect was calculated in gamma of acetylcholine equivalent. The procedure was as follows: 20γ of acetylcholine were first tested and compared with the effect of 200γ of physostigmine per ml. dissolved in Tyrode solution (19 experiments). Agitation of the physostigmine was necessary to obtain a clear solution. The evaluation of the results showed that 200γ of physostigmine produced an effect of 18.9γ of acetylcholine equivalent with a standard deviation of 3.31. Blood with no "tension substance" gave an average of 17.1γ of acetylcholine equivalent (79 different blood samples). These two experimental facts, (1) that 200γ of physostigmine and no "tension substance" gave an average of 17.1, and (2) that 200γ of physostigmine in Tyrode solution gave an average of 18.9γ, allow us to assert that physostigmine produces an effect equivalent to no more than 20.41γ of acetylcholine equivalent. In order to be on the safe side, we subtracted 20γ from the amount found. If acetylcholine is added to blood with physostigmine, it is able to preserve its activity as is shown by the following example: a sample of blood which did not show any "tension substance" was taken. In 5 ml. of this blood, one mg. of physostigmine was dissolved, then 200γ of acetylcholine were added to 1 ml. of this eserinized blood to produce a solution of 100γ per ml. The effect that 1 ml. of this blood produced in the rabbit's intestine was compared with the effect produced by a solution of acetylcholine containing 100γ per ml. The results measured in cm. showed that the effect of acetylcholine dissolved in eserinized blood was 0.4 cm. larger than the effect produced by acetylcholine dissolved in distilled water. These results indicate that the amount of physostigmine used was large enough to protect 100γ of acetylcholine. The greater effect obtained with acetylcholine in eserinized blood was due to the contracting effect of physostigmine.

We then compared the effect produced in the rabbit's intestine by two samples of the same blood to one of which physostigmine was added. Blood was extracted and 5 ml. were placed in a test tube containing 1 mg. of physostigmine. Slow agitation was necessary to mix the components. In 51 experiments we found a cholinergic effect present in both blood samples, provided that assays were made within a short time after extraction and that the amount was larger than 30γ in the sample containing physostigmine. However, this cholinergic substance was not found in the blood without physostigmine when the time lapse from the moment of taking the blood and the performance of the test was longer than 30 minutes, or when the concentration of the "tension substance" was not large. When blood was separated into red cells and plasma, a comparison was done between whole eserinized blood and plasma. The same phenomenon described above was observed: (1) substances were present in both samples when the amounts were greater and when the time lapse between extraction of blood and performance of the test was not long. (2) Effects obtained with blood eserine were greater and more frequently found. In some samples of blood this cholinergic material was present when none was found in the blood containing physostigmine. This seems to indicate that other contracting substances not related to tension states exist on some occasions in some patients.

The highly correlated incidence of the two effects obtained with plain blood and blood eserine permits us to believe that we were dealing with the same substance, and that the larger effect obtained with eserinized blood and the greater frequency of its appearance was due to the inhibition of cholinesterase produced by physostigmine.

Quantification of "tension substance." On adding physostigmine, a certain stabilization of the substance was achieved and a quantitative evaluation was attempted using crystalline acetylcholine as the reference standard. As it happens, in almost any pharmacologic test, a great variability in the response to a given dose of acetylcholine is observed. This variability occurred among rabbits of the same species as well as different species, and furthermore, in different strips of the same animal. A dose of 20γ will produce an increase of 2 cm. in one animal, and the same dose will elicit a different response (4 cm.) in another.

It is interesting to notice here the parallel resemblance observed in duplicate tests between the response to acetylcholine and to the "tension substance" present in the blood. For example, one gut gave a response of 4.9 cm. to 50γ of acetylcholine and a response of 5 cm. to the blood sample. The other duplicate gave a response of 2 cm. to the same amount of acetylcholine and a response of 2.1 cm. to the blood sample.

The "tension substance" produces an increase in the tonus of the contraction of the rabbit's intestine that is slower in onset and development than the one produced by crystalline acetylcholine. The effect of acetylcholine is an immediate contraction of the rabbit intestine. Blood containing the "tension substance" produces a more gradual change in contraction, and is recorded as a slow-grade curve, while the acetylcholine manifests its action in an almost vertical line (see Figure 6).

The following procedure was employed to estimate the amounts of "tension substance" in the blood. The intestine was treated with different concentrations of acetylcholine. Doses of 20γ and 50γ of

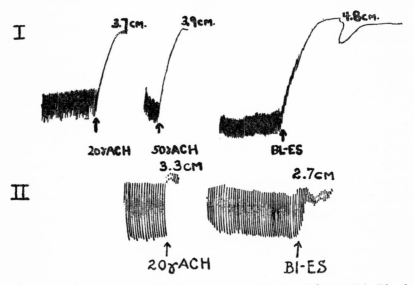

Figure 6. Quantitative Method of Measuring the "Tension Substance" in Blood
From Two Patients.

Key: 20γ ACH—20γ of acetylcholine
Bl-Es—Blood containing 0.2 mg. of eserine
Numbers on top are measured in cm. and numbers on bottom indicate the amount of acetylcholine and blood added.

I. Blood (plus eserine) of a very tense patient produced an increase of 4.8 cm. in tonus of contraction. Fifty γ of acetylcholine produced an increase equal to 3.9 cm., and eserine alone elicited an affect equivalent to that of 20γ acetylcholine. Therefore, the blood contained an amount greater than 30γ of acetylcholine.

II. Blood (plus eserine) of a non-tense patient produced an increase in tonus of contraction equal to 2.7 cm., which is less than the effect of 20γ of acetylcholine (effect of eserine alone). Therefore, the blood did not contain the "tension substance."

acetylcholine were added and then the effect of blood eserine was tested. The action of the blood was registered when a complete effect was obtained (on an average of 3.4 minutes). In our experiments, acetylcholine in the amount of less than 10γ produced an increase in the amplitude and in the tonus of the contraction of the rabbit intestine. However, doses of 10γ or more produced a decrease in the amplitude of the contraction and a great increase in the tonus. On this account, measurements were taken with only the increase in tonus being considered, and not the amplitude. The effect obtained with blood eserine in the rabbit intestine was similar to that obtained with acetylcholine; when the blood contained a greater concentration of "tension substance," a considerable increase in tonus is brought about with a loss of the amplitude of contraction. When the amounts of "tension substance" were small, the contractions of the intestine were maintained.

After the blood with physostigmine is added to the test object, the tonus of the rabbit intestine muscle usually is increased, and liberal washing and the passage of time are not successful in restoring the original tonus. The preparation is unsuitable for another test and a further control with acetylcholine cannot be done. Calculations of the action of the blood were made with the effect produced by the doses of acetylcholine added before the blood.

The quantitative evaluation was done comparing the effect produced by 20γ and 50γ of acetylcholine with the effect produced by the blood. Four different values have been obtained with the different blood samples:

1. Blood produced an increase in tonus measured in cm. that is less than or equal to the one produced by the 20γ of acetylcholine. In this case the "tension substance" was not present.
2. The increase in tonus produced by the blood is greater than the increase produced by 20γ of acetylcholine but less than that produced by 50γ of acetylcholine.
3. The increase in tonus produced by blood is exactly 50γ of acetylcholine.
4. The effect of the blood is greater than the one produced by 50γ of acetylcholine.

As happens in all quantitative tests, exact data are obtained when the amounts of the substance investigated are identical with those of the reference standard. The imaginary points between two known references are bound to be less exact than the known references. When the effect of blood corresponds to #1 or #3, no calculation is necessary. When the effect of blood corresponds to #2 or #4, two calculations have been applied in these cases: (a) a direct plot of the result of each experiment, and (b) a direct proportion measured by the effect produced by 50γ of acetylcholine.

Analysis of duplicate samples of the same blood have indicated the best way to measure the results. Measurements in centimeters of the effect of 20γ, 50γ of acetylcholine and the effects of the blood are taken. The results are more accurate when the tonus of the preparation does not change.

Results of the duplicate assays were analyzed by statistical methods, and showed no significant differences, giving a critical ratio of 0.23.

Effect of the "tension substance" on the frog. A parallel quantitative test was done between the abdominis rectus of the frog and the rabbit duodenum in order to study the similarity of the "tension substance" with acetylcholine. Acetylcholine produced an effect in both test objects. Seventy-three experiments of this type were performed; in 65 of them there was a positive correlation; in five tests the substance was found in the rabbit but not in the frog, and in three tests a response was found in the frog but not in the rabbit. Of the 65 tests in which a positive correlation was found, in 35 of them the substance was present in both tests and in 30 of them no effect was produced in either the frog or the rabbit (see Table 11). The high correlation

TABLE 11

PARALLEL QUANTITATIVE TEST OF FROG RECTUS ABDOMINIS AND RABBIT INTESTINE

	Tension substance	Resentment substance
Present in both tests.....	35	15
Rabbit only............	5	12
Frog only..............	3	20
In neither test..........	30	24

among the tests indicates that we are dealing with a substance which is active in both test objects. However, the amounts found in the frog are considerably less than those found in the rabbit. The maximum amount found in the frog corresponds to the maximum amount found in the rabbit, and vice versa. The results of this experiment showed that the "tension substance" can also be tested in the frog rectus abdominis muscle.

Effect of hyoscyamine. It is well known that atropine or its more active levo-isomer, hyoscyamine, blocks the effect of acetylcholine. In order to continue our study of acetylcholine and the "tension substance," the effect of hyoscyamine was studied. The effect of 1 ml. of blood before and after 50γ of hyoscyamine were added was studied. The results were that in some experiments no "tension substance" appeared without adding hyposcyamine, in others hyoscyamine completely prevented the effect, and in others both substances were present. In the latter cases, no correlation of the effect could be found before and after hyoscyamine. In some instances the amounts were greater before hyoscyamine, and in some instances they were smaller. The only explanation for that seemingly confusing result is that we were dealing with two different substances, one of which is blocked by hyoscyamine and the other which is not modified by that drug, and indeed requires hyoscyamine to bring out its action. This second cholinergic substance seems to be related to a different emotional state and we shall refer to it later.

In summary, we have found in the blood a substance which has the following properties: (1) it has an acetylcholine-like effect on the duodenum of the rabbit, and on the abdominis rectus of the frog; (2) it is protected or potentiated by physostigmine; (3) its action is blocked by hyoscyamine, and (4) when physostigmine was not used to inhibit the cholinesterase, this substance could be demonstrated only in the plasma which does not contain true cholinesterase, whereas none could be demonstrated in the red blood cells which do contain cholinesterase.

Amounts found. Following the method of calculation stated above, the amounts of the "tension substance" found in the blood of subjects and patients has varied from 0 to 70γ of acetylcholine equivalent. The results of 305 experiments have been: in 179 experiments amounts from 5 to 70γ have been found: in 126 determinations the substance has been absent. In the frog, amounts from 0 to 9γ of acetylcholine equivalent have been found.

Psychiatric and Biochemical Observations. This cholinergic substance was investigated in relation to emotional tension in patients and subjects in whom tension may or may not have been present. A correlation between the presence of the substance and emotional tension was established. In the blood of subjects and patients with mild tension, amounts from 5 to 15γ of acetylcholine equivalent were found. Moderate tension increased the amount from 15 to 30γ of acetylcholine equivalent. Marked tension produced amounts from 30 to 70γ.

A comparison of two samples of blood, one from a patient with marked tension, and the other obtained from a patient in whom emo-

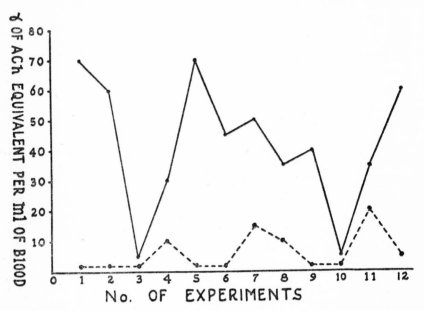

Figure 7. Comparison of Amounts of "Tension Substance" Found in Two Different Patients in Several Determinations. Dotted line indicates the results of 12 determinations in a patient who was mildly to moderately tense (Patient A). Solid line indicates the results of 12 determinations in a patient in whom tension was one of the main symptoms (Patient B).

tional tension was minimal or not detectable, is shown in Figure 6. Twelve determinations of the amounts of "tension substance" were made in two other cases. (See Figure 7.) Patient B showed greater amounts of tension (70γ acetylcholine equivalent) and the tension substance was present more constantly in the blood as compared with patient A, in whom the "tension substance" was never as high (less than 25γ) and who, in the majority of the tests, did not show any "tension substance."

Normal subjects. Psychiatric evaluation of tension and determination of "tension substance" in the blood was performed in 24 normal subjects. The blood of the same subjects was tested on different occasions. In total, 64 determinations of the "tension substance" were done in normal subjects in different emotional conditions. In 20 of these determinations "tension substance" was present. Different determinations in the same people indicate that on some occasions the "tension substance" was present and on others was absent. The maximal amount of "tension substance" was 70γ of acetylcholine equivalent. In some instances the situation that produced the tension was developed in our presence. The following example illustrates the point: a 23 year old single technician was being taught how to perform a vena puncture. She failed three times; then someone else tried and also failed. At that moment it was noticed that she was trembling. A test was performed on her and a great amount of "tension substance" was found (45γ). The "tension substance" developed within about 10 minutes after the first attempt. Other tests performed on the same person when no tension was present had been zero.

Another subject was a member of the staff who was taken for the study of the effect of 1 cc. of saline injection. Blood was taken before the injection and it showed no cholinergic substance; then he was left for one hour alone in a room. A second test was done after this time had elapsed, and revealed an increase in tension (17γ). On being questioned about it, he disclosed that he had been thinking about an involved conflict situation over which he could not make up his mind.

The injection of drugs evoked tension in two of eight cases. In each case, tension and corresponding amounts of "tension substance" were found before the injection (23γ and 25γ), while at two previous examinations no "tension substance" was found. These two subjects said that their desire to cooperate in the experiment conflicted with the fear that they would show undesirable traits of personality. It was observed in our group of control subjects that manifestations of anxiety with the injection of unknown drugs was more frequent than tension.

Psychiatric patients. In the psychiatric patient group, it was found that the "tension substance" varied from patient to patient and within the same person as can be seen in Figure 7. It was increased at one time or another in all the disease entities. The maximal amounts of "tension substance" found in this group did not differ from those found in normal subjects but occurred more frequently. Amounts greater than 30γ of acetylcholine equivalent have been found in 71 experiments.

An example may illustrate: the patient was a 23 year old girl who suffered from migraine and had been drinking heavily for six months. One cause for her tension was her father's objectionable behavior which had distressed her severely for many years. Migrainous attacks occurred frequently when she lived at home. Tension improved after receiving ambulatory psychotherapy. A sample of blood was taken when tension was not obvious and no cholinergic substance was found in the blood. During a one-hour interview she was induced to talk in detail about the intolerable situation with her father for which she had not been able to find a solution. Immediately following the interview, the tension substance in the blood was found to be marked (30γ). She complained of headache and when she returned home she became intoxicated.

Summary. A cholinergic substance has been found in two different test objects (rabbit intestine and frog rectus abdominis) in the presence of emotional tension. It varied significantly between patients and also in the same patient. Situations that produce emotional tension increase this substance in the blood. The substance has been found in normal subjects as well as in patients, and the amounts varied in relation to the intensity of the emotional tension.

Resentment

Psychological Determination. Resentment is an emotional reaction of bitterness about an injury and a desire for revenge. These hostile emotions are frequently repressed, while in others they are continually relived. The dynamic factors are to some extent conscious. Resentment is characterized by a feeling of being rejected, with corresponding feelings of loneliness and sadness. Resentment may be unacceptable to the subject and produce anxiety and humiliation. It can cause tension, in the struggle against this unacceptable emotion, or can become fear of the consequences if the hostile feelings were to be made overt. Others may become frightened by the observed expressions of resentment or react with anger. These responses may create additional emotional reactions in the resentful subject.

In this study, resentment has been classified as "mild," "moderate," and "marked." In a state of mild resentment, there are bitterness and hostility. When resentment is moderate, a critical attitude toward others is evident, expressed in sarcasm and complaints. Marked resentment is characterized by a desire for revenge, sometimes an indulgence in phantasies of revenge, suspiciousness, and sometimes paranoid misinterpretations (see Table 1).

Biochemical Findings in the Presence of Resentment. In 1946 it was observed by Milhorat and co-workers[8,23] that a cholinergic effect was obtained in the blood of patients only by adding hyoscyamine to the rabbit intestine. Experiments were carried out to observe the effect with blood before and after the addition of hyos-

TABLE 12

CONCOMITANCE OF "RESENTMENT SUBSTANCE" AND "TENSION SUBSTANCE"

Cases	Resentment subst.	Tension subst.
102	+	+
61	+	−
88	−	+
42	−	−

cyamine (Table 12). Four different results were obtained in 293 experiments:

(1) The cholinergic effect appeared only before hyoscyamine was added (88 experiments) and not after hyoscyamine was added.

(2) The cholinergic effect appeared only with hyoscyamine (61 experiments) and not before hyoscyamine.

(3) The cholinergic effect appeared before and after hyoscyamine, but the effects were different in magnitude and did not show any correlation (102 experiments).

(4) No effect was observed with or without hyoscyamine (42 experiments).

A working hypothesis was suggested; i.e., that the effect was produced by two substances,[8] one already described as "tension substance," stopped by hyoscyamine, and another, which appeared only when hyoscyamine was added to the sample. This hypothesis would explain the different effects obtained. However, the third effect, i.e., when the cholinergic effect was obtained before and after hyoscyamine, needs further clarification, as other hypotheses could account for the results obtained.

The cholinergic effect obtained after hyoscyamine could be due to the "tension substance" according to the following facts: (1) the amount of hyoscyamine added is not enough to stop completely the effect of the "tension substance"; (2) the "tension substance" is stopped by hyoscyamine, but the instance when the cholinergic effect appears after hyoscyamine is due to the presence of atropine esterase; (3) the "tension substance" is not stopped by hyoscyamine.

In order to study the validity of statements (1) and (3), experiments were done to determine what amount of hyoscyamine was necessary to stop the effect of 100γ of acetylcholine. Two amounts of hyoscyamine were tested: 10γ and 50γ respectively. Hyoscyamine produced a decrease in tonus of the contraction. The procedure followed was: 100γ of acetylcholine was tested first and the usual contraction was produced. After washing, 50γ of hyoscyamine was added; over this dose after 30 minutes, 100γ of acetylcholine dissolved in distilled water was added. After 10γ of hyoscyamine, 100γ of acetylcholine produced a slight increase in some cases, but 50γ of hyoscyamine completely stopped the effect. These results proved that 50γ of hyoscamine are able to stop the effect of 100γ of acetylcholine. These results eliminate the possibility that the amount of hyoscyamine is not enough to stop the effect of the "tension substance" completely; also the objection is eliminated that the cholinergic effect obtained with hyoscyamine is due to the destruction of hyoscyamine by the atropine esterase present in the black rabbits used (see explanation below). That is to say, that in some cases the effect with hyoscyamine was obtained because of the fact that this drug was destroyed by the atropine esterase, and the results would be the effect of only one substance.

Glick [19] showed that in certain species of rabbits, atropine esterase exists, and that this enzyme is genetically determined. The gene for it is in the same chromosome as the gene which determines the extent of the black coat. This enzyme is stopped completely by physostigmine; the entire reaction takes five hours. In our experiments, the following species were used: chinchilla, checker, and dwarf Dutch, which have some black in their coats. The fact that 50γ of hyoscyamine was able to stop the effect of 100γ of acetylcholine seems to indicate that atropine esterase did not exist in our rabbits, or if it did exist, its action was not potent or quick enough to destroy the effect of the amount of hyoscyamine added. The third possibility, that the "tension substance" is not blocked by hyoscyamine is eliminated by the number of cases (88) in which the "tension substance" is present only without hyoscyamine.

Effect of physostigmine on hyoscyamine. In order to investigate whether this "resentment substance" was also increased by physostigmine, experiments were carried out in vitro to study the effect of physostigmine on an intestine previously treated with hyoscyamine. As stated before, physostigmine produces a contracting effect on the rabbit intestine. In other experimental procedures, some authors have studied the inhibitory effect of hyoscyamine over physostigmine. Langley and Kito[22] claimed "that all the contraction in striated muscle produced by physostigmine which is considered to be of central origin may be decreased or stopped by a few milligrams of atropine." Schwetzer and Wright[25] said that the excitatory effect of eserine is slightly reduced in the atropinized animal, but, however, they concluded that eserine can produce marked central excitation following the injection of atropine.

In order to study the effect of hyoscyamine on physostigmine, the following procedure was used: 20γ of acetylcholine was added to the rabbit intestine to determine the sensitivity of the preparation. The physostigmine (0.2γ per ml.) produced in 20 experiments a minimal effect or no effect after hyoscyamine (50γ). The contracting effect of physostigmine was definitely decreased with the addition of hyoscyamine as can be seen in Figure 8.

Quantification of "resentment substance." On account of the variability of the response observed in different animals and in different strips, the effect obtained was quantified taking acetylcholine as the standard. The strips by which the resentment factor was going to be measured were treated in the following way. Twenty gammas of acetylcholine were added to the strip, which was then washed with 120 cc. of Tyrode solution. When the intestine had recuperated its contraction, the strip was treated with 50γ of hyoscyamine. One millilitre of blood eserine was added, and the effect measured in centimeters from the base line to the lower line (or tonus) and compared with the effect of 20γ of acetylcholine added previously.

Duplicate samples of the same blood were done in two different strips of the same rabbit. The results were calculated as acetylcholine equivalent. The difference between duplicates was not statistically significant.

Comparison with the "tension substance." (1) Amounts found: Analysis of the results obtained in the blood samples when both tension and resentment substances were obtained was done. The difference in amount found is statistically significant. Not only is the amount found significantly different, but when both substances are present there is not any correlation between either; that is to say, the "tension substances" could be found marked and the "resentment substances" low, and vice versa.

(2) Destruction: In the experiments done without physostigmine the "resentment substance" seemed to be more stable than the "tension substance." We have said before that "tension substance" protected with physostigmine could be recovered entirely after 30 minutes. In order to study the rate of destruction of the "resentment substance" and the effect of physostigmine in its protection and to compare the two substances, the blood was tested at different intervals of time. In plain blood, the "resentment substance" lost its activity in 30 minutes. In blood protected with physostigmine, the "resentment substance" lost its activity in 30 minutes.

These results point to the fact that physostigmine does not protect the "resentment substance," differing in this respect with the protection given to the "tension substance."

Effect of the "resentment substance" in the frog. A parallel quantitative assay was made using the rabbit duodenum and the abdominis rectus of the frog. The "resentment substance" was not shown by the latter test, and was only present in the rabbit duodenum previously treated with hyoscyamine.

The "resentment substance" differs from the previously discussed "tension substance" in that (1) they vary independently; (2) it is not only not blocked by hyoscyamine but needs that drug to evidence its effect; (3) physostigmine protects the "tension substance" and does not affect the "resentment substance," and (4) the "tension substance" affects the function of the abdominis of the frog whereas the "resentment substance" does not have any effect on that test object. It can be stated definitely that the "resentment substance" is not acetylcholine because it is not preserved by physostigmine, not stopped by hyoscyamine, and does not show the effect on the abdominis rectus of the frog.

Amounts found: Following the procedure described above, 314 samples of blood have been analyzed. Of these, the resentment factor has been found present in 169 and absent in 145. The amounts found in the 169 samples ranged from 4 to 30γ of acetylcholine equivalent. The blood produced an increase from 0 to 3.9 cm.

Psychiatric and Biochemical Observations. The "resentment substance" has been found to increase in normal subjects and in psychiatric patients, when on psychiatric observation emotional resentment is present. In mild resentment, amounts of "resentment substance" expressed as acetylcholine equivalent range from 2 to 8γ. In patients with moderate resentment, the blood contains amounts of 8 to 15γ, and in marked resentment amounts range from 15γ to 26γ. Figure 8 shows the effect of the blood of a very resentful person compared to the blood obtained from a non-resentful patient. The blood from the first person produced an increase of 3.4 cm. compared with the other where no effect was observed.

Normal subjects. Psychiatric evaluation of resentment has been done in six normal subjects. A total of 17 determinations was done in several different emotional states. In six of these determinations, the "resentment substance" was present. The maximum amount found in this group was 14γ of acetylcholine equivalent per centimeter. Different determinations on the same person indicate that the "resentment substance" was present whenever the emotion of resentment was found. The following case is an illustration:

A laboratory technician who had been with us for two years learned on the day before the test that another technician who had been here a shorter time was receiving a larger salary. She was pleasant and in a good mood on the day of the test, the incident of the day before apparently forgotten. However, resentment (7γ) was found in the blood test. Interviewed again, the subject stated that she had been angry. She did not feel she could express her anger to her constant

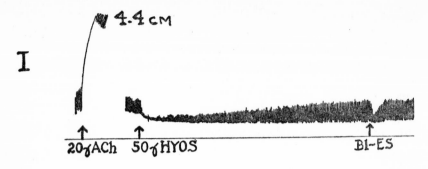

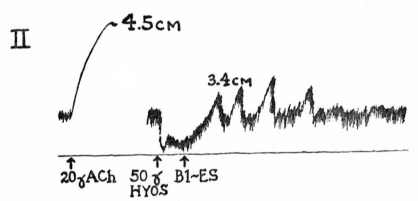

Figure 8. Quantitative Method of Measuring the "Resentment Substance" in the Blood From Two Patients.

    Key: ACH—Acetylcholine

           HYOS—Hyoscyamine

           Bl-Es—Blood containing 0.2 mg. of Eserine

           Numbers on top are measured in cm. The numbers on bottom indicate the amount of acetylcholine and blood added.

    I. Blood from a non-resentful patient. Blood produces no increase in the contraction.

    II. Blood from a very resentful patient. Blood produced an increase of 3.4 cm. in the tonus of the contraction equivalent to that of 15γ acetylcholine.

companion, the other technician. Similar results were obtained in other instances when staff members developed resentment which they were not willing to display.

    Psychiatric patients. In the psychiatric patient group it was found that the "resentment substance" varied from patient to patient and within the same person. Figure 9 shows nine and 10 biological assays performed in two persons respectively, one of whom was very resentful most of the time and the other mildly to moderately resentful. As can be seen, sometimes the resentful person did not present psychological resentment or "resentment substance" in the blood, and sometimes the more resentful person had amounts similar to those of the first one.

The maximal amount found in this group was higher than in normal subjects. No experiments, however, have been carried out to pro-

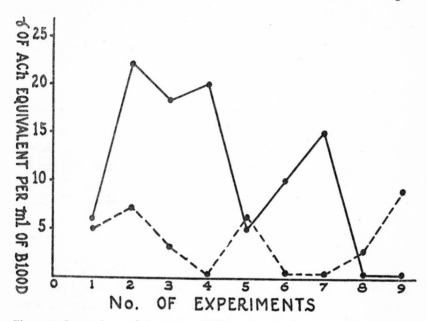

Figure 9. Comparison of Amounts of "Resentment Substance" Found in Two Different Patients in Several Determinations. Dotted line indicates the results of nine determinations in a patient who was mildly to moderately resentful. Solid line indicates the results of nine determinations in a chronic alcoholic patient who was markedly resentful.

duce resentment in normal persons. One hundred and forty-seven patients were examined in a total of 314 experiments. Resentment has been negative in 145, and increased amounts of varying degree have been found in 169. Amounts greater than 10γ have been found in 51 cases.

An example may illustrate the production of resentment in one patient. This 23 year old man suffered from a compulsion neurosis. Three determinations of blood showed mild resentment (from 6γ to

8γ), and marked tension (from 30γ to 50γ). In order to increase his emotional reaction, the nurses were instructed to stop him from performing his ritual. This was done, and in the three next assays the blood showed amounts that varied from 16 to 17 to 12γ of "resentment substance" in the blood, and "tension substance" remained high (30 to 60 to 45γ).

In summary, a contracting substance which correlates with emotional resentment has been found by means of the rabbit intestine technique. It varies with the intensity of the emotion and varies significantly from subject to subject, and within the same subject. It has been found that resentment-producing situations can develop it.

Study of Complex Emotional Reactions

Considering the whole individual in which the emotions and biochemical substances occurred, the following points must be analyzed: (1) the presence of more than one emotion and the interrelationships of one to another; (2) a comparison of the time lapse between the development of the emotions and of the substances in the blood; (3) frequency of the appearance of specific emotions and (4) physiological findings.

The blood studies have corroborated the psychiatric evaluation and simultaneous occurrence of two or more different emotions has been a source of difficulty as much from the psychiatric point of view as from the biochemical. Improvement of the psychiatric and biochemical methods has permitted a better evaluation of the different emotions and substances in the blood.

When the adrenergic substances were discussed it was mentioned that in some cases adrenergic and cholinergic substances were found simultaneously and that it was a source of error in the quantitative determination. In order to eliminate the possibility of error the whole blood was separated into red cells and plasma. (Mixture experiment in vitro.) The cholinergic substance was not found in the red cells and the quantitative determination of adrenergic substance was possible without error. The quantitative determination of nor-adrenergic substance in plasma was possible, allowing time for the cholinergic substance to be destroyed since the rate of destruction of nor-epinephrine is insignificant compared with the rapid destruction of the cholinergic substance. On the other hand, the cholinergic substance was preserved by means of physostigmine. From the psychiatric and biochemical points of view, seldom have we been able to find a single emotion, and this was only possible when the emotion was mild in intensity.

In every instance where anxiety was marked, tension, mild or moderate, existed; and vice versa, if tension was marked, mild anxiety was found. Sometimes both were marked. Tension, however, seemed more able to appear as a separate emotion than did anxiety. Resentment could be found alone; i.e., as the only marked emotion. Sometimes it was associated with tension; other times with anxiety, or all three emotions would be marked. As can be seen in Figures 4, 7, and 9, there are some patients who have a tendency to develop one particular emotion instead of another. In other words, if these patients are confronted with a disturbing situation, they develop anxiety mainly, while others develop tension in a similar situation.

Another difficulty arises from the fact that the presence of one emotion may give rise to the development of others. A further complication may arise with the use of drugs which, for instance, may reduce tension but be accompanied by an increase in anxiety (see page 105).

Analyzing the amounts of these three emotions in the group of normals, (24) it was found that the emotions of anxiety and resentment were never marked, and the respective substances in the blood were present in moderate amounts. However, tension reached concentrations that were equally as marked as those found in patients. These findings seem to correlate with statements in literature; tension could be present in healthy persons as a response to stress. When the injection of drugs involved normal people, (8 subjects) they reacted with mild anxiety. The results were compared with those obtained when the extraction of blood was involved. Of this group, only three reacted with tension. No resentment was found, which was expected, since they had volunteered for the experiment.

In the psychiatric group, (147) each of the three substances was found very much increased. Anxiety, tension, and resentment factors have been marked in all the psychopathologic entities studied.

It was of interest to study how long after the emotion was produced the concomitant substance could be recovered in the blood. Experimental productions of anxiety and tension prove that the substance could be recovered 10 minutes afterwards. Well controlled production of resentment proved to be a difficult task. The emotions of anxiety and tension disappeared rapidly when the disturbing factors had been abolished. However, resentment seems to be a long-lasting emotion; in three normal cases, resentment was found 24 hours after the emotional provocation. In alcoholics, we observed that the resentment was growing until it reached such a point that the craving for alcohol appeared.

The most common of the three emotions studied was tension which was found in 121 of 328 determinations. Marked degree of tension was found in normals but not marked anxiety and resentment. Marked amounts of anxiety (over 2γ) have been infrequently found in patients.

In order to understand the possible effect of these substances on the subject's physiology, consideration needs to be given to the fact that epinephrine and acetylcholine are interrelated in their mechanisms. Acetylcholine has been reported to increase the heartbeat. Epinephrine and nor-epinephrine depress the effect of acetylcholine. Nor-epinephrine and epinephrine affect the heart. The effects of epinephrine are potentiated by actylcholine. Furthermore, different individuals and different species act differently in response to acetylcholine (Altschul[1]).

The pulse rate was determined in 86 instances before blood was withdrawn. Analysis of the results indicate that no definite correlation exists between the pulse rate and the amount of nor-epinephrine or of "tension substance" in the blood. Individuals have particular pulse patterns, and the effect of adrenergic or cholinergic substances will depend on individual reaction. The following example will illustrate this point:

A relation between increased pulse and increased anxiety and tension has been observed. To differentiate which of the two substances act upon the pulse, cases in which only one of the substances was present were analyzed.

A patient with a pulse rate of 88 per minute and a concentration of nor-adrenergic substance in the blood of 2.8γ, and showing no tension or resentment, was given dibenamine, after which the pulse rate dropped to 76 and the anxiety factor to 1.1γ. This seems to indicate that pulse rate is an individual thing and that minimal or moderate amounts of nor-adrenaline raise the pulse rate considerably, whereas in others a maximal amount of nor-adrenergic substance produces the same increase in rate.

In a case where anxiety was not modified by mephenesin and tension increased, the pulse rate rose from 76 to 92 ("tension substance" increased by 13γ). This time the change seemed to be related to the increase of tension.

In a case having a pulse rate of 96 with 1γ of nor-epinephrine equivalent and 36γ of "tension substance" the pulse rate fell to 76 with no "tension substance," and nor-epinephrine equivalent increased to 1.5γ. When the nor-adrenergic substance was reduced to 0.5γ and "tension substance" increased to 24γ, the pulse rate rose again to 88. After a mephenesin injection, this same patient had no "tension substance," the nor-epinephrine equivalent was 1.5γ, and the pulse rate was 76 per minute. It is interesting that the same pulse rate was registered on both occasions when nor-epinephrine equivalent was 1.5γ.

In a patient where tension was constant, the pulse rate varied from 86 to 108 when nor-epinephrine equivalent increased from 0.7γ to 1γ.

The pulse rate of another patient dropped from 82 to 72 when "tension substance" disappeared (32γ to 0), and nor-adrenergic substance increased from 1.2 to 1.4γ.

In summary, the pulse rate has been correlated in some cases with an increase of nor-epinephrine equivalent, and in others with an increase of "tension substance."

The effect of "tension substances" on the perspiration of the hand was observed in some patients. Marked perspiration was brought about with marked tension, whereas no perspiration was found when the "tension substance" was absent. However, other patients with equal tension showed mild perspiration.

Headache was observed in one patient (see page 82) with a high degree of tension and 30γ of "tension substance." No complaints of headache were elicited when the "tension substance" was absent. The same tension did not give rise to the same complaint in other patients.

Trembling was found to be correlated with marked tension (see page 81). However, other patients did not tremble when the same degree of tension was present (Case C). These same patients did not have perspiration, trembling, or headache when tension was not present. A definite relationship was observed between the amount of tension and the perspiration, trembling or headache respectively; however, the same amount did not produce this effect on other patients.

These findings confirm in human beings what has been established in animals—that different individuals react differently to acetylcholine (Atschul[1]), and that it is a constitutional difference or different biochemical pattern (Williams[29]) as well as the emotions involved.

Effect of Alcohol on Emotions. In this study, a patient is considered to suffer from chronic alcoholism if he uses alcohol to such an extent that it interferes with a successful life (including physical, personality, and social aspects), and he is either not able to recognize this effect, or is not able to control his alcohol consumption although he knows its disastrous results. This takes into consideration undesirable effects on physical and mental health, on family and group relationships, and on work and other responsibilities. In addition, patients were studied who were excessive drinkers, and others who began to drink heavily when they suffered from a psychiatric disorder.

The majority of alcoholics in this study have psychoneurotic or psychopathic personalities. About one-half did not suffer from a well-defined psychiatric illness. Their personalities were rigid and somewhat compulsive; they were persons in whom self-reliance was not sufficiently developed. A strong need for power and an overestimation of their capacity, together with a feeling of inferiority and frustrated ability to judge performance were present. They were ambitious, but lacked the capacity for sustained effort. This type was chiefly resentful without anxiety. The other type responded quickly to situations with anxiety, having at the same time the inability to endure anxiety and being lacking in self-control.

Included also are patients in whom chronic alcoholism developed in the setting of schizophrenic or depressive illnesses.

The duration of drinking of the 57 patients studied had ranged from 10 months to 23 years. The psychiatric and biochemical investigations showed that during a period of several months, emotional variations occurred. The patients did not display these emotions in any marked form and they were usually unaware of them. Repeated observations of the same patient were made two to 26 times. Definite individual patterns of emotional behavior occurred. As stated above, in the majority of patients resentment seemed to be the most important emotion. In a smaller group anxiety and related tension were important and, less frequently, tension without anxiety. In no case has marked anxiety without tension been found.

The following routine was established with this group: during the first four weeks of hospitalization, patients were not permitted to leave the clinic. Afterwards they were permitted to visit the city and were urged to return to their regular work routine. Such patients worked from 9 a.m. to 5 p.m. and returned to the hospital for dinner. They were permitted to be absent Saturday afternoon and Sunday and spent weekends with their families or friends. Every evening when the patient returned to the hospital, his urine was tested for alcohol.

In two patients who had permission to visit the city, heavy alcoholic drinking occurred. When their records were analyzed it was found that the "resentment substance" had increased considerably during the two weeks before the use of alcohol and that the test afterwards showed absence of this substance in the blood.

Experiments to confirm this observation under supervised conditions were delineated. A control test using water instead of alcohol was done before giving alcohol to the patient. This experiment was done to study the effect that the change of environment, conversing with the nurse, and the passage of one hour had on the emotions. In this case, the patient was told that we wished to know his reaction to being with people in order to understand his emotional reaction better. The patient used for this experiment was an alcoholic with a psychopathic personality, in whom anxiety developed very easily. Before the test, he had moderate anxiety (1.5γ) and mild resentment (4γ). After the ingestion of water the blood showed a decrease from moderate to slight anxiety $(.75\gamma)$ and a slight increase in resentment (to 7γ). Since the results of this experiment showed no significant effect, alcohol was offered in the following manner to 11 patients. The formulation given to the patient by his own psychiatrist was: it was of interest for the physician to know the relation of his emotions to his craving for alcohol, and that an experiment involving the ingestion of alcohol was being offered in order to learn such effect. All of our patients willingly agreed and no emotion was elicited by the proposal of the experiment. Three to four hours after breakfast, the patient was moved to a pleasantly furnished experimental room outside the ward. The patient was accompanied by a nurse with whom he had never had contact previously. She asked him to drink six ounces of whiskey in the way that he habitually drank, diluted or undiluted, in amounts of two ounces every 10 minutes. Usually 30–50% water was added. The nurse remained with the patient during the whole experiment but did not make conversation if the patient did not feel like talking, but did engage in conversation if the patient wished to do so. After the patient had returned to his floor, the nurse recorded the content of the previous conversation.

Alcohol was given to 10 patients by the procedure described above.

TABLE 13

ALCOHOLIC PATIENTS BEFORE AND AFTER INGESTION OF ALCOHOL (WHISKEY)

Case	Amount	Nor-adrenergic subst.						Tension subst.*			Resentment subst.*		
		Red cells			Plasma			Whole blood			Whole blood		
		Be-fore	After		Be-fore	After		Be-fore	After		Be-fore	After	
			10 min.	22 hr.		10 min.	22 hr.		10 min.	22 hr.		10 min.	22 hr.
1	6 oz.	.4γ‡	.3γ	—	—	—	—	—	—	—	11γ	0γ	—
2	6 oz.	.8γ	.5γ	—	.4γ	.1γ	—	45γ	0γ		22γ	4γ	
3	4 oz.	.7γ	.4γ		.1γ	.05γ	—	39γ	0γ	—	3	—	—
4	2 oz.	1.0γ	.6γ	—	.15γ	—	—	13γ	0γ	—	14γ	8γ	—
5	6 oz.	.5γ	.9γ	1.0γ	0γ	.2γ	0γ	20γ	0γ	—	10γ	5.5γ	2.5γ
	6 oz.	1.0γ	.5γ	—	0γ	.1γ	—	0γ	0γ	—	2.5γ	6.0γ	—
6	6 oz.	1.9γ	.7γ	1.3γ	.5γ	.6γ	0γ	30γ	0γ		13γ	5γ	
7	6 oz.	1.3γ	1.0γ		.5γ	.5γ	.5γ	45γ	15γ		12γ	7.5γ	3γ
	8 oz.		1.0γ	.75γ		.5γ			0γ				0γ
8	6 oz.	3.0γ	1.8γ	—	.25γ	.5γ	—	38γ	30γ	—	11γ	14γ	—
9	4 oz.	0.4γ	0.5γ	0.5†γ	1.0γ	0.9γ	1.2†γ	29.5γ	28γ	0†	3.6γ	0γ	0γ†
10	6 oz.	1.25γ	0.5γ	0.75γ	0.7γ	0.2γ	—	13γ	6γ		5γ		0γ

* Measured as acetylcholine equivalent.
† After 30 minutes.
‡ Whole blood.

Analysis of the emotions and of the biochemical factors in the blood present before the ingestion of alcohol showed mild to moderate anxiety and moderate to marked resentment in all of them. Tension was present in different amounts in 9 of the 10 patients. No patient in this group showed signs of intoxication.

As may be seen in Table 13 and Figure 10, the effect of alcohol on the resentment factor in the blood was striking. Alcohol pro-

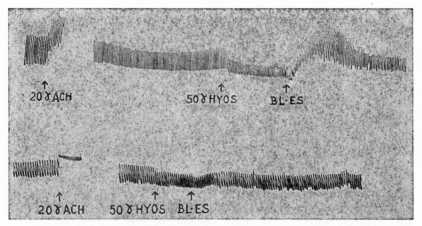

Figure 10. "Resentment Substance" Before and After Alcohol.
Key: 20γ ACH—20γ acetylcholine in 1 ml. of distilled water.
 50γ HYOS—50γ hyoscyamine in 1 ml. of distilled water.
 Bl-ES—1 ml. of blood with 0.2 mg. physostigmine.
Upper line: Resentment factor equivalent to 20γ of acetylcholine before ingestion of alcohol.
Lower line: Resentment factor equivalent to 2γ after the ingestion of 6 ounces of whiskey.

duced a decrease or complete disappearance of this resentment factor. This effect persisted to the point where, 22 hours after the ingestion of alcohol the concentration of the resentment factor was usually as low as that observed immediately after drinking, in some cases a slight increase to 2γ was observed during this period.

Of the 10 patients studied by this procedure, nine had tension substances in amounts ranging from 13γ to 45γ. Following the ingestion of alcohol, the "tension substance" disappeared completely from the blood streams of six patients. Anxiety was slightly decreased in some of the cases and not modified in others, except in one patient in whom anxiety was decreased from marked to moderate and tension was not modified.

The amount of alcohol given and the disappearance of the substances in the blood seem to be related. In most cases a complete disappearance of the "resentment substance" was produced with six ounces of alcohol; however, it was observed in one case in which the "resentment substance" was very high (22γ) that the alcohol produced a considerable decrease (4γ), but a craving for more alcohol was expressed. Because of these facts it was decided to perform a third test on another patient who also asked for more alcohol.

This patient (Case 7, Table 13) was an immature 19 year old psychopathic girl who had a great need for affection but who felt constantly rejected. She was anxious to do well. On November 1st, 1950, she presented moderate anxiety with no indication of resentment. The blood findings were 2γ of nor-epinephrine, no "tension substance," and mild "resentment substance" (3γ). On November 18th, increasing irritability was noticed but she felt less anxious. The blood findings were nor-epinephrine 1.3γ, "tension substance" 45γ, and "resentment substance" 12γ. Six ounces of alcohol were given to her, after which she was at ease, but had mild resentment and wanted to have another drink. In the blood a reduction of nor-epinephrine from 1.3γ to 1γ, was found; the "tension substance" dropped from 45γ to 15γ, and the "resentment substance" from 12γ to 7.5γ. Two additional ounces of alcohol were given and the patient felt relaxed and had no desire to drink further. No signs of tension or resentment were in evidence. The blood findings were: nor-epinephrine 1γ, and the tension and resentment substances had disappeared completely. Twenty-two hours later the patient still felt at ease but seemed mildly anxious. The blood finding showed a further reduction of nor-epinephrine (.75γ) and no tension and slight resentment (3γ) were found.

In two patients, anxiety seemed to be the essential emotion. Both were immature psychopathic persons with a longing for affection and feelings of rejection. Neither of them was a chronic alcoholic patient, but both resorted to alcohol to alleviate anxiety and the resulting tension. Dependence on alcohol was merely one of the psychopathologic symptoms.

One of these patients was a 40 year old physician (Case 3). When returning from service and finding difficulty in starting a practice, he developed anxiety, and in February 1949, the picture of a full-fledged anxiety neurosis developed. This man has always been a quiet, reserved, insecure person, dependent on his family, and had never married. In seven tests he showed at times moderate resentment and marked tension, and usually mild to moderate anxiety. On June 6, 1950, an experiment was performed. He received four ounces of whiskey, felt exhilarated, not anxious, was relaxed, and had lost the feeling that "something was hanging over him."

Before alcohol:

nor-adrenergic substance 0.7γ "tension substance" 39γ
"resentment substance" 3γ

After alcohol:

nor-adrenergic substance 0.4γ "tension substance" 0γ
"resentment substance" trace

The psychiatric analysis of the patient as well as this experiment indicated that resentment did not play a role in his drinking. The need to obtain relief from tension was related to his anxieties.

The second case (Case 4) presented moderate anxiety (1γ), slight tension (13γ), and moderate resentment (14γ). After the ingestion of alcohol, tension and anxiety disappeared while resentment was only slightly reduced (8γ).

Special mention should be given the following case. This 38 year old woman had been drinking heavily for 20 years (Case 8). Her diagnosis was chronic alcoholism in a psychopathic personality. She felt ashamed of her drinking but refused to consider it a problem, and was unwilling to cooperate fully in treatment. When asked to participate in the experiment she was afraid that we would let her appear drunk in front of the other patients, and she was very resentful towards us. Before drinking the alcohol she presented marked anxiety (3γ), tension (38γ), and moderate resentment (11γ). After having drunk six ounces of whiskey, she seemed less anxious but became suspicious. The blood showed a considerable decrease in anxiety (to 1.8γ) and a decrease of "tension substance" (to 30γ). The "resentment substance" was increased by the amount of 3γ (from 11γ to 14γ).

Another 32 year old patient (Case 5) had had mild anxiety (.5γ), moderate tension (20γ), and resentment (10γ) before taking alcohol; afterwards he felt depressed and was very anxious on account of this depression. Tension was shown by the test to be abolished and resentment decreased, although anxiety had increased (.9γ). This was the only subject in whom anxiety increased with alcohol. The next day the anxiety was only moderate (1γ) and he was again given six ounces of whiskey. This time the anxiety decreased (.5γ) but mild resentment was shown (6γ).

In summary, alcoholic patients presented resentment as a predominant emotion. This emotion was especially intense when an urge to drink was present. Before alcohol was given experimentally all of them had resentment to a moderate or marked degree. Tension was present in approximately two-thirds of the cases studied and anxiety was not as important in some of them. Alcohol decreased or abolished completely the emotion of resentment as well as the biochemical substance that accompanied the symptoms; it also decreased anxiety and tension when these latter emotions were present.

The results of these experiments stimulated the following question: why do not other patients who suffer from emotional disturbance seek relief from alcohol since alcohol produces such relief in the alcoholic patient? Comparing the personalities of alcoholic patients with those of subjects with other nosologic entities, it was observed that alcoholics seem to be more resentful individuals. This was confirmed by the biochemical study which showed that the "resentment substance" was higher and more persistent in alcoholic patients than in non-alcoholic subjects.

In order to answer the question formulated above, alcohol was given to patients who did not suffer from chronic alcoholism and the effect on them was observed. Five non-alcoholic patients (three males and two females) were studied. The psychiatric diagnosis of these patients were: A—compulsion neurosis, B—anxiety hysteria, C—psychopathic personality with anxiety neurosis and morphine addiction, D—psychoneurotic depression, E—psychopathic personality with mild depression.

The analysis of their emotions showed that, compared with the alcoholic group described above, these patients showed considerably less resentment. As a group they showed more anxiety and tension (Table 14).

TABLE 14

NON-ALCOHOLIC PATIENTS BEFORE AND AFTER INGESTION OF ALCOHOL (WHISKEY)

Case	Amount	Nor-adrenergic subst.						Tension subst.*			Resentment subst.*		
		Red cells			Plasma			Whole blood			Whole blood		
		Before	After 10 min.	22 hr.	Before	After 10 min.	22 hr.	Before	After 10 min.	22 hr.	Before	After 10 min.	22 hr.
A	6 oz.	.66γ	1.0γ	1.0γ	.33γ	1.0γ	.75γ	28γ	31γ	37γ	7.0γ	1.4γ	9γ
B	6 oz.	1.0γ	.9γ	—	.6γ	.4γ	—	26γ	28γ	—	17γ	0γ	—
C	6 oz.	1.0γ	.9γ	—	.4γ	.6γ	—	45γ	28γ	—	5.5γ	3γ	—
D	6 oz.	2.3γ	.7γ	—	.6γ	.3γ	—	0γ	0γ	—	6.4γ	4.5γ	—
E	4 oz.	2.8γ	3.3γ	—	.5γ	.25γ	—	38γ	31γ	—	5.6γ	7.9γ	
	6 oz.		.7γ		.5γ				25γ			0γ	

* Measured as acetylcholine equivalent.

Alcohol was given to them following the same procedure used with the alcoholic group. Alcohol modified tension in two cases. Case C showed a decrease of 17γ and Case E of 13γ. In two cases where marked anxiety was present a considerable reduction was observed. Case D showed a decrease from 2.3γ to 0.7γ and Case E from 2.8γ to 0.7γ. In the other three who had had moderate anxiety before, no modification was found. The effect of alcohol on the "resentment substance" in non-alcoholic patients was doubtful since the resentment was mild, ranging from 5.5 to 7.0γ in four patients. In Case B resentment was marked (17γ) and was abolished with ingestion of alcohol.

If we compare these results with those of the alcoholic group, the greatest difference is seen in the effect of alcohol on the tension factor. In the alcoholic group, tension, when present, was abolished and in the non-alcoholic group was not reduced as much. Alcohol decreased the resentment factor in the alcoholic and non-alcoholic groups. However, in the non-alcoholic group resentment was the least intense of their emotions and did not seem to play an important role in their psychiatric disorder. Anxiety, when moderate or marked, was decreased in both groups. However, the decrease of the anxiety factor in the alcoholic group seems to be more constant than in the non-alcoholic group, where it was not reduced in three cases.

If we analyze the cases closely, some interesting data are obtained. Case A, a 28 year old man with obsessive-compulsive features, complained of tension in the struggle against his compulsions. He said that alcohol did not relieve his symptoms and he would drink only after persuasion. Before taking alcohol he had mild anxiety $(.66\gamma)$, marked tension (28γ), and mild resentment (7γ) (directed mainly against the nurses who had prevented him from carrying out his compulsions). After the ingestion of alcohol, there was an increase in anxiety (1γ) and tension (31γ), and the mild resentment decreased (1.4γ). During the afternoon he felt nauseated and intoxicated. This was the only case of the whole group where intoxication was provoked by the amount of alcohol given. A test the next day showed a further increase of tension (37γ), while anxiety remained the same (1γ), and resentment was slightly increased (9γ).

In another patient of this group (Case C), the tension was reduced with the drinking from 45γ to 28γ. This case was a 40 year old woman who in one period of her life had been a heavy drinker but had stopped the use of alcohol after she became a morphine addict.

The two patients in whom anxiety was decreased under the influence of alcohol had used alcohol to alleviate their symptoms (Case D—psychoneurotic depression, and Case E—psychopathic personality with mild depression). Alcohol made them feel more at ease but did not change the depressed mood to cheerfulness.

The two other patients (Case A—compulsion neurotic, and Case B—anxiety hysteria) never drank; alcohol failed to decrease their anxiety.

In summary, alcohol did not reduce emotional tension or the "tension substance" among five non-alcoholic patients studied.

Effect of Various Drugs on Emotions. Since alcohol had not produced relief in this group of non-alcoholic patients, a comparative study of the effect of other drugs was made: mephenesin, sodium amytal, dexedrine, dibenamine, and morphine. A preliminary report of our findings is presented here.

A comparison of the effect of alcohol with that of mephenesin, dexedrine, and sodium amytal was made in the same patients. The effect of mephenesin was likewise compared with that of alcohol, sodium amytal, dexedrine, and dibenamine. These comparisons are seen in Table 15. We were interested mainly in studying the effects of different drugs on the same patient.

TABLE 15
EFFECT OF DIFFERENT DRUGS IN THE SAME PATIENT

| Case | Drugs | Time† | Amount | Nor-adrenergic substance | | Tension substance* | | Resentment substance* | |
| | | | | Red cells | | Whole blood | | Whole blood | |
				Before	After	Before	After	Before	After
A	Whiskey	30	6 oz.	0.66γ	1γ	28γ	31γ	7.0γ	1.4γ
A	Mephenesin	120	.5 gm.	—	—	30γ	39γ	3.6γ	6γ
A	Dexedrine	30	15 mg.	1.0γ	0.99γ	28γ	0γ		
B	Whiskey	30	6 oz.	1γ	0.9γ	26γ	28γ	17γ	0γ
B	Mephenesin	60	.5 gm.	0.82γ	0.81γ	33γ	0γ	12γ	9γ
C	Whiskey	30	6 oz.	1γ	0.9γ	45γ	28γ	5.5γ	3γ
C	Morphine	30	.03 gm.	1.5γ	1.0γ	27γ	44γ	0γ	0γ
E	Whiskey	30	6 oz.	2.8γ	0.7γ	38γ	25γ	5.6γ	0γ
E	Sod. amytal	‡	.5 gm.	0.8γ	0.9γ	32γ	7γ	8.5γ	0γ
F	Whiskey	30	6 oz.	1.25γ	0.5γ	13γ	6γ	5γ	0γ
F	Sod. amytal	‡	.5 gm.	0.5γ	0.5γ	36γ	0γ	0γ	0γ
G	Mephenesin	60	.5 gm.	1γ	0.75γ	31γ	0γ	3.1γ	1.3γ
G	Sod. amytal	‡	.5 gm.	1.2γ	0.8γ	33γ	0γ	2γ	2γ
H	Mephenesin	60	.5 gm.	1.7γ	1.5γ	30γ	0γ	3γ	9γ
H	Dibenamine	90	240 mg.	2.3γ	0.5γ	36γ	24γ	0γ	0γ

* Measured as acetylcholine equivalent.
† In minutes.
‡ Immediately.

Mephenesin was given to two of the five non-alcoholic patients. In one patient (B) it caused a disappearance of tension after one hour (33γ to 0). Anxiety was not modified (.82γ to .81γ) and the moderate resentment decreased slightly (12γ to 9γ). In the other patient (A), mephenesin failed to produce any effect. After two hours, the tension had increased slightly (from 30γ to 39γ). Dexedrine was then given to this patient. The patient said dexedrine was the only drug that made him feel better. As can be seen in the table, dexedrine succeeded in relieving tension (28γ to 0).

Patient E was given sodium amytal, which succeeded in decreasing tension (32γ to 7γ), while alcohol in the same patient had produced a reduction from 38γ to 25γ.

To patient C who was diagnosed a morphine addict, morphine was given, and whereas alcohol had produced a decrease in tension (from 45 to 28γ), 30 minutes after the injection of ½ gr. of morphine, "tension substance" had increased from 27γ to 44γ. The patient had been withdrawn from morphine several weeks previously. To be given morphine distressed her considerably because she became aware of her still existing desire for the drug. This emotional reaction was not accompanied by guilt, and her anxiety was changed little (from 1.5γ to 1.0γ).

In summary, mephenesin, dexedrine, and sodium amytal caused a decrease of the "tension substance" when alcohol had failed to do so.

A comparison of the effect of mephenesin with dexedrine in one patient indicated that the latter substance was active when mephenesin was ineffective. Comparisons between mephenesin and sodium amytal were done in a depressed 56 year old man, (Case G). Both drugs abolished the "tension substance." Mephenesin decreased the "tension substance" from 31γ to 0, and sodium amytal from 33γ to 0.

Mephenesin and dibenamine were given to a 32 year old woman (Case H) who suffered from a severe psychoneurosis with tension, depression, and depersonalization. It is interesting to observe that dibenamine abolished the "tension substance" after 1½ hours (from 36γ to 0), but a new increase was found after three hours (24γ). Anxiety and the nor-epinephrine-like substance was reduced from 2.3γ to .5 after three hours. Mephenesin abolished the tension after one hour (from 30γ to 0), but anxiety remained unchanged (from 1.7γ to 1.5γ).

Effect of mephenesin on alcoholic and non-alcoholic patients— Mephenesin was given to 10 patients, two of whom had increased alcohol consumption when depressed. The second blood determination (between 20 and 30 minutes) did not show any appreciable modification of nor-adrenergic substance, "tension substance" or "resentment substance" (four cases). It was therefore decided to do a second test at one hour and 15 minutes and at two hours on the other 6 patients. Results obtained with the longer time interval were a decrease of the "tension substance" from a mean of 33.9γ to 13.4γ. Anxiety and resentment were not modified. However, in three of the patients the tension was unmodified and in three patients there was a decrease but not a complete disappearance. In the two patients who had found that alcohol offered them relief, a reduction of tension and "tension substance" was produced by mephenesin.

Mephenesin did not affect the "resentment substance." In one case the decrease was slight (12γ to 9γ). However, only one of the patients on whom this experiment was performed had marked resentment (20γ) and it was not affected (20γ). The others had mild resentment (4 to 5γ) which was also not affected, while in others the resentment seemed to increase (from 3γ to 9γ).

Mephenesin did not seem to modify anxiety. In only one patient was there a considerable reduction, which was probably not due to the drug but rather to psychological reasons. This 20 year old man (anxiety neurosis) was taken to the experimental room without being given an adequate explanation. When the blood was taken he became very apprehensive and anxious, and he refused to take the mephenesin pill unless his own doctor were called. After reassurance by his own psychiatrist, he took the pill. Nor-epinephrine decreased considerably in this subject (from marked 2.4γ to mild 1γ).

Further studies of the effect of mephenesin on the emotions and substances in the blood were made in collaboration with Dr. Louis J. West. A placebo was used to abolish the effect of suggestion that the ingestion of drugs can produce. (The Squibb Co. furnished us with a placebo which was identical in form and taste to the mephenesin tablets.) The doses used were large and proportional to body weight. The results obtained were similar to what was described before; some of the emotional tension and "tension substance" was reduced with the ingestion of mephenesin. An interesting observation was made in relation to the anxiety and nor-adrenergic substance. It was found that not only was anxiety not reduced, but it seemed to have been increased.

One of the patients was a 32 year old woman who suffered from anxiety neurosis and tension headaches. These headaches were relieved by large amounts of sherry. On the morning of the test she showed marked anxiety and tension, and mild resentment. (The chemical findings were: nor-adrenergic substance 1γ, "tension substance" 35γ, "resentment substance" 0.) After having received mephenesin (2 gm.), her anxiety and resentment increased and tension disappeared. (The chemical findings were: nor-adrenergic substance 1.8γ, "tension substance" 0, "resentment substance" 3γ.)

Another patient was a 55 year old successful man who had been a heavy drinker for many years. The patient showed moderate anxiety (1.0γ), marked tension (30γ), and mild resentment (2.3γ). After mephenesin had been given, the patient's anxiety seemed clinically the same but the chemical substance had increased to 1.7γ. Tension and resentment disappeared (0). In a second test the same patient showed similar findings.

Effect of sodium amytal on alcoholic and non-alcoholic patients— It was described before that (1) the effect of sodium amytal on non-alcoholic patients was more effective than alcohol, and (2) sodium amytal was just as effective as mephenesin in reducing emotional tension and "tension substance" in one patient who suffered from a depression and used alcohol excessively during his illness. The effect of sodium amytal was studied in a chronic alcoholic patient who showed marked tension (36γ) at the moment of the test. This was reduced to zero 10 minutes after .5 gm. of sodium amytal had been administered intravenously.

A total of four patients were studied in this way. In all of them tension was reduced and the "tension substance" disappeared in the blood 10 minutes after the injection. However, these four patients presented tension (30γ to 40γ) as the main emotion. They had only mild anxiety (.5 to 1.2γ) and mild resentment (0 to 8.5γ), and the effect of sodium amytal on these two substances could not be appreciated because of the small amounts present before the injection.

In summary, mephenesin and sodium amytal reduced emotional tension and the concomitant substance in the blood of alcoholic and non-alcoholic patients.

CONCLUSION

The significance of the emotions of anxiety, tension, and resentment was studied in relation to alcohol consumption in patients who were chronic alcoholics or excessive drinkers. The definition of these emotions, subjective descriptions and objective signs as used in this study, are outlined in the beginning of this presentation.

Anxiety is accompanied by the presence in the blood of a substance similar to nor-epinephrine in its effect on the rabbit duodenum, and the rat colon and uterus. Like nor-epinephrine, it is not inhibited by ergotamine. Nor-epinephrine and epinephrine were recovered from the red cells after injection of these drugs in patients. Nor-epinephrine and epinephrine are able to summate their effects with the nor-adrenergic substance produced in anxiety.

Anxiety was observed to be mild to moderate in normal subjects, and marked in some of the psychiatric patients. The concentration of the "anxiety substance" in the blood corresponded to the intensity of the emotional reaction.

The substance is decreased significantly by dibenamine. Alcohol and sodium amytal produce a slight reduction in the nor-adrenergic substance. Mephenesin has no effect on this substance.

Tension produces a cholinergic-like substance, the effect of which may be demonstrated by the frog and rabbit preparations. The effect is increased by physostigmine and prevented by hyoscyamine.

The amount of this substance was marked in normal and psychiatric subjects. Experimentally-produced emotional tension increased the "tension substance" in the blood. In some instances, mephenesin, sodium amytal, and dexedrine reduced the concentration of this substance in the blood. Dibenamine also reduced the substance, although this was explainable as a secondary phenomenon of reduction of nor-epinephrine.

Tension was completely abolished in alcoholic patients and slightly modified in non-alcoholics by the ingestion of six ounces of whiskey. In these experiments the "tension substance" in the blood disappeared in the alcoholic patients and was slightly decreased in the non-alcoholics.

Resentment produces a contracting substance which is manifested when tested on the rabbit duodenum previously treated with hyoscyamine. This substance had no effect on the frog abdominis rectus muscle.

Amounts of the "resentment substance" were consistently higher in alcoholic patients than in non-alcoholic subjects. This "resentment substance" was reduced significantly in alcoholic patients by alcohol, and not by the other drugs investigated. In non-alcoholic patients resentment was affected less by consumption of alcohol than in alcoholic patients.

A comparison of the effects of alcohol in alcoholic and non-alcoholic patients showed that emotional tension as well as the "tension substance," and in others resentment as well as the "resentment substance" were reduced more significantly in the alcoholic group.

Both emotional tension and "tension substance" were reduced in the alcoholics and non-alcoholics by certain other substances; mainly, mephenesin, sodium amytal, and dexedrine. No drug was found to decrease the resentment and "resentment substance."

BIBLIOGRAPHY

1. ALTSCHUL, R.: Cholinergic sensitivity. *J. Nerv. & Ment. Dis., 99:*895, 1944.
2. BAIN, W. A., GAUNT, W. E. and SUFFOLK, S. F.: Observations on the inactivation of adrenaline by blood and tissues in vitro. *J. Physiol., 91:*233, 1937.
3. BÜLBRING, E. and BURN, J. H.: Liberation of noradrenaline from adrenal medulla by splanchnic stimulation. *Nature, 163:*363, 1949.
4. CANNON, W. B. and BACQ, Z. M.: Studies on the conditions of activity in endocrine organs. *Am. J. Physiol., 96:*392, 1931.
5. CANNON, W. B. and DE LA PAZ, D.: Emotional stimulation of adrenal secretion. *Am. J. Physiol., 28:*64, 1911.
6. CHANG, H. C. and GADDUM, J. H.: Choline esters in tissue extracts. *J. Physiol., 79:*255, 1933.
7. DIETHELM, O., DOTY, E. J. and MILHORAT, A. T.: Emotions and adrenergic and cholinergic changes in the blood. *Arch. Neurol. & Psychiat., 54:*110, 1945.
8. DIETHELM, O., FLEETWOOD, M. F. and MILHORAT, A. T.: The predictable association of certain emotions and biochemical changes in the blood. In *Life Stress and Bodily Disease.* Baltimore, Williams & Wilkins, 1950.
9. DIETHELM, O. and JONES, M. R.: Influence of anxiety on attention, learning, retention and thinking. *Arch. Neurol. & Psychiat., 58:*325, 1947.
10. EULER, U. S. V.: A sympathomimetic pressor substance in animal organ extracts. *Nature, 156:*18, 1945.
11. ———: A substance with sympathin E properties in spleen extracts. *Nature, 157:*369, 1946.
12. ———: A specific sympathomimetic ergone in adrenergic nerve fibers (sympathin) and its relations to adrenaline and nor-adrenaline. *Acta physiol. scandinav., 12:*73, 1946.
13. ———: Sympathin E and nor-adrenaline. *Science, 107:*422, 1948.
14. FELDBERG, W. and ROSENFELD, P.: Der Nachweis eines acetylcholinartigen Stoffes im Pfortaderblut. *Arch. ges. Physiol., 232:*212, 1933.
15. FLEETWOOD, M. F.: Determination of adrenergic substance in blood related to anxiety. *Am. J. Physiol., 166:*314, 1951.
16. FLEETWOOD, M. F. and DIETHELM, O.: Emotions and biochemical findings in alcoholism. *Am. J. Psychiat., 108:*433, 1951.

17. GADDUM, J. H., PEART, W. and VOGT, M.: The estimation of adrenalin and allied substances in the blood. *J. Physiol., 108:*467, 1949.
18. GLICK, D.: Studies on specificity of choline esterase. *J. Biol. Chem., 125:*729, 1938.
19. ———: Further studies on specificity of choline esterase. *J. Biol. Chem., 130:*527, 1939.
20. HOLTON, PAMELA: Noradrenaline in adrenal medullary tumors. *Nature, 163:*217, 1949.
21. JALON, DE P. G., BAYO, J. B. and DE JALON, M. G.: *Farmacoterap. actual, 2:*313, 1945.
22. LANGLEY, J. N. and KATO, T.: The physiological action of physostigmine and its action on denervated skeletal muscle. *J. Physiol., 49:*410, 1914.
23. MILHORAT, A. T. and DIETHELM, O.: Substances in blood of patients during emotional states. Effect on isolated rabbit intestine. *Fed. Proc., 6:*165, 1947.
24. MILHORAT, A. T., SMALL, S. M., DOTY, E. J. and BARTELS, W. E.: Probable mechanism by which somatic changes in certain emotional states are mediated. *Proc. Soc. Exper. Biol. & Med., 53:*23, 1943.
25. SCHWEITZER, A. and WRIGHT, S.: The action of eserine and related compounds and acetylcholine on the central nervous system. *J. Physiol., 89:*165, 1937.
26. SELYE, H. The Physiology and Pathology of Exposure to Stress. *Acta. Inc. Med. Pub.,* Montreal, Canada. 1st Ed., 1950.
27. WELSH, J. W.: The pituitary responses of frog's heart and rectus abdominis to acetylcholine. *J. Cell. & Comp. Physiol., 23:*59, 1944.
28. WEST, J. B.: The estimation of adrenaline in normal rabbit's blood. *J. Physiol., 106:*418, 1947.
29. WILLIAMS, R. J., *et al.:* Individual metabolic patterns, alcoholism, genetrophic diseases. *Proc. Nat. Acad. Sc., 35:*265, 1949.
30. ZELLER, E. A. and BISSEGGER, A.: *Helvet. chim. Acta., 26:*1619, 1943.

FAMILIAL AND PERSONAL BACKGROUND
OF CHRONIC ALCOHOLICS

MANFRED BLEULER, M.D.

INTRODUCTION

The plan for this study originated from the assumption that psychiatry is in need of new and systematic research on the families and on the premorbid personalities of patients with practically all mental conditions. It is true that a great amount of work has been done along these lines. Some well known results of these studies belong to the general psychiatric knowledge of our days, but on the whole the really important and helpful conclusions of family and personality studies in psychiatry are still rather scanty. Among the many reasons for this partial failure of genetics in psychiatry, one seems to be outstanding. The findings on the families and premorbid personalities of mental patients have frequently been misinterpreted on the basis of prejudices and one-sided oversimplifications. Workers who were interested in heredity usually took it for granted that a familial incidence was due to hereditary factors. They forgot the possibility that a morbid attitude on the part of a relative might influence a person quite independently of heredity, by education, by frustration of many kinds, by identification, and so on. The opposite is true for many students of interhuman relationships who frequently assume only psychological influences of one relative on another, rejecting the possibility of hereditary factors. The fact needs to be remembered that the observation of the familial incidence in a morbid condition in itself never allows a decision to be made whether this incidence is due to hereditary or environmental factors or to the interrelationship of both. Neither is it permitted to draw definite conclusions from the observation that a morbid condition frequently arises in persons with certain premorbid peculiarities, like schizophrenia in schizoid persons. The

110

premorbid peculiarities might well be a predisposition or an early manifestation of the morbid process, or they might be connected with it in many other ways. We are in need of studies which do not only count the number of different morbid conditions among the relatives of mental patients, but which consider *at the same time* the influence of the morbid relatives on the patient's environment, particularly his early identifications.

The questions which arise in a modern study of the familial and personality background of psychiatric patients are therefore much more differentiated than formerly, as might be illustrated by the following schema (Table I):

TABLE I

DIFFERENT RESEARCH PROGRAMS IN PSYCHIATRIC FAMILY STUDIES

1. *Older approach*—assumption that a mental condition is an inherited damage little dependent upon environmental influences.	2. *Older approach*—assumption that a mental condition is the result of environmental influences little dependent on heredity.	3. *Modern approach*—attempt to study heredity and environment in their interrelationships or even as an entity.
First task: To count the morbid conditions in the families of the index cases and to investigate the stable premorbid personality background of the index cases.	To study the environmental influences, particularly the early influences of father and mother, on the patient.	Both as under 1 and 2. The morbidity of the relatives has to be studied as a possible stress for the patient. On the other hand, the environmental stress has also to be examined as a sequel of the patient's and the relatives' constitution. The interrelationship between the patient's environment and the cases of disease among the patient's relatives has to be studied in detail.
Ultimate task: To discover a Mendelian formula which demonstrates the hereditary transmission of the disease and the predisposing constitution.	To understand the personality make-up and the disease as a result of the discovered environmental situation.	How is the patient's environment formed by his inborn reaction pattern and how are his personality and his morbid condition developed by his environment?

The present study should be a contribution to the view-point among psychiatrists who no longer consider constitution and psychological development independently of each other, but in their mutual relationships, and even as concepts which can hardly be separated. This study is a part of the research program on alcoholism at the Payne Whitney Psychiatric Clinic[15,16] and a part of the research program of the University of Zürich Psychiatric Clinic Burghölzli. For the past nine years, the Burghölzli group has tried to improve its understanding of the genesis of different groups of psychotics; for instance, of schizophrenics, by studies which compare constitution and individual facts.[4,6,7,8] Similar research on other conditions than those studied as yet is needed for comparison.

SELECTION OF PATIENTS

The cases studied were all severe alcoholics. The diagnosis in all of them was defined to fit the definition of chronic alcoholism which was presented in the introduction of this book. All alcoholics under treatment in the Payne Whitney Clinic from October 1949 to February 1950 were originally included in the study, and this material was supplemented by eight cases under treatment at the Westchester Division of The New York Hospital in April 1950. There were originally 57 American cases included in this study. Seven were not included in the final evaluation because the work with the patients could not be completed either on account of unforseen interruption of the treatment, or on account of the impossibility of checking the patient's statements sufficiently by more objective information, or on account of doubts in regard to the chronicity and severity of alcoholic habits. *Finally therefore, 50 cases of chronic alcoholism from the Payne Whitney Clinic and the Westchester Division of The New York Hospital were evaluated.**

The thorough and detailed records of the Payne Whitney Clinic and the Westchester Division of The New York Hospital were utilized for the study. All the patients had been treated psychotherapeutically by the hospital staff, the majority of them for many months. The experiences occurring during psychotherapy were utilized in the study. In nearly all cases the physicians were in close touch with some of the relatives and their knowledge of them was very helpful. The author completed the data which the therapist had obtained by personal interviews with the patients, which took, on the average, eight

---

* In another chapter a study of 50 alcoholics of Zürich is added to the American study.

to 10 hours (the least time spent with one patient was two hours, the longest 20 hours). Forty-one relatives of patients were also questioned by the author for a period of one-half to five hours and an attempt was made to obtain the case records of all the relatives who had been treated in mental hospitals.

Among the 50 cases were 34 males and 16 females. At the time of our examinations, 27 were married,* seven divorced, two separated, one widowed, and 13 single. The age distribution is as follows:

20–30 years	7 patients
30–40 years	14 patients
40–50 years	18 patients
50–60 years	10 patients
60–70 years	1 patient

Because of the policy of admission to the Payne Whitney Clinic and the Westchester Division of The New York Hospital, the patient's educational and intellectual level was far above the average of the general population. Among the males were six physicians, four priests and ministers, one lawyer, two university professors of languages, three writers and journalists, four business men in high positions, nine employees in business, one professional army officer, one commercial artist, and three college students. The professions of the female patients before their marriages were as follows: one writer, four employees and secretaries, two teachers, two nurses and social workers, one dressmaker, five with no profession, and one college student. The professions of the husbands of the married female patients were: four physicians, one university professor of natural science, three writers, one independent business man, four business men in high positions, one employee. All the patients were of average or above average intelligence.

Forty-nine of the patients were white; one was a Negro. Forty-seven were born in the United States, one in Canada, one in Mexico, and one in Austria. Of the 100 parents of the patients, 81 were born in the United States, one in Australia, three in Austria, four in Canada, one in England, two in Finland, one in France, one in Germany, three in Ireland, one in Italy, one in Mexico, and one in Switzerland.

---

* Four of these had previously been divorced.

Thirty-two patients were Protestants, 14 Catholics, one Jewish, and three without religion.

The alcoholism of the 50 patients had started at the following ages:

15–20 years	8 cases
20–30 years	17 cases
30–40 years	16 cases
40–50 years	7 cases
50–60 years	1 case
61 years	1 case

The duration of the alcoholism at the time of the examination was:

1– 5 years in	16 cases
5–10 years in	14 cases
10–20 years in	11 cases
more than 20 years in	9 cases

In all the patients, minor physical impairment caused by alcohol or alcohol and avitaminosis had occurred such as tremor, gastritis, slight signs of damage to the liver. In none of the patients did there exist very severe alcoholic physical diseases like advanced liver cirrhosis, optic atrophy, pseudo-paresis, etc. Two patients had suffered from a characteristic alcoholic hallucinosis, and two patients had gone through mild forms of delirium tremens. One patient had convulsions with unconsciousness and enuresis in connection with alcoholic excesses. Pathologic intoxications occurred in four patients. None of the patients suffered from a severe chronic alcoholic psychosis. Mild forms of alcoholic deterioration and Korsakow's psychosis had occurred in six patients. The alcoholism of one patient took for many years the form of a characteristic dipsomania. Thirty-five patients showed no signs of psychosis or of intellectual impairment of an organic kind. They all showed, however, a clear-cut change of the personality as is usually seen in severe alcoholism.

The fact that all of the patients had mild physical signs of alcoholism and at least some changes of character, but none of them severe physical alcoholic invalidism, or severe chronic alcoholic psychoses, is a result of selection. Only patients in whom the alcoholism was not only revealed by the history of the patient's drinking and social attitude, but also by at least mild and temporary physical or mental changes were chosen for the study. On the other hand, the most severe and hopeless cases of alcoholism with chronic psychoses and physical invalidism were excluded from admission by the Payne Whitney Clinic and the Westchester Division of The New York Hospital, which are eager to admit for treatment patients with a good prognosis. For the same reason, the duration of the alcoholism of the patients was relatively short (under five years in 32 per cent, under 10 years in 60 per cent, and more than 20 years in only 18 per cent).

In short, *the present study concerns a selection of 50 alcoholics of mostly North American descent and on an average social and intellectual level which is higher than the general population. Their alcoholism is of a marked, but not extreme, degree.*

INCIDENCE OF PSYCHIATRIC DISORDERS AMONG THE RELATIVES OF THE ALCOHOLICS

A conclusive study of the families of patients of any kind cannot restrict itself to the mere enumeration of psychiatric conditions among the relatives. The number of the relatives with psychopathologic disorders must be compared with the number of healthy relatives. The age of every relative has to be considered by means of the technique of the Munich and Scandinavian schools.[14,33,40,52,58] Furthermore, the findings on the families of patients selected in one special way have to be compared with those of patients with the same diagnosis selected in a different way, in order to exclude casual findings because of a certain selection of the index cases. The family findings on a group of mental patients need to be compared with those of the average population. The material must be worked up in such a way as to exclude unconscious selection; particularly, the possibility that the families with a high incidence of psychiatric disorders are more carefully studied than the healthy families has to be excluded. Such an error is made, as a rule, by the routine hospital examination, because the physician is not interested in a complete enumeration of healthy relatives, but rather in information about relatives with mental illness. One of the purposes of the author's personal interviews was to exclude such a selection as will be found in all clinical records if no special research interest in the families exists.

It was possible to gather sufficient data on all the parents, siblings, half-siblings, children, nephews, and nieces, husbands, wives and step-parents of the 50 alcoholics. The information collected about them seemed to be reliable so that one could safely assume that all persons included* could be classified as mentally healthy, borderline cases, or morbid from the social point of view. The majority of the grandparents, the uncles and aunts, the cousins and the step-siblings could be evaluated. In 168 of the 200 grandparents sufficient information in regard to their mental health could be gathered. Sufficient information in regard to all uncles and aunts could be elicited in 36 of the 50 index cases and in regard to the cousins in 26 of them. Of other relatives (great-grandparents, children of the cousins, wives and husbands of the uncles, aunts and cousins, etc.) only a minority were known. On account of the fact that this latter knowledge was incomplete, it was not included in the statistical study, but frequently helped in the understanding of the individual cases. In the nearest relatives of our patients, the possibility of a selection because of a greater interest on the part of the examiner and his informants in abnormal than normal individuals can be excluded. In the more distant relatives, on the other hand, this possibility is recognized since it is impossible to determine if the informant has a tendency to forget the existence of the normal or of the abnormal relatives.

A first survey of the closer relatives of the 50 alcoholics is given in Table II.

A study of these figures, together with known facts from the study of the families of other groups of psychiatric disorders, gives the following impressions: (1) Among the relatives of alcoholics there are more alcoholics than among the relatives of persons from the average population, or of schizophrenics, or other psychotics. The high percentage of alcoholics, however, also concerns the close relatives by marriage (husbands, wives and step-parents of alcoholics) and not only the blood-relatives—an observation which is highly important in the following discussion; (2) The incidence of schizophrenia corresponds to its occurrence in the average population, the incidence of manic-depressive psychoses is somewhat higher, and the incidence of epilepsy lower than in the average population. Before these impressions are taken for granted and discussed, however, they

---

* Except perhaps some children, who died shortly after birth.

TABLE II

SURVEY OF CLOSE RELATIVES OF FIFTY AMERICAN ALCOHOLICS

	Total	Schizophrenia	Probable Schizophrenia	Manic-depressive Psychoses[1]	Involutional Depressions	Other Depressions	Senile and Arterio-sclerotic Psychoses	Epilepsy	Other Organic Psychoses	Psychoses with Unknown Diagnosis	Alcoholism	Probable Alcoholism	Alcoholic Psychoses[2]	Feeble-mindedness	Neurotic and Psychopathic Personality Alterations	Suicide
Parents..........	100	1	—	4	2	1	10	1	2	1	14	—	1	1	22	2[3]
Siblings..........	114	1	—	1	1	1	—	1	—	—	10	—	—	2	12	—
Half-siblings.....	17	—	—	1	—	1	—	1	—	—	2	—	—	—	1	—
Children.........	63	—	—	—	—	—	—	1	—	—	—	—	—	1	13	—
Grandparents.....	168	—	—	—	—	8	—	3	1	—	12	—	—	—	11	1[4]
Uncles and aunts..	333	—	2	1	—	—	7	—	1	2	24	1	2	2	27	2[5]
Cousins..........	337	1	1	1	—	—	—	—	1	—	15	1	—	7	17	—
Nephews and nieces.........	119	—	—	—	—	1	—	—	—	—	1	—	—	4	8	—
Wives and husbands......	46	1	—	—	—	—	—	—	—	—	8	1	—	—	6	—
Step- and fosterparents...	16	—	—	—	—	—	—	—	1	—	2	—	—	—	1	1[6]
All relatives......	1313	4	3	8	3	4	25	4[7]	8[8]	4	88	3	3[9]	17[10]	118	6

Comments:

[1] Cases without hospital treatment included.

[2] Are also included among "alcoholics."

[3] Both also included among manic-depressive psychoses.

[4] Sudden suicide without known reasons.

[5] One included under alcoholics, 1 included under other organic psychoses (suicide during typhus delirium).

[6] The grandfather being the fosterfather of the patient, this case is the same as the suicidal case among "grandparents."

[7] Three cases of epileptic seizures in childhood, 1 case of epileptic seizures during uremia, no genuine epilepsy.

[8] One case of morphine delirium, 1 case of delirious state during cardiac insufficiency, 1 case of delirium with typhoid fever, 2 cases of organic deterioration with pernicious anemia, 1 case of organic deterioration with Paget's disease, 1 case of general paresis, 1 case of brain tumor.

[9] One case of delirium tremens, 1 case of Korsakow psychosis, 1 case of Korsakow psychosis after delirium tremens.

[10] Seven morons, 7 imbeciles, 3 idiots.

have to be checked by exact numbers, by calculation of the average error, and by the presentation of comparative figures.

Family studies on alcoholics using the same technique as in this investigation have been published only by Brugger.[14] He presented in 1934 the result of a study of the families of 88 chronic alcoholics in Basal and Munich. The alcoholics studied by Brugger never had delirium tremens or alcoholic hallucinosis—just as with the large majority of patients studied here. His patients, however, were not chosen from private hospitals, but from public institutions and have, for the most part, poor social backgrounds and intelligence ranging from average to mildly feeble-minded. Material regarding the families of healthy persons with the same social and intellectual backgrounds as the 50 alcoholics studied here does not exist. However, the families of 200 mentally healthy patients of a surgical ward in a Swiss hospital were studied in the same way as those 50 alcoholics.[5] Together with Rapoport and Zurgilgen,[10,11,62] the author also studied the families of 100 tuberculous, but mentally healthy, patients in Switzerland. The study of these 300 families offers an opportunity to compare the figures drawn from the study of 50 alcoholics with the findings in an average population. It should not be forgotten, however, that the mentally healthy patients come from quite another social background than the alcoholics of the present study. In 1929–30, families of 100 schizophrenics at the Westchester Division of The New York Hospital were studied.[4] These patients came from a social class very similar to that of the alcoholics of the present study. Figures for comparison, therefore, taken from the families of alcoholics and schizophrenics of a similar social background are available. It will prove useful for the discussion of some points to refer also to a study of 100 Swiss schizophrenic patients with a social background entirely different from the schizophrenics studied in The New York Hospital, but similar to the alcoholics studied by Brugger. It is not necessary to repeat here detailed indications in regard to the collection of this latter material. The reader is referred to the original publications for these details.

Further material for comparison with the figures of the present study will be available in the near future: Benedetti, of the Burghölzli Psychiatric Clinic, has worked up 100 cases of alcoholic hallucinosis, coming from an unselected Swiss population, in the same

way as presented here.[2] In addition, chronic alcoholics in the Burghölzli Clinic are at present studied in a similar way to that in the
Payne Whitney Clinic. A part of this study is presented in a second
chapter.

The consideration of the ages for the calculation of the different
rates of morbidity is done by the shortened procedure of Weinberg[58]
and Ruedin,[40] which has, particularly for schizophrenia, proved to
be reliable. This technique has been applied by many Scandinavian,
German and Swiss authors, but only by a few English and American
authors, among them Slater[48] and Kallmann.[25] That procedure can
be illustrated by the calculation of the probability of schizophrenia
among the siblings of the alcoholic patients. Among 114 of these
siblings, one is schizophrenic. This proportion (1:114) is not significant in itself, because it has quite a different meaning when all
siblings are children or when they are old people. The large majority
of the siblings who become schizophrenic will become sick between
the ages of 17 and 40. For statistical purposes, one can assume that
nearly all of the siblings under the age of 17 who will ever be schizophrenic, have not fallen sick as yet at the time of the study. On the
other hand, the large majority of the siblings over 40, who will ever
be schizophrenic, have already fallen sick at the time of the study. A
further statement has proved to be nearly exact: half of the siblings
between 17–40 who will ever become schizophrenic, have already
become sick at the time of the study. (For the discussion of this technique see Ruedin[40] or Luxenburger[33].) One therefore has to relate
the single case of schizophrenia among the siblings of alcholics not
with all 114 siblings, but only with the 44 siblings over 40 years of
age and with half of the 42 siblings between 17 and 40 years of age;
i.e., with 65 siblings. While the rough percentage of schizophrenia
among all siblings is 0.9%, the corrected percentage is

$$\frac{100.1}{65} \quad 1.5\%$$

The difference in the given example is of course practically meaning-
less on account of the smallness of the absolute numbers. It is, however, quite remarkable in the material of comparison with much
larger absolute figures.

The corrected percentage of the incidence of manic-depressive psychoses is calculated by the same method. For the manic-depressive psychoses, however, half of the relatives between 20–60 and all the relatives above 60 are taken into account. To calculate exact corrected percentages for the incidence of epilepsy in the different relatives would be much more complicated. Since the very low incidence of epilepsy among the relatives of these alcoholics becomes quite clear without such a calculation, and since epilepsy, on the average, starts much earlier in life than schizophrenia and manic-depressive psychoses, only the percentage of epileptics in all relatives above 10 years is indicated. The parents of feeble-minded children frequently do not realize the feeble-mindedness before school age. Statements from parents that a small child is of normal intelligence are very unreliable. The percentage of feeble-mindedness among all the relatives above 10 years of age is therefore presented.

The comparison of the incidence of schizophrenia, manic-depressive psychoses, epilepsy, and feeble-mindedness among different relatives of the alcoholics and in the material of other investigations is given in Table III.

As for schizophrenia,* the following conclusions are obvious: (1) There is no statistically significant difference between the frequency of schizophrenia in different grades of relatives. The seemingly wide differences in the corrected percentages are all calculated on very small figures and are not significant. (2) *In the families of 50 alcoholics here studied, there are no more schizophrenics than in the average population.* The differences in the percentages are largely within the error of the small number. The same statement is true for the alcoholics studied by Brugger, who have a notably different social background from that of the present group. It cannot be assumed, therefore, that the low incidence of schizophrenia in the families of these alcoholic patients is due to their social selection. (3) *The frequency of schizophrenia in the relatives of alcoholics is much lower* than in the relatives of schizophrenics. This difference is not statistically significant for the comparison of the corrected percentage of

---

* In the above figures are included only the well-established schizophrenics, as in the figures of the material for comparison. It is not necessary to present the figures which include the probable cases both in the present material and in the material for comparison; their calculation led to exactly the same conclusions as the consideration of the well-established cases alone.

schizophrenics in any single grade of parenthood of alcoholics and schizophrenics. It is, however, statistically certain, if we consider the differences in all the different parenthoods together.

As will be discussed later, among the 50 alcoholic *index-cases* there are two schizophrenics. The mother of one of them is also a schizophrenic. If schizophrenic alcoholics had been excluded from the study, there would be no schizophrenics among the parents of the alcoholics. *The data obtained demonstrate that there is no increase of schizophrenia in the relatives of non-schizophrenic alcoholics as compared with the average population.*

Nobody in literature seems to have maintained that there is a common constitutional background of alcoholism and schizophrenia. From this point of view, the finding of the same number of schizophrenics in the relatives of alcoholics as in the average population was to be expected and is of no special interest. There are, however, modern hypotheses which admit very similar psychological reasons for alcoholism and for schizophrenia. They have to do with early feeding experiences. This study demonstrates that a hypothesis must be wrong or incomplete if it accepts the same reasons in the parent-child relationship for both alcoholism and schizophrenia. If, for instance, the same defective nursing attitude of the mother were responsible for both alcoholism and schizophrenia, one would expect more schizophrenics among the siblings of alcoholics than in the average population (and also more alcoholics among the siblings of schizophrenics than in the average population).

Manic-depressive psychoses occur more frequently among the relatives of the alcoholics here studied than in the average population and than among the relatives of the different groups of schizophrenics examined. The same is not true for the alcoholics studied by Brugger, who had a lower social and intellectual background than the present group of alcoholics. A constitutional relationship between alcoholism and manic-depressive psychoses can therefore be supposed only for a social and intellectual selection of alcoholics. It is interesting to observe that two out of eight manic-depressive psychoses in the families of alcoholics occur in the relatives of the only alcoholic who is a manic-depressive. Two of the other cases occur in alcoholics in whom frequent and short depressive changes of mood play an important role in the evolution of their alcoholism.

TABLE III

FREQUENCY OF SCHIZOPHRENIA, MANIC-DEPRESSIVE PSYCHOSES, EPILEPSY AND FEEBLE-MINDEDNESS IN THE FAMILIES OF FIFTY AMERICAN ALCOHOLICS COMPARED WITH THE RESULTS OF OTHER INVESTIGATIONS ON OTHER GROUPS

	Absolute Numbers of Relatives	Absolute Numbers of Schizophrenics[1]	Corrected Percentage of Schizophrenics[2]	Absolute Numbers of Manic-depressives	Corrected Percentage of Manic-depressives[2]	Absolute Numbers of Epileptics	Percentage of Epileptics	Absolute Numbers of Feeble-minded	Corrected Percentage of Feeble-minded[2]
Relatives of the 50 alcoholic patients of this study:									
Parents..................	100	1	1.2	4	4.7	1	1.0	1	1.0
Siblings.................	114	1	1.3	1	1.3	1	1.0	2	2.0
Half-siblings............	17	—	—	1	(14)	1	(7.1)	—	—
Children................	63	—	—	—	—	1	(1.6)	1	(2.0)
Grandparents............	168	—	—	—	—	—	—	—	—
Uncles and aunts.........	333	—	—	1	0.4	—	—	2	0.7
Cousins.................	337	1	0.5	1	0.7	—	—	7	2.1
Nephews and nieces.......	119	—	—	—	—	—	—	4	0.6
Husbands and wives......	46	1	0.3	—	—	—	—	—	—
Step-parents............	16	—	—	—	—	—	—	—	—
Total..................	1313	4	0.4[3]	8	1.1[4]	4[5]	0.3	17	1.5
Relatives of 88 alcoholics in Bâle and Munich studies by Brugger:									
Parents..................	142	1	0.8	—	—	—	—	—	—
Siblings.................	354	4	1.9	1	0.5[6]	3	0.8	6	2.5[7]
Relatives of 200 nonpsychiatric surgical patients in Switzerland studied by M. Bleuler:									
Parents..................	400	1	0.3	3	0.6	—	—	2	0.5
Siblings.................	1111	5	1.0	1	0.2	4	0.5	14	1.6
Relatives of 100 schizophrenics of similar social background as the alcoholics studied by M. Bleuler:									
Parents..................	200	4	2.0	—	—	—	—	—	—
Siblings.................	351	9	4.8	—	—	—	—	1	0.3
Relatives of 100 schizophrenics in Switzerland studied by M. Bleuler:									
Parents..................	200	11	5.6	4	2.2	—	—	5	2.5
Siblings.................	492	26	10.1	—	—	6	1.5	16	4.1
Uncles and aunts.........	877	13	2.1	4	0.7	3	0.4	14	2.1
Cousins.................	1837	18	1.9	4	0.5	4	0.2	38	2.5

TABLE III (*Continued*)

Comments:

[1] The figures on schizophrenia include only cases with a well-established diagnosis. (This is also true in the material dealing with comparisons.) If the cases with probable, but not absolutely certain diagnoses are included, the percentage rises in the present study in the same way as in the studies which are mentioned for comparison. The conclusions mentioned in the text are the same, whether one considers the definite or the probable cases of schizophrenia.

[2] "Corrected" percentage means that the age of the relatives is taken into account and that from the total number of the relatives those who are still too young to have become sick before the time of the study are subtracted. The "corrected" percentages are, of course, higher than the rough percentage of all cases of disease among all the relatives.

[3] The average error of this figure is $\sqrt{\dfrac{0.4 \cdot 99.6}{740}} = 0.2$. If we take as usual the average error multiplied by 3 as the utmost possibility of mere casual variations, we can assume that it is proven that schizophrenia among alcoholics of the same selection as in our material is between 0 and 1 per cent.

[4] The average error of this figure is $\sqrt{\dfrac{1.1 \cdot 98.9}{740}} = 0.3$. It has been proven that among our alcoholics manic-depressive psychoses occur in a frequency between 0.2 and 2.0.

[5] No case of idiopathic epilepsy occurred among them.

[6] Brugger regards as the usual age of onset 16–50 years compared with 20–50 years of the other authors. This and minor other differences in the statistical calculations are insignificant in the final figures and discussions.

[7] Only imbeciles were counted and not morons as in the other figures.

One patient who became an alcoholic in a severe and long-standing depression, diagnosed as reactive, had three relatives who also showed severe reactive depressions, during which they drank excessively. It seems clear therefore that periods of depression related to constitutional depressive features play a role in the genesis of alcoholism in some patients.

Idiopathic epilepsy does not occur in the relatives of alcoholics considered in the present study. Even if one counts the case of symtomatic epileptic seizures in uremia and the three cases of a period of seizures in childhood as epilepsy, there are still no more epileptics in the relatives of these alcoholics than in the average population. Brugger found epilepsy more frequent among the alcoholics of low social and intellectual background than in the average population. His figures, however, are too small to be statistically reliable. Our findings throw a new light on the frequent statements in the older literature that epilepsy and alcoholism arise from the same constitutional background or that alcoholism frequently causes epilepsy in the offspring. The very low incidence of epilepsy in the relatives of intelligent alcoholics argues against these assumptions.

The differences in the incidence of *feeble-mindedness* in the relatives of this group of alcoholics, in that of Brugger, and in other material of comparison are not statistically significant. If the old assumption that alcoholism frequently causes feeble-mindedness in the offspring is true, it would have been expected that feeble-mindedness would be less frequent in the average population than in these families with so much alcoholism in all generations.

The incidence of *alcoholism* in the relatives of the index-cases is shown in Table IV.

As to the material utilized for comparison, the following points must be kept in mind: The surgical patients studied in Switzerland by the author as representing an average population come from a part of the country which suffers even more than most other regions from a high incidence of alcoholism. The incidence of alcoholism as revealed by inquiries is, in accordance with this statement, considerably higher than in the studies of other examples of the general population. The chronic alcoholics studied by Brugger in Switzerland have, on the average, a modest intellectual and social background as compared with the alcoholics studied by the author. On the other hand, the schizophrenics studied by the author in The New York Hospital come from the same social class as the alcoholics of this study, and have about the same high intellectual background. Quite a number of writers reached, with other techniques, the conclusion that alcoholism is frequent among the parents and other close relatives of alcoholics, for instance, Wall,[55] Williams,[59] Dublineau and Duchenne,[17] Haggard and Jellinek.[22]

The figures show clearly that the incidence of alcoholism in the parents and siblings of our alcoholics is higher than in the general population and even many times higher than in the relatives of schizophrenics of the same social and intellectual background. On the other hand, it is interesting that the frequency of alcoholism among the relatives of the intellectual American alcoholics of high social position is (within the limits of the casual variation of the small numbers) just the same as with the alcoholics of a much poorer intellectual and social background whom Brugger studied. It should be noted, furthermore, that alcoholism is more frequent in the siblings

TABLE IV
FREQUENCY OF ALCOHOLISM IN THE FAMILIES OF FIFTY AMERICAN ALCOHOLICS COMPARED WITH THE RESULTS OF OTHER INVESTIGATIONS

	Number of Relatives Above 10 Years	and Number of Alcoholics Among Them	Percentage of Alcoholics Among the Relatives Above 10 Years	Number of Male Relatives Above 10	and Number of Alcoholics Among Them	Percentage of Male Alcoholics Among the Relatives Above 10 Years	Number of Female Relatives Above 10	and Number of Alcoholics Among Them	Percentage of Alcoholics Among the Female Relatives Above 10 Years	Number of Relatives Above 40 Years	and Number of Alcoholics Among Them	Percentage of Alcoholics Among the Relatives Above 40	Number of Male Relatives Above 40	and Number of Alcoholics Among Them	Percentage of Alcoholics Among the Male Relatives Above 40	Number of Female Relatives Above 40	and Number of Alcoholics Among Them	Percentage of Alcoholics Among the Female Relatives Above 40
Relatives of the 50 Alcoholics of this Study:																		
Parents...	100	14	14	50	11	22	50	3	6	95	13	43.7	49	11	22.4	45	2	4.4
Siblings...	101	10	10	51	6	11.8	50	4	8	56	9	16.1	27	6	22.3	29	3	10.3
Half-siblings	14	2	14.3	6	1	16.6	8	1	12.5	14	2	14.3	6	1	16.6	8	1	12.5
Children..	41	0	—	21	0	—	20	0	—	—	—	—	—	—	—	—	—	—
Grandparents.	168	12	7.1	85	9	10.6	83	3	3.6	164	12	7.3	83	9	10.8	81	3	3.7
Uncles and aunts...	302	25	8.2	146	22	15.1	156	3	1.9	257	23	8.9	119	20	16.8	138	3	2.2
Cousins...	315	16	5.1	159	9	5.7	156	7	4.5	148	14	9.4	73	9	12.3	75	5	6.7
Nephews & nieces	63	1	1.6	31	0	—	32	1	3.1	8	0	—	4	0	—	4	0	—
Husbands & wives	46	9	19.6	14	4	28.6	32	5	15.6	26	6	23.1	11	4	36.4	15	2	13.3
Step-parents.	16	2	12.5	9	2	22.2	7	0	—	13	0	—	6	0	—	7	0	—
Relatives of 84 Alcoholics in Bâle and Munich Studied by Brugger:																		
Parents...	142	21	14.8	70	17	24.3	72	4	5.5	127	20	15.7	61	16	26.2	66	4	6.1
Siblings...	239	27	11.3	106	24	22.6	133	3	2.3	190	26	13.7	83	23	27.7	107	3	2.8

TABLE IV (*Continued*)

	Number of Relatives Above 10 Years	and Number of Alcoholics Among Them	Percentage of Alcoholics Among the Relatives Above 10 Years	Number of Male Relatives Above 10	and Number of Alcoholics Among Them	Percentage of Male Alcoholics Among the Relatives Above 10 Years	Number of Female Relatives Above 10	and Number of Alcoholics Among Them	Percentage of Alcoholics Among the Female Relatives Above 10 Years	Number of Relatives Above 40 Years	and Number of Alcoholics Among Them	Percentage of Alcoholics Among the Relatives Above 40	Number of Male Relatives Above 40	and Number of Alcoholics Among Them	Percentage of Alcoholics Among the Male Relatives Above 40	Number of Female Relatives Above 40	and Number of Alcoholics Among Them	Percentage of Alcoholics Among the Female Relatives Above 40
Relatives of 200 Non-psychiatric, Surgical Patients in Switzerland Studied by M. Bleuler:																		
Parents...	400	32	8	200	26	13	200	6	3	377	31	8.2	192	25	13.0	185	6	3.3
Siblings...	866	20	2.3	436	20	4.6	430	0	—	256	18	7.0	144	18	12.5	112	0	—
Relatives of 100 Schizophrenics of Similar Social Background as the Alcoholics Studied by M. Bleuler:																		
Parents...	200	4	2	100	3	3	100	1	1	192	4	2.1	95	3	3.2	97	1	1
Siblings...	294	3	1	150	2	1.3	144	1	0.7	113	3	2.7	54	2	3.7	59	1	1.7

and parents of alcoholics than in grandparents, uncles, aunts, cousins, nephews and nieces. This observation demonstrates that the frequency of alcoholism in the relatives has a certain relationship to the alcoholism of the index case and is not common to the general level of the families selected. It should be taken into account, however, that alcoholism among husbands and wives of alcoholics is particularly high. (The numbers are large enough for this general statement, but they would not be large enough for a more detailed evaluation.) *This demonstrates that psychological and social factors must be considered even more than the possibility of heredity.*

The morbid development of personalities is very difficult to count. The main difficulty is the delimitation from so-called normal development in personality. In order to differentiate between these two groups, the social point of view was used. In doubtful cases the determining factors were success or failure in professional career, in marriage, and in other responsibilities. No attempt was made to differentiate between constitutional and neurotic deviations in personality. The theoretical and practical difficulties in making such a distinction are well known. Under the vague term of morbid personality developments are mainly included severe and long-standing neurotic developments and so-called psychopathic personality disorders. One is able to compare the figures on morbid personality in the families of the alcoholics of this study only with the corresponding figures of the studies on other index cases. The distinction between "normal" and "morbid" personality development is too dependent upon the author's individual approach to allow the comparison of figures of different authors.

The number of morbid personality developments among different relatives of the alcoholics of the present study compared with an average population and with the relatives of schizophrenics are as shown in Table V.

It is an interesting result that morbid personality deviations among the relatives of these alcoholics are much more frequent than in an average Swiss population. They are just as frequent as in the relatives of schizophrenics who were chosen in the same country and in the same social group as these alcoholics. One has to be very cautious however in generalizing such a statement and in considering the facts as true for all alcoholics, which were found in the group of selected alcoholics of high intellectual and social background and of American descent. Neither can one consider the surgical patients from Switzerland as representative of average populations outside of Switzerland. However, some other findings can be added which make it probable that the results are of general significance and not restricted to a selected group of alcoholics:

1. It could be argued that the high incidence of morbid personality developments among the American alcoholics and schizophrenics of a high social and intellectual background is not due to the fact that the index cases are schizophrenics or alcoholics but to the fact that

TABLE V

FREQUENCY OF MORBID PERSONALITY DEVELOPMENT IN THE FAMILIES OF FIFTY AMERICAN ALCOHOLICS COMPARED WITH THE RESULTS OF OTHER INVESTIGATIONS

	Relatives of the 50 Alcoholics of This Study			Relatives of 200 Non-psychiatric Surgical Patients in Switzerland			Relatives of 100 Schizophrenics of Similar Social Background as the Alcoholics of This Study[1]		
	Number of Relatives Above 10 Years	Number of Psychopathic Developments Among Them	Percentage of Psychopathic Developments Among Them	Number of Relatives Above 10 Years	Number of Psychopathic Developments Among Them	Percentage of Psychopathic Developments Among Them	Number of Relatives Above 10 Years	Number of Psychopathic Developments Among Them	Percentage of Psychopathic Developments Among Them
Parents.............	100	22	22	400	6	1.5	200	41	20.5
Siblings.............	101	12	11.9	866	16	1.8	294	35	11.9
Half-siblings..........	14	1	7.1						
Children............	41	13	31.7						
Grandparents........	168	11	6.5				360	34	9.4
Uncles, aunts........	302	27	8.9				667	71	10.6
Cousins.............	315	17	5.4						
Nephews, nieces......	63	8	12.7						
Husbands, wives......	46	6	13.0						
Step-parents.........	16	1	6.2						

[1] In the original paper the alcoholics had been included among the morbid personalities. For the purpose of this table, they have been excluded.

there might generally be found more morbid personality developments in a highly intelligent, than in an intellectually poor population. (Such an assumption is more probable because feeble-minded persons with morbid personality developments were included under the feeble-minded and not under the morbid personality developments; one has also to take into account that a morbid personality might be more easily recognized in an intellectual personality than in a primitive one.) However, it is interesting to remember that even more morbid personality developments were found among the relatives of Swiss schizophrenics with low social background than in the American schizophrenics of high social background (29% among the parents and 17.1% among the siblings older than 10 years). One should therefore not overestimate the influence of the different social backgrounds in the discussion of the high incidence of morbid personalities among the relatives of the alcoholics of this study.

2. Brugger[13] has described the psychopathic personality developments among the relatives of alcoholics and in an average population in Munich and Basle with a rather low social background. (The percentages which he indicates includes also alcoholics; since he gives a short description of every morbid personality, the number of morbid personalities in his series excluding alcoholics can be counted.) In accordance with the present findings, Brugger observes more morbid personalities among the parents and siblings of alcoholics than in the average population. The difference in the material of Brugger, drawn from a low social background, however, is much less marked than the difference in material of the author, drawn from a high social background. *It seems therefore that alcoholism in well-educated people of superior intelligence has better etiologic correlation with morbid personality developments than alcoholism in an average population.*

In summary, there is no evidence of an increased incidence of any non-alcoholic psychosis and of oligophrenia among the relatives of alcoholics. This is particularly true of schizophrenia, which occurs among the relatives of alcoholics in the same frequency as in the average population. The frequency of epilepsy and manic-depressive psychoses among the relatives of alcoholics is dependent on the social level of the families studied; epilepsy and manic-depressive psychoses occur with the same frequency among the relatives of alcoholics and of non-alcoholics, if both of them are chosen from the same social level.

On the other hand, alcoholism occurs much more frequently among the relatives of alcoholics than among the relatives of schizophrenics or among the general population. Morbid (psychopathic and neurotic) personalities occur among the relatives of alcoholics more frequently than among the general population. They occur among the relatives of alcoholics about as frequently as among the relatives of schizophrenics.*

---

* After this manuscript had been finished, Curt Amark published an excellent study on the incidence of mental derangements in the parents and siblings of alcoholics. His material, collected in Sweden, is very extensive and has been worked up with par-

These findings lead to the conclusion that the genetic background of alcoholism as a whole has nothing in common with the genetic background of schizophrenia, manic-depressive psychoses, epilepsy and oligophrenia, but has much in common with the genetic background of morbid (psychopathic and neurotic) personalities.

PERSONAL CONSTITUTION OF THE INDEX CASES

I. Physical Constitution

The distribution of the *physical types* as described by Kretschmer[29] among the 50 index cases runs as follows: 21 asthenics, 19 pyknics, six athletics, four not characteristic. No statistically-proved difference from the average population can be drawn from these small figures. However, they suggest an increase of pyknic body types and a smaller number of athletics than in the average population. If the difference proved true in a larger body of material, it would be explained by the selection of alcoholics: among an intellectual population, to which most of the index cases belong, athletic constitution is rarer than in the average population; on the other hand the correlation of the population of high social level, from which the index cases were selected, with manic-depressive disturbances makes the high incidence of pyknic constitution intelligible.

More interesting are the results of the study of the *endocrine condition* of the index cases:* none of them suffered from severe endocrine disorders, but 14 of them showed definite signs of endocrine

---

ticularly careful statistical methods. The conclusions of Amark are the same as those of the present study: The frequency of schizophrenia, manic-depressive psychoses, epilepsy and oligophrenia among the parents and siblings of Swedish alcoholics is the same as in the general population; on the other hand, psychopathy and alcoholism are increased in the relatives of the Swedish alcoholics. (AMARK, CURT: *A Study In Alcoholism,* Stockholm, 1951.)

* The endocrine studies on our patients include the taking of a thorough anamnesis regarding the endocrine conditions (the development of puberty, the course of pregnancies and the climacterium was known in every case) and a thorough general physical examination with particular consideration of body proportions, hair distribution, skin, voice, thyroid, male genital organs, gynecological findings, evidence of hypoparathyroidism. In every case routine laboratory work was done, frequently including basal metabolism-rate, cholesterin determination of the blood, blood sugar and sugar tolerance tests. There were, however, no special laboratory examinations, such as vaginal smear, determination of pregnandiol and 17 ketosteroid excretion. A study of some selected alcoholics with complete endocrine examinations has been started recently.

disturbance of mild degree and four more at least suspicious signs of such. The endocrine disturbances were:

Two cases (male and female) of distinct but mild hyperthyroidism. In one case, the alcoholism and the hyperthyroidism developed at the same period. In the other case, the hyperthyroidism had made treatment necessary for one year, but it had disappeared more than 10 years before the beginning of alcoholism.

One case (male) of questionable hyperthyroidism: The diagnosis had been made by a physician one year before the author's examination of the patient, and four years after the onset of his alcoholism. The symptoms, however, on which the diagnosis was based, were not marked enough to prove it.

One case (male) of hypothyroidism during puberty, which made medication necessary for two or three years and which disappeared later. (The mother of this patient suffered from hyperthyroidism.)

One case (male) who showed a mild diabetes mellitus for half a year before the author's examination. The alcoholism had started 15 years before and had been very much improved within the last two years. The patient also suffered from adiposity. His beard had started to grow only after his 20th year and he did not start shaving until 21. He still has an unusually light beard (as does his brother).

Two cases (male) with acromegaloid body configuration. One of them had shown at puberty a very irregular growth. The other still shows an abnormally light beard. One of them had spells of thirst.

Four cases (one male, three female) with physical infantilism: In three of them the infantilism was seen in the appearance of the face, the hands, or the whole skeletal proportions, and in an infantile voice. The male case showed a late growth of the beard and started shaving only at 19. He still has an abnormally light beard. The fourth case had a normal general bodily type, but infantile genitalia. The diagnosis of the gynocologist was "hypoplasia of the genital tract." She had an abnormally small uterus and ovaries. She suffered for many years from prolonged bleeding (16 days).

Three cases (two male, one female) of still other abnormalities of development in puberty than those already mentioned: An exceptionally early puberty with full development of the sexual signs, ejaculation and frequent intercourse between 10 and 11, in one case; a classic anorexia nervosa starting at puberty in a girl (as the relations of the anorexia nervosa and the endocrine glands are still unclear, the case is counted only as a possible and questionable endocrine disturbance); a marked adiposity in puberty with the diagnosis of a complex endocrine disorder during puberty in a male case (this case, however, can only be counted as a questionable endocrine disorder. There exists serious doubt that such cases of adiposity have any endocrine basis).

Two cases (male and female) with heterosexual stigmata: One in a woman who had a very male type of hair distribution with hirsutism of the face, practically no breasts, and male facial features. In the man the fat distribution and the muscular development was of a female type, but he was counted only as a questionable endocrine disorder since there were no other signs of heterosexuality.

One case (female) of manopause at 22 with severe climacteric symptoms at this early age. Under endocrine treatment menstruation recurred for short periods later in life, but ceased completely at 38.

One case of severe climacteric complaints, which were closely connected with the onset of alcoholism.

A numerical evaluation of these facts is hardly possible; the necessary studies of non-alcoholic index cases of the same age and sex distribution and receiving the same kind of medical attention do not exist. It is questionable that the incidence of endocrine disturbances among alcoholics is higher than in non-alcoholics, although the impression seems to indicate it. It is, on the other hand, interesting to study in every individual case the possible connection between alcoholism and endocrine disturbance. Such a study revealed:

No correlation between alcoholism and endocrine disturbance could be elicited in two cases of hyperthyroidism (one of them questionable), and in the only case of hypothyroidism. In these cases the thyroid condition was cured many years before the alcoholism started. On the other hand, in the third case hyperthyroidism developed at the same time as the alcoholism. The hyperthyroidism was in relation to anxiety, which was one of the manifest causes of the alcoholism. There existed a marked tremor, which was partly caused by hyperthyroidism and which increased the patient's anxiety in his professional duties and induced him to drink.

All the four cases of physical infantilism were combined with extremely marked psychoinfantilism, characterized by: shyness (in all cases, in one of them with stuttering in childhood, in another case with great difficulties in his relations with superiors), uncertainty with a tendency to overscrupulousness (in all cases), lack of independence and exaggerated dependence on parents, husbands, wives or older friends (in all cases), rapid changes of mood (in all cases), lively imagination (in three cases), infantile psychosexual development (in all cases), great suggestibility (in all cases). The study of the psychodynamics of the alcoholism revealed in all cases a close relationship between alcoholism and psychoinfantilism: alcohol was used in order to overcome shyness with superiors, friends and members of the other sex; it was also used, because patients could not stand being alone; alcohol helped the patients to live out their aggressiveness and their sexuality which they repressed in a sober state on account of their self-consciousness and shyness. The awareness of their physical infantilism added to their feeling insecure and led to their drinking. In the patient with diabetes, this disease had no visible correlation with the alcoholism; his delayed and pathologically scanty beard growth coexisted, however, with a marked psychoinfantilism.

The female patient with masculine physical traits suffered from marked premenstrual tension, which possibly was related to her endocrine derangement and increased her tendency to drink. There might also be a relationship between her physical constitution and her lack of female interests, particularly her dislike of any housework; she made it clear that her alcoholism meant to her an escape from her duties as a housewife. The male patient with slight feminine physical traits had strong homosexual tendencies and was not satisfied with his marriage. He lacked masculine professional initiative and was very passive. These personality traits played an important role in the development of his alcoholism. He fled in intoxication from his dissatisfaction in his married life and lived out his homosexual tendencies in an intoxicated state.

The case of early physical puberty in a male was connected with a pathologically early and strong sexuality. The first alcoholic excesses were in association with the sexual excesses. Increased sexuality and drinking habits remained linked ever since then. The patient with the adiposity (treated during puberty) showed an extremely passive personality, revolted in a passive way—just doing nothing—against his father, did not care about proper schooling and later as regards his professional career, "just let it go"; if nothing was asked of him, he showed a childish and sweet temperament. The question is open as to whether his psychopathic traits have to do with a pituitary, or (more probably), diencephalic disturbance. It is certain that his passivity and irresponsibility were main factors in the development of his alcoholism. The girl with anorexia nervosa developed alcoholism in direct causal relationship with anorexia. Just as other patients of this kind at times secretly eat certain food (particularly vegetables) in too large an amount, she had the habit of drinking when hungry.

The acromegaoloid constitution is in the majority of cases complicated by certain personality disturbances. A large accumulation of material which made this evident has been published from the Zürich Clinic.[9,28,53,57,60,61] The main characteristics are changes of mood or impulsiveness, which start and disappear suddenly without apparent external cause. The kinds of moods and instincts are very different. There might, for instance, arise attacks of hunger, of thirst, of sexual excitement, as well as of anxiety, depression, or apathy. Poriomanic and dipsomanic behavior is not rare. The habitual mood is often characterized by indifference and cheerfulness, a personality without deep responsibility and without inner warmth. The habitual mood can also be anxious and hypochondriacal. (For more details see M. BLEULER: Untersuchungen aus dem Grenzgebiet zwischen Psychopathologie und Endokrinologie, *Arch. Psych. 180:*H.¾, 1948.) It is understood that these disturbances are the same as those in the milder forms of diencephalic lesions, for instance, in mild cases of encephalitis lethargica. Both of the acromegaloid index cases show a morbid personality which fits into the characteristics of personality derangements in the acromegaloid constitution. In both cases it is apparent that the alcoholism is to a large extent influenced by the sudden changes of mood as well as by the lack of responsibility and warmth in social contacts.

In the two women with pathologic climacterium the alcoholism arose in close connection with the menopausal tension and feelings of inferiority with the loss of womanhood.

In this short survey I merely wished to point out *that there do exist causal interrelations between physical endocrine derangements, personality derangements, and alcoholism.* I want to emphasize, however, that I leave open the question as to what is primary and what is secondary. Some observers might claim that the somatic infantilism or the hyperthyroidism, for instance, lead to character complications like psychoinfantilism of anxiety and tension and that these difficulties cause the alcoholism. Others might argue that both infantilism and hyperthyroidism can be the sequelae of a morbid psychological development. In the experience of the author many other interrelationships also exist. This variety of possibilities may be illustrated by the following schematic presentation, which, however, is far from being complete:

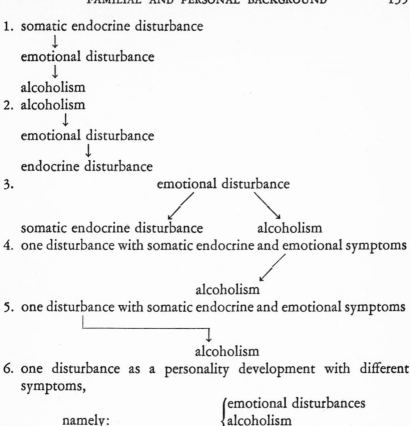

1. somatic endocrine disturbance
   ↓
   emotional disturbance
   ↓
   alcoholism
2. alcoholism
   ↓
   emotional disturbance
   ↓
   endocrine disturbance
3.   emotional disturbance

   somatic endocrine disturbance   alcoholism
4. one disturbance with somatic endocrine and emotional symptoms

                          alcoholism
5. one disturbance with somatic endocrine and emotional symptoms

                          alcoholism
6. one disturbance as a personality development with different symptoms,

       namely: {emotional disturbances
                        {alcoholism
                        {somatic endocrine disturbance

It is not the purpose of this paper to discuss these possibilities of causal interrelationship. (Many years of study in the fields of endocrine psychiatry have led to the assumption that any of them might be true in certain cases.) The facts revealed by this study only emphasize that there do exist some causal relationships between alcoholism and somatic endocrine derangements in a certain number of alcoholics.

To summarize, *14 of the 50 alcoholics show mild, but distinct endocrine derangement and four more show questionable endocrine derangements. A causal interrelationship between alcoholism and endocrine derangement seems probable in 12 cases and questionable in three. In three cases there is no causal interrelationship between alcoholism and endocrine derangement.*

One physical condition which at times seems to have something to do with the psychodynamics of alcoholism is *tremor*. It is a common statement of alcoholics that they are forced to drink in order to get rid of their tremor. This tremor, as a rule has an alcoholic origin. Four of the 50 alcoholic patients, however, suffered long before the onset of their alcoholism from a marked tremor. In two cases this tremor was essentially a familial tremor (one index case, the mother and two sisters suffered from it; the other index case had the tremor in common with his father and a sister). In a third case, the tremor was partly a symptom of hyperthyroidism; it occurred, however, in the paternal family of the patient without hyperthyroidism (three paternal aunts had tremor, while hyperthyroidism occurred in the maternal family). The tremor is probably in this case of mixed hyperthyroid and familial origin. Another patient suffered from paralysis agitans with tremor. In the first three patients, the psychodynamics of alcoholism were apparently very much influenced by the tremor. All these three patients considered their tremor as the main reason for drinking. In order not to appear ridiculous during their professional duties (as physician and clergyman) or in society, they tried to stop the shaking by drinking. They suffered from periods of anxiety, in which the fear of shaking, being weak, and ridiculous played a major role. The coexistence between tremor, fear, and alcoholism is an interesting example of the interrelationship of emotion and emotional muscular responses. Tremor suggests fear and increases fear, even when it is not caused by fear.

Eleven of the 50 index cases had suffered from *severe and chronic or recurring physical diseases* of the most varying kinds: peptic ulcer, colitis ulcerosa, pleural empyema, pulmonary tuberculosis (accompanied by severe allergic conditions), paroxysmal tachycardia and chest deformity, paralysis agitans, iridocyclitis, osteomyelitis, rheumatic polyarthritis, ichthyosis, a continuous chain of different physical disturbances. In nearly all of these cases the psychic trauma, which was caused by those ailments, was shown to play a role in the dynamics of alcoholism.

II. Personality

As mentioned before, the selection of the index cases excluded any persons with low intelligence. The intelligence of all index cases was about average or above average.

In this discussion the degree of personality disturbance before the onset of the alcoholism will be considered first and then the types of these disturbances.

A distinction is made between normal personalities, morbid personalities without psychoses, and psychotic personalities. Interposed between the normal personalities and the morbid personalities without psychoses is a further group of borderline cases. "Morbid" and "normal" are only considered from the practical point of view: a study was made as to whether the patients suffered subjectively from their personality, if their personality make-up enabled them to take over the essential duties of life (during education, in making a living, in being responsible towards parents, husbands, wives or children); and if they were a burden to others on account of some personality derangement. There exists, of course, a wide field between a normal personality make-up and a clearly morbid personality without psychosis, in which the opinions of different psychiatrists would disagree. There are, on the other hand, certain personalities which can be classified easily and without much doubt as normal or morbid. (There also exist many borderline cases between morbid personalities without psychoses and psychotic personalities; borderline cases of this kind, however, did not occur among the index cases.)

The personalities of the 50 index cases before the onset of their alcoholism were judged as follows:

10 had normal personalities (six males, four females)
20 were borderline cases between normal personalities and morbid personalities without psychoses (12 males, eight females)
18 were clearly morbid personalities, but without psychosis (14 males, four females)
2 had suffered from psychoses (one male, one female).

It is quite evident that *morbid personalities and borderline cases between the normal and morbid are much more frequent among the alcoholics studied here than in an average intelligent population, but that a manifest morbid personality, on the other hand, is not a compulsory condition for alcoholism.*

Of the two patients who had suffered from psychoses, the female patient had gone through three depressive episodes of a manic-depressive psychosis before the onset of alcoholism, which had started during her fourth depression. The second psychotic patient had been suffering for years from chronic schizophrenia before the beginning of alcoholism. Another index case developed an acute catatonic psychosis, from which he recovered, during alcoholism.

No attempt is made to classify all personalities of the patients into a certain schema as for example the schema of Jung,[23] Kretschmer,[29] Kahn,[24] Schneider[41] or Sjoebring.[45-47] Each personality is described briefly in the way which seems most appropriate, independent of classification.

Among the morbid personalities without psychoses there is first a group of four patients whose difficulties consist mainly of transient depressive moods; they fit into the conception of cycloid psychopaths in the sense of Kretschmer. Their depressions are much more frequent and severe than the elated moods. They do not, however, reach a psychotic degree which would justify the diagnosis of manic-depressive psychosis. Three patients showed severe compulsive and obsessional neuroses before the onset of alcoholism. (One of them suffered at the same time from a typical compulsive neurosis of anorexia nervosa.) In three patients the main derangements are well described by the old conception of hysterical reaction. (In all of them there was hysterical symptomatology; in one case there were mainly sensations of being choked, in another violent emotional outbursts, and in the third sudden blindness with anxiety and respiratory distress.) One case is a marked homosexual, spending a good deal of his time seeking homosexual partners in spite of being married. He is at times capable, however, of heterosexual emotions. In a group of six patients the main difficulty consisted of a lack of sufficient contact with other people, particularly of the opposite sex. They are shy, shut-in, seclusive, inclined to states of anxiety in connection with human relationships of any kind, and feel very tense in the presence of others. From the point of view of their inner isolation they could easily be called schizoid. They are, however, very conscious of this isolation, feeling a strong urge to break through it and to mix with other people. There is no lack of an inner inclination for society as in the classical schizoid personality. The tension between the shyness and the urge for close association with other people is felt as being constant torture. They are moody and always unsatisfied. They like to describe their mood as "being disgusted with everything." There is, as a rule, not only a lack of personal relations with other people, but also a lack of active interests.

In the borderline cases the main difficulties suggesting a mild morbidity were the following ones: mild or very temporary obsessive and compulsive traits in two cases; infantile traits in one case; mild homosexual features (with stronger heterosexuality) in four cases; a mildly elated, restless, and overactive mood in the direction of a mild hypomania in three cases; a slight social irresponsibility with egoistic and materialistic attitude in three cases; an exaggerated premenstrual tension in one case; insecurity with stuttering in childhood, which disappeared during adolescence long before the onset of alcoholism in one case; in five cases there was a lack of human relationship with shyness and dissatisfaction in a mild degree; furthermore, two of them suffered from ejaculatio praecox.

In all of these cases the mentioned personality difficulties played an apparent and important role in the psychogenesis of the alcoholism of the patient: drinking caused the patient to break through the shyness or overscrupulousness and enabled him to be social without feelings of inferiority, to satisfy his sexuality, or at least to obtain relief from his usual tension; the homosexuals, while drinking, withdrew from their wives, joined male company, and at times found the courage for homosexual contacts. For the socially irresponsible, materialistic patients, drinking became a symbol of unrestrained materialism.

It seemed particularly interesting to study the personalities of the patients who were considered normal before the onset of their alcoholism. They too, of course, had personal difficulties. One man was a cheerful, syntonic character, but with little independence. He had had an unhappy development in as far as he had become accustomed very early to prostitutes and had never felt a strong sexual attraction to girls whom he might have been able to marry. Another man was somewhat shy and shut-in, not to the degree, however, that his life had been unhappy before the onset of his alcoholism. He was married to a much more active wife and there existed a tension beween his retiring and her active temperament. Another man seemed to be well adjusted, sociable, cheerful, syntonic in a normal sense. A certain inner insecurity was, however, demonstrated by mild and temporary aberrations of sexual potency. Another man showed, within normal limits, a marked scrupulousness with mild obsessive coloring. Another man, who seemed cheerful and quite happy, suffered from a lack of interest and inability to love women other than "pick-ups." In another man, there seemed to his friends to exist a very even, happy and well balanced mood, while he himself complained of a chronic sadness and lack of satisfaction. Of the female patients, two showed a superficial personality, inclined to many social activities, but without deep interest and deep relationships with other people. One female patient showed an overactive temperament. She had marked infantile personality traits, which, however, were of no practical importance before the onset of alcoholism.

A summary of the personality derangements and peculiarities of the 50 alcoholics is given in Table VI:

TABLE VI

CLASSIFICATION OF PERSONALITY DEVELOPMENT OF FIFTY AMERICAN ALCOHOLICS

Kind of Derangement and Peculiarity	Psychotic	Psychopathic Personality	Borderline Cases	Within Normal Limits	Total
Schizophrenia	1	—	—	—	1
Depressions of manic-depressive psychosis or cycloid personality	1	4	—	—	5
Hypomania	—	—	3	2	5
Shut-in, moody tense in society	—	6	5	2	13
Compulsive and obsessive traits	—	3	2	1	6
Social irresponsibility	—	—	3	2	5
Homosexuality	—	1	4	—	5
Infantilism	—	1	1	1	3
Hysteria	—	3	—	—	3
Miscellaneous	—	—	2	2	4
Total	2	18	20	10	50

In going through such a survey, *we are not only struck by the frequency of personality disorders in intellectual chronic alcoholics, but also by the variety of these disorders. It appears as if almost any personality disorder could form the background of chronic alcoholism.* There are two large groups of personality derangements among alcoholics, both of which relate to the mood and the emotionality: the first group belongs to the manic-depressive or cycloid disorders; the second concerns retiring persons who feel moody and dissatisfied in their isolation, but tense and anxious in society. There are other groups of compulsive personalities, homosexuals, socially irresponsible types, and of infantile and hysterical make-up.

For the classifications of this survey, the most outstanding traits in the personality make-up were considered. There were, of course, many combinations; for instance, that of homosexuality and infantilism, or of irresponsible attitude and hypomania.

Special attention was paid to the *sexual adjustment* of the index cases: In all of the 16 females and in 32 of the 34 males, it could be sufficiently studied. In three of the 32 males potency was severely damaged. (One man of 35 years of age had never been able to have sexual intercourse on account of ejaculatio praecox in spite of many trials; in one man of 41, sexual intercourse had always been very difficult and unpleasant for him and his wife because of ejaculatio praecox; the third man of 42 had at times satisfactory sexual relations, but was greatly disturbed by, and very much afraid of, impotence.) The other 29 males had none or only mild and temporary disturbances of potency. Of the 16 female patients, there were eight who had never experienced an orgasm and had been completely frigid; five patients had had orgasm on rare occasions, but had shown for the most part complete frigidity. (Of the eight patients with severe frigidity, six had been married and two were single; their ages at the time of the examination were between 29 and 51 years.) Of the 32 male patients severe homosexuality had been a problem throughout adult life in three cases (all of them were also capable of heterosexual activities); in three further cases there had been frequent homosexual relations (particularly under the influence of alcohol), while the main sexual pattern was heterosexual. Among the 15 female patients, one had shown severe homosexual activities throughout adult life and one had had milder and temporary homosexual problems. As to other sexual perversions of long-standing and severe nature the following should be mentioned: severe and permanent masturbation in two adult men, for whom masturbation meant much more satisfaction than sexual intercourse; one case of several heterosexual perversions, and one clear case of sadistic attitude with frequent beating of his wife. There was one woman who had been educated to and accepted sadistic and masochistic activities directed toward her husband.

It is again impossible to say whether this number of sexual difficulties is higher than that in intellectuals of the same age in our population. Statistically there are certainly no real differences; it is possible, however, that sexual difficulties occur somewhat more frequently in alcoholics. (It has to be kept in mind that only the sexual behavior before the outbreak of severe alcoholism was decisive for the classification, that only severe sexual aberrations were used for classification.) It is particulaly interesting that overt homosexual tendencies are hardly more frequent among these alcoholics than in the average population.

One is more impressed with the pathological aspect of the sexual pre-alcoholic life of the alcoholics, if one considers the *ability to love* ("Liebesfähigkeit"). Many of the patients never experienced a real love relationship; they were never emotionally bound to any sexual partner, did not suffer when terminating their relationships, and never felt an urge to take over responsibilities and sacrifices for a mate. The majority of them had many merely sexual and temporary affairs and only felt sexual satisfaction, never love, for their mates. The minority of them had little sexual desire, and hardly ever had sexual relations and never love experiences. Some of them tried to build up relations on an intellectual basis, desiring to be married for social reasons, for instance, but remained very cold and distant to their mates. Of the 32 males only 10 had shown the ability to love, 17 were definitely unable to love, and five were borderline cases. Of the 16 females a relatively much higher number, 10, were able to love, five were not, and one was a borderline case. *If we include the ability to love in the classification of the sexual life, the number of sexually normal persons among these alcoholics becomes very small: only eight of the 32 males and six of the 16 females had a normal or a fairly normal sex life; in the large majority the sex life (particularly the ability to love) is severely and chronically disturbed.* The former statement concerning the great frequency of personality derangements in the premorbid personality of chronic intellectual alcoholics is reflected in the findings of sexual difficulties.

ENVIRONMENT DURING CHILDHOOD AND ADOLESCENCE

As a result of the selection of the index cases on a high social level the *material conditions* during their childhood and adolescence were much above average. None of them was ever hungry; none had to be ashamed in school because he was not properly dressed and cared for, and only one lived in an unhygienic and overcrowded apartment.

On the other hand, a very large number of these patients came from broken homes. If a *broken home* is defined as one in which the parents were separated or divorced before the patient was 20, or when one or both of the parents had died before he was 20, then 22 of the 50 patients came from broken homes. If one considers a home broken when the loss of one parent by divorce, separation, or death occurred before the patient was 17, still 20 of the 50 patients came from broken homes. The cases of broken homes are distributed as indicated in Table VII:

TABLE VII

BROKEN HOMES IN THE LIFE HISTORIES OF FIFTY AMERICAN ALCOHOLICS

Home Broken by	Age of patient when home was broken				
	0–5 Years	5–10 Years	10–15 Years	15–17 Years	17–20 Years
Separation of parents..............	3	1	—	—	1
Divorce of parents................	—	1	2	2	—
Death of one parent..............	5	1	4	1	1
Total...........................	8	3	6	3	2

The percentage of 40 or 44 of the patients coming from broken homes seems higher than in the average population. Ruth and Theodor Lidz and Pollock,[31,38] for instance, find about the same number of broken homes in the histories of schizophrenics (38%) and feel that these are very high numbers compared with depressives (20 and 16.7%) and medical students (17.4%).* One has to be careful, however, in interpreting the numbers: Prout and White[39] found broken homes before the age of 15 in 28% of both mothers of schizophrenics and mothers of normal people, as compared with 34% in this study; the difference is not statistically significant.

In each patient a careful study was made with regard to the home conditions up to his 20th year. The relationship with the parents or step-parents, the siblings or foster siblings, with servants who handled the nursing and education of the children, with other family

---

* Home broken before the age of 19.

members living in the same home, and the school environment was considered. For statistical purposes a distinction was made between home conditions which were distinctly favorable and those which were without any doubt grossly unfavorable. There remained a group of borderline cases in which the home conditions might be considered as fair. Grossly unfavorable home environments are of such a marked degree that there would no doubt be general agreement as to what type of case this term might be applied. On the other hand, there might be some dispute about the application of "favorable" or "fair."

As an example of a grossly unfavorable home environment, the following excerpt of a case history is given:

" . . . She was frequently told by her father that she had been an unwanted child, and that her mother had been very mean to her in her infancy. Although her father was a successful engineer and businessman, dying a millionaire, he subjected the family to the strictest economical measures, making them think he was poor. The parents had always had 'terrific arguments and violent quarrels' together. No reaction to the births of the younger siblings is recalled, but she was jealous of the youngest and only boy, who attracted most of her father's attention, and she frequently joined with her sisters in throwing stones at him. The patient, being the most attractive of the girls, was her father's favorite. The father treated her somewhat in the same way as his own girl friends, but he was always afraid that she might indulge in sexual relations and become pregnant. He showed her more attention, but would also frequently pull up her dress and beat her across the thighs until she became 16. He spanked and whipped the patient frequently. She lied frequently and he said 'he was going to beat it out of her.' He was jealous of all suitors except her eventual husband, and would pull her dress up in front of her boy friends before dates to see whether she had her panties on. As a child he would pinch her and her sisters and their friends on the thighs and buttocks to such an extent that their friends would not enter the house. He would parade nude around the house and the patient recalls an early aversion to his pubic hair and also his genitalia. He was openly unfaithful to his wife, and when the patient was 10, her mother rejected sexual relations with him, and after some violent arguments during which he would beat her, her father left the house, returning only at weekends, at which times the mother would leave. He would lock his room at night, telling the children that their mother was crazy and would surely kill him if she got the chance. The patient resented her mother for what she regarded as a hostile attitude towards her because of the attention she received from her father.

The mother was a most miserable housekeeper and neglected everything in the household, even the nursing of the children. She liked only her son, but disliked the daughters. She was 'always puttering about the house doing nothing.' She did not care for the patient when she was sick. She was sloppy about herself. The children felt that she was sneaky, opening the children's letters secretly, for instance. Childhood was punctuated by frequent changes of home throughout the country. The patient attended public schools until the second year of high school. She was a below-average student but would change report cards, one for the father to sign, and then back to the original for her teacher, until discovered when she accidentally omitted the second change. She attended two prep schools, being dropped from the first. She attended a school for kindergarten teachers from which she graduated but never taught, working instead in a store . . . "

According to this classification, 19 or 38% of the patients grew up in a grossly unfavorable home environment; in 16 or 32%, the home environment could be considered as favorable; in 15 or 30%, the home environment was considered to be fair. The distribution of favorable, fair, grossly unfavorable environments in the parents' homes and in broken homes is indicated in Table VIII:

TABLE VIII

QUALITY OF EARLY ENVIRONMENT OF FIFTY AMERICAN ALCOHOLICS

| | Home Environment | | | |
	Favorable	Fair	Poor	Total
With both parents.....................	10	10	10	30
In broken homes:				
With father alone...................	1	—	—	1
With mother alone.................	—	4	3	7
With father and step-mother..........	—	1	1	2
With mother and step-father..........	—	1	2	3
With two step-parents..............	1	1	1	3
With step-father alone..............	1	—	1	2
With step-mother alone.............	1	—	1	2
Total.........................	14	17	19	50

Only 10 out of the 50 alcoholic patients were brought up by both parents in favorable circumstances. Thirty out of 50 were brought up either in broken homes or under unfavorable circumstances by both parents. (Breaking up of the home until the age of 17.) Ten more were brought up by both parents under fair circumstances. A typical situation in the broken home of the alcoholics could not be discovered. Father or mother, with or without step-parent, foster parents, and foster father, or foster mother took care of the child after it had lost one or both parents. There are no differences in the care of the later alcoholics after the breaking up of their homes if we distinguish between males and females, which has not been done in the above table.

A further study was done with regard to the patients' attitudes toward the parents. The result of this study is summarized in Table IX.

Such a survey is open to very severe criticism: 1. It suggests a statistical evaluation while the numbers are much too small to allow any detailed statistical conclusions. 2. The evaluation of the quality of the parent picture is highly subjective and unreliable. The table has therefore only a very limited value in itself. It seems to me, however, to be a contribution to future research work. When the numbers can be added to those of other studies, they will have more meaning. By comparing the author's subjective impressions of the patients' parent-pictures with those of other investigators in the same field, the qualifications as to a general agreement will become clarified. The limited extent of our knowledge makes it necessary to add the conclusions of different research workers in order to reach definitive results. The criticism of the table of one of them would be justified if unproven conclusions were drawn from it. This criticism is however unjustified if the table is presented merely as a contribution to a future symposium of similar studies of different workers.

The classification presented of different parent-pictures has not been chosen on the grounds of a theoretical consideration. I have chosen the classification which was easiest to apply to my patients' descriptions. Most of the applied qualifications were repeatedly and clearly given by the patients themselves. It is admitted that it would be easy to present a more logically founded classification. The patients' descriptions, however, would hardly fit in with such a classifi-

TABLE IX
ATTITUDE OF FIFTY AMERICAN ALCOHOLICS IN REGARD TO THEIR PARENTS

FATHER PICTURE

Favorable and normal — 12 (8 males, 4 females)

Unfavorable	Borderline cases	Abnormal
Rejected		
As too strong & domineering	—	2 males
Too weak & effeminate	3 (2 males, 1 female)	5 (3 males, 2 females)
Too vague & distant	8 (males)	6 (5 males, 1 female)
Overaccepted		
Admired	3 (2 males, 1 female)	—
Highly ambitendent		
Loved and feared	2 (1 male, 1 female)	6 (1 male, 5 females)
Loved and held in contempt	—	3 (2 males, 1 female)
Total	16 (13 males, 3 females)	22 (13 males, 9 females)

MOTHER PICTURE

Favorable and normal — 17 (10 males, 7 females)

Unfavorable	Borderline cases	Abnormal
Rejected		
As too strong or masculine	4 (3 males, 1 female)	3 (1 male, 2 females)
Too weak & helpless	3 (2 males, 1 female)	5 (4 males, 1 female)
Too vague & distant	3 (1 male, 2 females)	5 (males)
Overaccepted		
Loved and pitied	5 (4 males, 1 female)	2 (males)
Highly ambitendent		
Loved and feared	2 (1 male, 1 female)	1 (male)
Total	17 (11 males, 6 females)	16 (13 males, 3 females)

TO BOTH PARENTS

Favorable and normal — 5 (2 males, 3 females)

Unfavorable	Borderline cases	Abnormal
To father, normal; to mother, disturbed	5 (4 males, 1 female)	3 (males)
To father, disturbed; to mother, normal	7 (6 males, 1 female)	4 (1 male, 3 females)
To both parents, disturbed	5 (3 males, 2 females)	21 (15 males, 6 females)
Total	17 (13 males, 4 females)	28 (19 males, 9 females)

cation. As in the case of any classification of subjective impressions, the one presented here is highly defective. For instance, any parent-picture can be qualified as "highly ambivalent." In my material it was true, however, that the conscious attitude of the patients as it was presented during an interview of several hours showed great differences in the grade of overt ambivalence. Most patients had consciously arrived at a somewhat uniform attitude toward a parent; of hate, fear, contempt, admiration or love, for instance. There was only a minority in whom love and fear or pity and hate, etc., were consciously of similar intensity. Only the latter were qualified as highly ambivalent. This does not exclude the fact that marked ambivalent attitudes could be discovered in each patient and certainly would even be more visible if the time spent with them could have been increased. The most difficult qualification concerned the question as to whether a parent-picture was "favorable and normal" or "unfavorable and abnormal." A group of borderline cases had to be interposed. These pictures are characterized by the most terrible experiences of cruelty, neglect, shameful, or overprotective behavior of the parents. The entire emotional life of these patients is damaged by the unfavorable parent-picture.

In order to illustrate the classification it is mentioned that the home environment described on page 147 led to an abnormal attitude of high ambivalence (love and fear) towards the father, and to a completely rejected mother-picture, which was considered as too weak and defective by the patient.

The tabulation of the parent-picture shows clearly one fact: *Unfavorable and abnormal parent-pictures prevail among our alcoholic patients.* Only five of the 50 patients have favorable and normal pictures of both parents. In 33 patients, on the other hand, one or both parent-pictures are unfavorable to an abnormal degree or the pictures of both parents are at least on the borderline between favorable and abnormally unfavorable. These findings confirm those of Wall and Allen.[55,56]

The findings further demonstrate that one has to be careful with regard to generalization: *The kind of disturbance of the parent-picture varies greatly in different cases.* Both in male or in female alcoholics the father-picture or the mother-picture can be too domineering or too weak. Just as important as an over-domineering or a very weak parent seems to be the vague picture of a parent who was mostly absent from the environment. There is no typical constellation visible in the figures; such as, for instance, a feared father and an overprotective mother for male alcoholics, etc. This does not exclude the possibility that some more or less typical constellations can be found in other and more extensive material. It only shows that almost any combination of unfavorable attitudes to father and mother may be found in some alcoholics.

It was further considered *how frequently the alcoholic patients have been under the influence of alcoholics during their childhood and adolescence before 20.* All 14 alcoholic parents have had a direct and apparent influence upon the 13 alcoholic index cases (one of them had two alcoholic parents). In at least two other index cases the father drank too much and was frequently seen intoxicated by the patient, but the degree of his abuse of alcohol was not sufficient to call him an alcoholic. (There was no alcoholic physical or mental damage nor any apparent social sequel due to alcohol elicited.) One further case had two alcoholic stepfathers: Therefore, 16 of the 50 index cases were under the influence of drinking parents or stepparents during long periods of their childhood and adolescence. Six further index cases were impressed at an age before 20 by the alcoholism of an uncle, an aunt, a grandparent, or a cousin. Some of them had frequently watched the alcoholic excesses of these relatives, and shared their fathers' and mothers' worries on account of the alcoholic relatives. Two further male index cases had been in a long-standing and intimate relationship with an alcoholic father or mother of a girl friend during adolescence. Four other index cases had long-standing friendships with alcoholic comrades before 20. One watched the alcoholism of a neighbor very closely and with strong emotional response for a long period. *As a whole, 29 of the 50 index cases had before the age of 20 long-standing and intimate contact with persons who had alcoholic problems.* We know (see page 124) that alcoholism in the parents of the alcoholic patients is more frequent than in the average population, but there is no material to compare the frequency of experience, of alcoholics with alcoholics other than the parents, with those of the average population. As a whole, early experiences of these alcoholics with alcoholic adults seem to be very frequent, occurring in 29 of the 50 cases. On the other hand, it is by no means a regular finding in alcoholics: 21 of the 50 patients had not had close relationships with any alcoholics in their childhood and adolescence. The majority of this second group can hardly remember having ever been confronted with an alcoholic or the problem of alcoholism in childhood and adolescence.

The early experiences of our patients show up even more unfavorably if one considers not only the relationship with alcoholics, but also include other severe kinds of personality disturbances: as the table on page 117 shows, 60 cases of psychoses and severe personality troubles (alcoholism included) occurred among the 100 parents of these alcoholics. Many of these disturbances started at an older age and were not yet noticeable when the patients were children and adolescents. *Thirty-three of the 50 alcoholic patients, however, were exposed for long periods before the age of 20 to psychoses and severe personality disturbances of one or both of their parents.* This is certainly an abnormally high number. Three other patients were greatly exposed in childhood or adolescence to the influence of psychotic, psychopathic, or alcoholic behavior of relatives other than father and mother. Four further patients were exposed, as already mentioned, to long-standing influences of alcoholic persons without blood-relationship. *There are only 10 of the 50 patients who had not suffered from a long-standing, unhappy influence of morbid personalities before the age of 20.*

Such a survey clearly demonstrates that the possibilities of unfavorable early identifications with important sequelae on the personality occur in alcoholism, as stated by Wall,[55,56] Bergler,[3] Sillman[44] and others.

INTERRELATIONS BETWEEN CONSTITUTION AND ENVIRONMENT

Hypothetically, a very easy way to distinguish constitutional from environmental influences seems to be by the study of alcoholics with poor constitution and healthy environmental experiences and of alcoholics under environmental stress but with a sound constitution. One could argue that alcoholism in a constitutionally-sound personality under environmental stress proves the significance of environmental factors and vice versa. The clinical facts, however, clearly demonstrate that such a consideration is not helpful. At once it is observed that in all alcoholics who have morbid parents or siblings, the morbidity of these parents and siblings has an important influence upon the environmental experiences of the patients. There were no constitutionally tainted alcoholics in this study whose psychodynamic development was not greatly influenced by the knowledge of, and the experience with, the morbidity of their near relatives. On the other hand, in every patient who had been apparently damaged by a poor environment, this environment proved to be poor in close connection with morbidity in the family or the morbid personality of the patient himself. *An independence of constitution and environment could never be found.*

In every individual case there can be made both a constitutional and an environmental hypothesis of the genesis of alcoholism; *in every single case, however, one reaches a much better understanding of the genesis of alcoholism if one takes into account the interrelationship of constitution and environment than if one studies both factors independently.* This statement may be illustrated by a brief summary of the genetic conclusions about alcoholism in some of the individual cases studied:

1. The alcoholism of a young female patient had started after her marriage. Judged in a superficial way, this marriage had seemed to be most promising. The husband was socially and professionally a very successful man with a warm and sympathetic personality and much consideration for the patient. The patient was of average intelligence and full of ambition to do well in life. Curiously enough, she emphasized that she became alcoholic because of jealousy of the husband's brilliant career and feeling bitter in regard to her own modest contribution to her family's success. She went through spells of anger because she was socially less esteemed than her husband. She also felt very dissatisfied by having to do housework, but neither was she able to do intellectual work in a satisfactory way. This attitude becomes understandable if one takes into consideration her own parents. Her mother had been a high-strung, active and aggressive woman. She had dominated the patient's father in her contact with him, but the father had retired into a seclusive admiration of nature and into loneliness. Apparently the patient's mother's attitude was formed by her own early experience: The patient's maternal grandmother was a "grande dame," an aristocrat, educated at a king's court, who had married a capable and rich, but unpretentious and plebian husband whom she had treated as socially inferior throughout their married life. The father had been educated, domineered and mishandled by a stepmother who had disliked him. He had defended himself against the stepmother in much the same way as he later defended himself against his wife—by being gentle and shy, but also by retiring into an introverted and romantic attitude. From the environmental study, one can conclude that the patient had identified herself with her domi-

neering and proud mother, her maternal grandmother, and paternal grand step-mother, but failed to achieve this identification in her own marriage on account of the personal and intellectual superiority of her husband. Her drinking meant to her much of a compensation of this failure, a revenge against the too successful husband and an expression of her frustrated male attitudes. Constitutionally, she could be diagnosed as suffering from an inborn ambitious and domineering activity which could not be realized on account of an average intelligence and the lack of warmth and originality of her personality. It can be considered that the occurrence of similar personality characteristics in her mother and her grandmother demonstrates inherited personal difficulties as the basis of her alcoholism. Constitution might have been shaped by the environmental factors, but the opposite is also possible. Most likely the interrelationship of both constitutional and environmental factors is responsible for the unhappy outcome.

2. In one male patient the alcoholism seemed to a great extent to be the expression of a hypomanic, overaggressive, and over-active attitude. He loved uninterrupted activity, both social and professional; his relations with other men seemed to be intensified and deepened by drinking in common; he made friends of his customers in indulging in social drinking with them, and he made customers of his friends with whom he drank. The personality of his father and grandfather had also been characterized by a hypomanic temperament and seen from this point of view the patient's alcoholism has an hereditary basis. But he was also married to a cold, demanding, hysterical woman who drove him out of the home by her cruel and egoistic behavior. His choice of a hysterical wife was certainly a result of his identification with his father. His father, a very warm, successful, and active personality had found fulfillment of his activity in spoiling and nursing the patient's mother, who had hysterical traits very similar to those of his wife. While the father had reached happiness through his care of the hysterical mother, the hysteria of the patient's wife was much worse than his mother's and made a happy life impossible. From a psychodynamic point of view, the marital situation can be explained by the patient's early identification with his parents and the alcoholism as an expression of the complete failure of his adaptation to life on the basis of these identifications. It is interesting to note that the father's relations with the mother seemed again to have been a copy of his father's (the patient's grandfather's) relations with his wife.

3. Another alcoholic patient had a brilliant, domineering, strong and very strict father, a greatly honored man in a brilliant society. His mother

was a sociable, intelligent, and over-active person, who was, however, quite dependent on her husband. The patient's brother created tremendous educational problems in his childhood, was in constant protest against paternal authority, and fought lively against discipline and restrictions. The patient, on the other hand (who was two years his brother's junior), was very obedient, diligent, and seemed to be no problem. The family's prognosis for the future life of the patient's brother was poor, but excellent for the patient. This situation was reversed after the two young men had left school and were faced with the problems of learning and practicing a profession. The brother did well, became a very successful businessman, took over the father's business and his leading social position after his death, and became a well-to-do prominent man as his father had been. The patient, on the other hand, felt anxious as soon as he was faced with any professional responsibility. He ran away from all work and duty because he suffered from feelings of inferiority, was extremely shy with girls, and indulged in solitary drinking when he had escaped from responsible situations and felt empty, dissatisfied, lonely, aimless, and anxious. Both brothers' developments can be explained by their personal reaction to the early home environment, but the sharp difference between these reactions suggests a constitutional background. The patient showed signs of shyness and passivity ever since his early childhood, while his brother was active and energetic although exposed to the same kind of stress as the patient.

4. Another alcoholic index case is the son of an alcoholic. His father had constant extramarital relations, was untidy, loud and aggressive at home; he was also suspicious and shut-in. The mother and the children reacted to the father's challenge by rejecting him and shutting him out from the common life. "Everyone withdrew, when he appeared." The mother was a hard worker, did very well from an economic point of view, cared a great deal for her children, but her display of affection toward them was poor. "The ordinary picture you have of a Scotsman would describe her." The patient developed very well intellectually and made a good academic career. He remained quite immature, however, in his emotions. He always felt insecure, inferior, anxious, and had compulsive personality features. Intellectually he was of his mother's opinion, but obtained no emotional satisfaction from the contact with her. He longed to break through the wall between the family and his father, but never could, and was very much afraid of his father. He married a wife who treated him much the same as his mother had treated his father. She did not show him overt affection, withdrew from him, refused to have much in common with him and domineered him. He felt

that his drinking was greatly due to the rejection by his wife and a form of protest against her since he was too timid to react in any other way. His personality development could be easily understood by the ambivalence to both parents; he identified himself consciously with his mother, but was emotionally frustrated by her unaffectionate attitude. He feared and rejected his father, but was secretly very much attached to him. His marital situation can easily be understood as a projection of his emotional identifications. He looked for a wife somewhat similar to his mother, but was frustrated by the cold attitude of such a wife. He felt anxious and unhappy in the role of his father and could not display the same brutality as his father had done. Drinking meant to him revenge against his wife, and at the same time, an attempt to complete the reconstruction of his early family situation, and an escape from his feelings of inferiority. There can also be found, however, much evidence that the patient's alcoholism has inherited constitutional roots. His family is tainted on either side by alcoholism (father, maternal grandmother, maternal uncle). His personality could be described as a schizoid psychopathy with compulsive traits, and schizoid psychopaths were very frequent in his father's and his mother's family. His alcoholism might just as well be the expression of his schizoid, psychopathic personality as of his psychological development. Furthermore, he is of an acromegaloid constitution and has many mental symptoms common in acromegaloid conditions, of which spells of increased thirst are most important for the explanation of his alcoholism. In this patient again, we cannot distinguish whether or not the environment has entirely formed his personality, or if his environment has been formed by the constitutional personality deviations of the patient and his relatives. (One small point is worth mentioning. The patient's father drank whisky to excess outside the home. The mother thought that drinking beer at home might be harmless and protect him from alcoholism. The patient's later alcoholism consisted in drinking beer at home to excess.)

There is not a single case among the 50 alcoholic index cases, in which the familial constitution did not cause a great emotional stress for the patient and the whole family group and in which, on the other hand, the emotional stress could not be understood as the underlying psychodynamics of the morbid personality development.

Familial constitution, personal constitution, environment, and personal development in alcoholics are not factors which can be separated from each other; they only exist in close interrelationship and have to be studied as an entity. A similar conception is evident in the teachings of Diethelm[15,16] on alcoholism. It is also one of the leading ideas of other workers on alcoholism such as Moore,[35,36] Wall,[55,56] Williams[59] and others.

CONCLUSIONS AND DISCUSSION

1. The results of this study demonstrate *the inadequacy of the older speculations in regard to causal connections between alcoholism and epilepsy and oligophrenia:* The older literature maintained that alcoholism leads to epilepsy and oligophrenia in the following generations, it also stated that a so-called "degenerative process," which was thought to cause epilepsy and oligophrenia, was the main constitutional background of alcoholism. These conceptions have been partly forgotten; however, one at times encounters some traces of them even in the most modern literature. Much evidence against the essential genetic interrelationship between alcoholism, epilepsy, and oligophrenia has been gathered within the last decades. It can not be stated, however, that the lack of such an interrelationship has been proved with unquestionable methods.

Among the relatives of this group of intellectual alcoholics are no more epileptics and oligophrenics than in the average population, in spite of the great frequency of alcoholics in all generations. *Alcoholism in one generation has not caused epilepsy or oligophrenia in the next generation.* This statement confirms former findings of Boss[12] and Bleuler.[5]

On the other hand, there is no doubt that oligophrenia or epileptic deterioration may be a causal factor in the genesis of alcoholism of some patients. In the parenthood of the alcoholics here studied, however, a correlation between alcoholism, epilepsy, and oligophrenia is completely lacking. This is an indication that epilepsy and oligophrenia must not be overestimated as predispositions to alcoholism.

2. Schizophrenia, manic-depressive psychoses, schizoid and cycloid psychopathies may be, in some cases, the background against which alcoholism develops. Among an intellectual group of alcoholics, manic-depressive personality traits are particularly frequent, just as they are more frequent in any educated group than in a group of a low intellectual standing. However, the present study (compared with studies on other groups of alcoholic index cases with the same technique) clearly demonstrates that *schizophrenic and manic-depressive*

psychoses are not more frequent in the relatives of alcoholics compared with the general population. This statement does not seem interesting since a hereditary link between alcoholism, schizophrenia, and manic-depressive phychoses has not been suspected. It is, however, interesting for dynamic psychiatry: The present group of alcoholics (as well as their siblings and a great number of their other relatives) had been submitted to situations of heavy and longstanding emotional stress during childhood and youth. The relationship with the parents was severely disturbed in the majority of the alcoholics. Furthermore, the sexual development was, in the majority of cases, unsatisfactory, or clearly morbid. As a matter of fact, the group of alcoholics studied (and most of their siblings and many of their relatives) were exposed during childhood to much the same stress situations as are frequently thought to be causal factors for psychoses, particularly for schizophrenia. There does not exist, however, an increased frequency of schizophrenia among these alcoholics, their siblings and their other relatives. This is certainly an instructive experience, which demonstrates how carefully one has to build up theories about the psychodynamics of schizophrenia. In the present study one deals with a group of 50 alcoholics and 1313 of their relatives who, on the average, have gone through more intensive stress situations during childhood than an average group of the population —but the frequency of schizophrenia is not increased among them.

This observation is certainly not in contradiction to the hypothesis of the importance of certain stress situations in the genesis of schizophrenia. It is, however, in contradiction to an oversimplification in this direction; it proves that not every stress situation, not every emotional frustration, not every disturbance of the relationship with the parents during childhood, and not every sexual maladaptation is a predisposition for schizophrenia. If early stress situations play an important role in the genesis of schizophrenia, they must be of another, or more special, nature than the stress situations to which the group of the population here studied was exposed, or they must exist in combination with certain constitutional or other factors, in order to be pathogenetic in schizophrenia.

3. The findings in the group of alcoholics studied demonstrate that endocrinological disturbances frequently play a causal role in the development of alcoholism. This is confirmed by some experimental and clinical observations of other investigators such as Goldberg,[19]

Goldfarb and Berman,[20] Gross,[21] Palmer,[37] J. J. Smith,[49-51] Tintera and Lovell,[54] and others. The present observations illustrate the importance of findings in endocrine patients regarding thirst and tension states. It is a well known fact that alternations of thirst exist during physiological periods of endocrine* conditions. The studies of the Zürich Psychiatric Clinic on the psychopathology of different endocrine disturbances revealed a great frequency of tension states in endocrine patients quite similar to those which are described by so many alcoholics. It has been shown, for instance, that acromegaloid persons frequently suffer from episodic agitation and tension, which may lead to poriomania, to uncontrolled sexual behavior, and also to dipsomania. *The finding of a frequent relationship between alcoholism and endocrine disturbances among the studied alcoholics certainly stresses the importance of the present interest in the endocrine roots of alcoholism.*

The same findings, however, also warn against exaggeration and oversimplification of the endocrinological theories of alcoholism: *Clinical evidence of endocrine disturbances cannot be found in the majority of alcoholics, but only in a minority. Furthermore, the endocrinological findings in alcoholics are extremely different from each other and cover practically the whole field of endocrinopathology.* It does not seem possible to consider just one, or a few, endocrinological factors as causal factors in alcoholism (such as hypoglycemia or adrenocortical hypofunction) and to neglect others. Such a one-sided conception does not fit in with the observation of most endocrinological findings in alcoholism.

The present observations also warn against the conception that endocrine influences act only on a mere metabolic (and not a psychological) basis in the genesis of alcoholism. The metabolic effects of endocrine disturbances are most frequently connected with marked emotional upsets. The question always to be considered is whether the endocrine disturbance helps to cause alcoholism merely by metabolic processes or by its emotional effects. In the group studied, emotional tensions were frequently connected with endocrine disturbance and the psychological action of the endocrine disturbance in the genesis of alcoholism becomes quite clear.

4. One observation stands out in this material: *alcoholism is most frequently a symptom of a morbid personality development. The con-*

---

* Changes (pregnancy, menstruation) and in the varied morbid endocrine.

stitutional background of alcoholism is identical with the constitu-
tional background of neurotic and psychopathic personality develop-
ments. All the findings in this group lead to the following statements:

a. The majority of alcoholics studied has been exposed to the same
kind of stress which is generally acknowledged to be the basis of
morbid personality developments; namely, conflict with the parents
and between the parents in their childhood.

b. The alcoholics themselves frequently show personality disturbances of some kind, particularly disturbances in the process of
sexual maturation.

c. Among the relatives of the alcoholics—many of whom had been
exposed to similar stress situations as the alcoholics themselves—both
alcoholism and the various kinds of morbid personality developments
occur in great frequency.

These findings confirm strongly the opinion of many modern authors, who emphasize the importance of the personality and its development into alcoholism (Diethelm,[15,16] Karpman,[26] Moore,[35,36]
Wall,[55,56] Williams,[59] Farago,[18] Seliger,[43] Lawn[30] and many others).

While the results of this study clearly show the outstanding importance of the personality development in the genesis of alcoholism,
they warn, on the other hand, against statements regarding one
special kind of personality derangement as the unique or main cause
of alcoholism. The roots of alcoholism are to be found in very different types of personality maladaptation. In many alcoholics, infantile traits are prominent; in others there exists a compulsive personality; in still others a depressive or hypomanic or cycloid maladaptation prevails; in a large group the morbid personality is expressed by
the emotions of tension and anxiety in social contacts and of dissatisfaction and loneliness when isolated from society; in some alcoholics
homosexual problems are active, etc. Generalized statements in
regard to the leading role of just one condition in the genesis of
alcoholism do not contain the whole truth. It is certainly right to state,
for instance, that an ambivalence regarding homo- and heterosexuality
is an important problem in many alcoholics. However, it would be
quite wrong to state that homosexuality is the main, or unique, sexual
problem of alcoholics. Many other sexual maladjustments play a similar important role, particularly infantilism.

Many previous authors have emphasized the importance of one or several personal characteristics which are encountered in this material. The importance of infantilism as a predisposition for alcoholism is stressed by Amark[1] and Lindberg.[32] Sillman[44] found all his alcoholics suffering from moodiness and anxiety. Karpman[27] and Wall[55] describe the various sexual aberrations of female alcoholics, which correspond to these findings. Farago[18] finds among 43 of 61 drug (mostly alcohol-) addicts the lack of ability to form mature love relationships with sexual partners, or nearly the same proportions as in this material. The importance of homosexuality in alcoholism has been demonstrated by the early psychoanalytic school. The great variety of personal predisposition is also mentioned by Diethelm[15,16] and is statistically demonstrated by Malzberg.[34]

As to prophylaxis and therapy of alcoholism, the findings on the group studied point out the *importance of psychotherapy*. This psychotherapy must consider the whole personality. *A therapy which does not consider the whole personality derangement cannot be acknowledged as a causal therapy of alcoholism.*

The attempt to find a specific character structure and specific psychodynamics has failed for alcoholism just as for many other troubles arising as symptoms of a morbid personality development. The question remains to be answered as to what causes lead to the choice of alcoholism as an expression of the morbid personality. The present study gives two leads in regard to this question: At first the positive and negative identification with alcoholic relatives, particularly with the parents, seems to play an important role in the choice of alcoholism as the outstanding symptom of the morbid personality. In some cases there might be endocrinological reasons which connect tension and anxiety states with thirst.

5. One aspect of the present study seems to be interesting not only in regard to alcoholism but also to general psychiatry: The findings here presented demonstrate that alcoholism is a highly familial morbid condition. The older psychiatry took it for granted that a familial incidence was due either to heredity or to environmental influences, and that hereditary and environmental factors could be easily separated. In sharp contradiction to such a conception, the present study shows that *in alcoholism one deals with the result of a very close interrelationship of heredity and environment.* It is superficially possible to explain alcoholism either by the hypothesis of

hereditary primary personality derangements or by the hypothesis of a maladaptation to environmental stress. A satisfactory explanation, however, can be given, if one considers the influence of the inherited personality pattern in forming the environment and the environment in acting on the individual personality. Constitution and environment in the genesis of alcoholism cannot be separated.*

This illustrates a situation which holds true not only for alcoholism,

---

* The classic method which genetic science offers in order to distinguish the influence of environment and of heredity is, of course, the twin method. This method, however, could not solve the problem presented. It is built up on the assumption that monozygotic twins are identical in their hereditary constitution, but just as different as dizygotic twins in regard to the environment in which they grow up. With regard to psychodynamics, this latter assumption is entirely wrong. It would only be right if the emotional environment of a man was not influenced by his personality make-up. As a matter of fact, one might say that personality forms its environment and is formed by its environment. A high correlation of psychological symptoms in monozygotic twins can be due to both; to the identical hereditary constitution and to the similar environment which both identical twins have created.

The inadequacy of the twin method with regard to the separation of constitutional and environmental causes of alcoholism is well demonstrated by a monozygotic pair of twins in this material. Both of them showed an alcoholism of a very similar kind and a very similar degree. If someone is prejudiced by hereditary hypotheses he will be inclined to see in this fact a clear evidence of the importance of heredity in alcoholism. If one considers the facts from a psychodynamic point of view, however, quite a different conclusion is arrived at. In both twins, alcoholism was connected with a feeling of disgust with common interhuman relationships and tendencies to withdraw from ordinary life and from loneliness to a unique and brilliant, but unknown kind of activity. Both twin brothers had been gifted much more than their parents and siblings and had worked themselves up from a primitive social life to highly intellectual activities. They lost any close touch with people of their former group. In their new social contacts, however, they felt insecure and lonely and longed for the warmth of the old home. They were able to build up relationships on a highly intellectual basis with other men, but not on an emotional basis with women. Their high intellectual ambition forbade contacts with people of the same origin, but their emotions were still linked up with them. In their new situation they created the most curious social relations, tried to be comrades to queer old ladies, felt hurt in military service by the authority of non-intellectual superiors, etc. They failed in both heterosexual adaptation and in homosexual activities. They also had a marked problem of being emotionally dependent on each other. As a matter of fact, they suffered from exactly the same kind of environmental stress, gone through acquaintances and failed in friendships with the same or similar persons of both sexes, were in the same way intellectually distant from and emotionally close to their parents and siblings. From this point of view, the alcoholism of which they suffered in common was a reaction of the same kind of emotional stress. They had not only the same inherited constitution but also the same adaptation problems, and their common alcoholism can be regarded as an hereditary disease as well as an adaptation difficulty.

but also for the majority of psychiatric conditions. In many of them, for instance, in the group of schizophrenic disorders, the study of the family history on the basis of heredity has failed entirely to lead to satisfactory knowledge. With all the work of the last decades on the relatives of schizophrenics, the nature of schizophrenia could not be explained; neither has it been possible to find, up to the present, a specific situation of environmental stress as the explanation of a schizophrenic development. Much more promising were the studies which considered in some small groups of schizophrenics, or in the individual schizophrenic, the interrelationship of constitution and environment.

The speculative assumption of an independence of heredity and environment in psychiatry has proved to be a great hindrance to therapeutic and prophylactic progress. We must learn that both in life and in psychiatric practice constitutional and environmental influences are not to be separated.

Modern psychotherapy arises from the understanding by the therapist and by the patient himself of the patient's personal development. Such an understanding must be based on the study of the environmental influences on a certain personality. The knowledge of the personal reaction patterns and their influence upon the formation of the environment is needed to complete the study of the influence of the environment with its stress situations of the personality.

The close interrelationship between constitutional and environmental factors in the genesis of alcoholism is a warning against the old speculative attempts to consider constitution and environment as separate facts in psychiatric research and psychiatric treatment.

SUMMARY

1. A group of 50 chronic alcoholics of North American descent and of a superior intellectual and social background were studied and information was collected about their 1313 relatives.

2. Among the relatives of the alcoholic index cases no more cases of schizophrenia, manic-depressive psychoses, epilepsy, and oligophrenia were found than in an average population of the same social level. On the other hand, there was much more alcoholism among the siblings, parents, and husbands and wives of these alcoholic index cases than in the average population. There were also more morbid per-

sonality developments of neurotic or psychopathic nature among the close relatives of the alcoholics studied than in the average population. The statement on the increased number of alcoholics and morbid personality developments on the one hand, and that concerning an average number of schizophrenics, manic-depressive psychoses, epileptics and oligophrenics, on the other hand, can be generalized, since it holds true also for alcoholics studied by Brugger in Switzerland, and since different groups of the relatives of non-alcoholics studied with the same technique can be compared with the present findings.

3. In more than a fourth of the studied cases of alcoholics there is clinical evidence of some endocrinological disturbance. Causal interrelationship between these endocrinological disturbances and alcoholism can be demonstrated in most of the cases; the kind of interaction between endocrine difficulty and alcoholism is variable.

No characteristic body type of the alcoholics studied has been found.

Tremor is not only a common sequel of alcoholism, but can also influence the psychodynamics of alcoholism.

4. In 20 of the 50 alcoholic index cases the personality development before the onset of alcoholism was clearly morbid; only 10 of them could be considered as clinically normal personalities before they started to drink. Twenty were borderline cases. The most varied types of personality disorders were observed in the index cases before the onset of their alcoholism. Most frequent were those persons who felt tense and anxious in society and unsatisfied and lonely when they were alone; also frequent were cyclic, depressed, or hypomanic personalities, then compulsive personalities, persons with infantilism, and persons with homosexual problems. Sexual adjustment was sound in only 14 of the alcoholics before the onset of their alcoholism, while it was severely impaired in the other 36 cases. Most frequently there was the impossibility of forming a real love-relationship with the other sex; also frequent was impotence and frigidity and homosexual trends. There also occurred various other sexual maladjustments.

5. The home conditions during the childhood of the alcoholic index cases proved to be very poor. Only 10 of the 50 alcoholics were brought up by both parents in favorable circumstances. Thirty of them were brought up in broken homes or in unsatisfactory circumstances by both parents.

The majority of the alcoholics studied had very unfavorable and clearly morbid relations with one or both parents. Only five of the 50 patients had a favorable and sound picture of both parents. The type of disturbance in the relations with the parents was varied and no rules could be formulated with regard to it. The father picture and the mother picture were disturbed in about the same frequency; both pictures could be described as a too strong, severe, and dominating attitude or by a too weak and dependent attitude, or by ambivalent attitude, or by being too protective towards, or too distant from, the patient.

6. Twenty-nine of the 50 alcoholics had before the age of 20 long-standing and intimate contact with persons with alcoholic problems. On the other hand, it often occurs that older alcoholics have never met any alcoholics during their childhood and adolescence. Many of them, however, were under the long-standing influence of morbid personalities of another kind than alcoholic. There were only 10 of the 50 alcoholics who had not suffered from a long-standing unhappy influence of morbid personalities before the age of 20.

7. In the cases studied it proved to be quite impossible to separate hereditary from environmental influences. There was a close causal interrelationship between environmental and hereditary factors. The environment seemed to form the personality and the personality formed the environment.

8. The following *conclusions* were drawn: (a) Family studies in alcoholism reveal no evidence of the old hypothesis that alcoholism causes epilepsy or oligophrenia in the offspring; (b) Any hypothesis which postulates the same kind of stress as the essential cause of both schizophrenia and alcoholism must be wrong or incomplete, since the increased stress situation in a group of alcoholics here studied leads only to increased frequency of alcoholism but not to increased frequency of schizophrenia; (c) There do exist important endocrinological factors in alcoholism. They are, however, not evident in all cases of alcoholism; the kind of endocrinopathology is extremely varied and endocrinological disturbances do not only cause a disposition towards alcoholism by the metabolism, but also by its action on the emotions; (d) The genetics of alcoholism are very closely related to genetics of abnormal personality developments and alcoholism has to be considered mainly as a symptom of abnormal personality development. For this reason, a therapy acting on the personal development seems to be the most promising in alcoholism; (e) The study of the

constitution of alcoholics reveals a situation characteristic of the majority of psychiatric conditions: Environment and inherited constitution cannot be separated and considered as independent causal factors. Environment and constitution are closely interrelated. It is important for psychiatric research and therapy to consider hereditary and environmental influences together and to drop the older speculative assumption that genetic research and therapy could be based only on constitutional research or on environmental research.

BIBLIOGRAPHY

1. AMARK, C.: Nagra synpunkter pa miljöförhallanden och konstitutionella faktorer vis kronisk alcoholism. *Sv. Läkartidn.* 25:1644, 1946.
2. BENEDETTI, G.: Die Konstitutionspathologie der Alkoholhalluzinose und das Problem der Anlage zu den alkoholischen Psychosen. In preparation.
3. BERGLER, EDMUND: Personality traits of alcohol addicts. *Quart. J. Stud. Alcohol,* 7:356, 1947/48.
4. BLEULER, M.: Vererbungsprobleme bei Schizophrenen. *Z Neurol.,* 127:321, 1930. *J. Nerv. & Ment. Dis.,* 74:993, 1931.
5. —— Psychotische Belastung von körperlich Kranken. *Z. Neurol.,* 142:780, 1932.
6. —— Krankheitsverlauf, Persönlichkeit und Familienbild Schizophrener und ihre gegenseitigen Beziehungen. Leipzig, Georg Thieme, 1941.
7. —— Das Wesen der Schizophrenieremission nach Schockbehandlung. *Z. Neurol.,* 73:553, 1941.
8. —— Die spätschizophrenen Krankheitsbilder. *Fortschr. d. Neur. & Psych.,* 25, Jg., 259, 1943.
9. —— Untersuchungen aus dem Grenzgebiet zwischen Psychopathologie und Endokrinologie: Akromegaloid: *Uebersicht. Arch. Psych.* 180, H.3/4, 282, 1948. Ein Genialer mit akromegaloider Körperkonstitution. do. p. 303.
10. BLEULER, M. and RAPOPORT, L.: Untersuchungen über die konstitutionelle Verwandtschaft von Tuberkulose und Geisteskrankheiten. *Z. Neurol.,* 153:649, 1935.
11. BLEULER, M. and ZURGILGEN, B. A.: Tuberkulose und Schizophrenie. *Wiener med. Wchnschr.,* 99, Jg., 31/32, 357, 1949.
12. BOSS, M.: Zur Frage der erbbiologischen Bedeutung des Alkohols. *Mschr. Neurol.,* 72:264, 1929.
13. BRUGGER, C.: Zur Frage einer Belastungsstatistik der Durchschnittsbevölkerung. *Z. Neurol.,* 118:459, 1929.
14. —— Familienuntersuchungen bei chronischen Alkoholikern. *Z. Neurol.,* 151:103, 1934.
15. DIETHELM, OSKAR: Research Project on the Etiology of Alcoholism. *Quart. J. Stud. Alcohol,* 9:72, 1948.
16. —— *Treatment in Psychiatry.* Springfield, Ill., Charles C Thomas, Publisher, 1950.
17. DUBLINEAU, J. and DUCHENNE, H.: Analysis of one hundred cases in a special psychiatric service for alcoholic patients in the Paris area. Encéphale, 2:275, 1940. Abstract in: *Arch. Neurol. & Psychiat.,* 46:1946, 1941.
18. FARAGO, ISTVÀN: Zur Frage der Entstehung von Suchtkrankheiten. *Mschr. Psychiat. & Neurol.,* 117:98, 1949.

19. GOLDBERG, L. and STOERTEBECKER, T. P.: Antinarcotic effect of estrone on alcohol intoxication. *Acta Physiol. Scandinav.* 5:289, 1943.

20. GOLDFARB, ALWIN I., and BERMAN, SIDNEY: Alcoholism as a psychiatric disorder. I. Endocrine pathology of animals and men excessively exposed to alcohol, its possible relation to behavior pathology. *Quart. J. Stud. Alcohol,* 10:415, 1949.

21. GROSS, M.: The relation of the pituitary gland to some symptoms of alcoholic intoxication and chronic alcoholism. *Quart. J. Stud. Alcohol,* 6:24, 1945.

22. HAGGARD, H. W. and JELLINEK, E. M.: *Alcohol Explored.* Garden City, Doubleday, 1942.

23. JUNG, C. G.: *Psychologische Typen.* Zürich, Rascher & Cie., 1921.

24. KAHN, EUGEN: Die psychopathischen Persönlichkeiten. In: Bumke Oswald: *Handbuch der Geisteskrankheiten,* 5.Bd., Berlin, Springer-Verlag, 1928.

25. KALLMAN, F. J.: *The Genetics of Schizophrenia.* New York, J. J. Augustin, 1938.

26. KARPMAN, BENJAMIN: The chronic alcoholic as a neurotic and a dreamer. *J. Nerv. & Ment. Dis.,* 94:17, 1941.

27. —— *The Alcoholic Woman.* Washington, The Linacre Press, 1948.

28. KNOEPFEL, H. K.: Untersuchungen aus dem Grenzgebiet zwischen Psychopathologie und Endokrinologie. Fünf akromegaloide Schizophrene und Psychopathen mit ihren Familien. *Arch. Psych.* 180, H.3/4, 332, 1948. Statistische Verarbeitung von 23 Fällen bereits beschriebener akromegaloider Schizophrener und Psychopathen und ihrer Familien. do. p. 361.

29. KRETSCHMER, E.: *Körperbau und Charakter.* Heidelberg-Berlin, Springer-Verlag, 1950.

30. LAWN, HAROLD J.: The study and treatment of alcoholism in the 5th SC. Rehabilitation Center. *Am. J. Psychiat.,* 102:479, 1945/46.

31. LIDZ, RUTH WILMANNS and LIDZ, THEODORE: The family environment of schizophrenic patients. *Am. Psychiat.,* 106:332, 1949.

32. LINDBERG, BENGT T.: Psycho-Infantilism. *Acta Psychiat. et Neur.,* Suppl. 61, 1950.

33. LUXENBURGER, H.: Zur Methodik der empirischen Erbprognose in der Psychiatrie. *Z. Neurol.,* 117:543, 1928.

34. MALZBERG, B.: A study of first admissions with alcoholic psychoses in New York State, 1943–1944. *Quart. J. Stud. Alcohol.* 8:274, 1947/48.

35. MOORE, MERRILL and GRAY, M. G.: A comparison of alcoholism and drug addiction with particular reference to the underlying psychopathological factors. *J. Criminal Psychopath.,* 3:151, 1942.

36. —— Alcoholism: Some contemporary opinions. *New England J. Med.,* 224:848, 1941.

37. PALMER, H. D.: The Hypoglycemic State in Alcoholism. Mentioned in: MOORE, MERRILL: Alcoholism: Some contemporary opinions. *New England J. Med.,* 224:848, 1941.

38. POLLOCK, H. M., MALZBERG, B. and FULLER, R. G.: *Hereditary and Environmental Factors in the Causation of Manic-Depressive Psychoses and Dementia Praecox.* State Hosp. Press, Utica, New York, 1939.

39. PROUT, G. T. and WHITE, M. A.: A controlled study of personality in mothers of schizophrenic male patients. *Am. J. Psychiat.,* 107:251, 1950.

40. RUEDIN, E.: *Studien über Vererbung und Entstehung geistiger Störungen.* Berlin, J. Springer, 1916.

41. SCHNEIDER, KURT: Die psychopathischen Persönlichkeiten. In: Aschaffenburg's *Handbuch der Psychiatrie.* Leipzig-Wien, 1923.

42. SCHULZ, B.: *Die Methodik der medizinischen Erbforschung.* Leipzig, Georg Thieme, 1936.
43. SELIGER, R. V.: The psychiatrist looks at contemporary alcoholism. *Am. J. Psychotherapy,* 2:383, 1948.
44. SILLMAN, LEONARD R.: Chronic Alcoholism. *J. Nerv. & Ment. Dis.,* 107:127, 1948.
45. SJOEBRING, H.: Den individualpsykologiska frageställningen inom psykiatrien. Uppsala, 1913.
46. ———— Psykisk konstitution och psykos. *Sv. Läkaresällskapets Handlingar,* 45:462, 1919.
47. ———— Det konstitutionella problemet. *Förh. vid Nord. Psykiatr., Kongr.,* 1922.
48. SLATER, E.: The inheritance of manic-depressive insanity and its relation to mental defect. *J. Ment. Sc.,* 82:626, 1936.
49. SMITH, J. J.: A medical approach to problem drinking. *Quart. J. Stud. Alcohol,* 10:251, 1949.
50. ———— The role of the adrenal gland in alcoholism. In: MOTE, I. R.: *Proceedings of the First Clinical ACTH Conference.* Philadelphia, Blakiston Co., 1950, p. 566.
51. ———— The treatment of acute alcoholic states with ACTH and adrenocortical hormones. *Quart. J. Stud. Alcohol,* 11:190, 1950.
52. STROEMGREN, E.: Zum Ersatz des Weinberg'schen abgekürzten Verfahrens. Zugleich ein Beitrag zur Frage von der Erblichkeit des Erkrankungsalters bei der Schizophrenie. *Z. Neur.,* 153:784, 1935.
53. SULZER, H. J.: Zur Frage der Beziehungen zwischen dyskrinem und schizophrenem Krankheitsgeschehen. Ein akromegaloider Schizophrener und seine Familie. *Arch. Klaus-Stiftg.* Zürich, 18:461, 1943.
54. TINTERA, J. W. and LOVELL, H. W.: Endocrine treatment of alcoholism. *Geriatrics,* 4:274, 1949.
55. WALL, J. H.: Psychotherapy of alcohol addiction in a private mental hospital. *Quart. J. Stud. Alcohol,* 5:547, 1944/45.
56. WALL, J. H. and ALLEN, E. B.: Results of hospital treatment of alcoholism. *Am. J. Psychiat.,* 100:474, 1944.
57. WANDER-VOEGELIN, MARGRIT: Schizophrenes und endokrines Krankheitsgeschehen: Akromegaloide Schizophrene und ihre Familien. *Arch. Klaus-Stiftg.* Zürich, 20:257, 1945.
58. WEINBERG, J.: Zum Problem der Erbprognosebestimmung. Die Erkrankungsaussichten der Vettern und Basen von Schizophrenen. *Z. Neurol.,* 112:101, 1938.
59. WILLIAMS, ROGER J.: The etiology of alcoholism: a working hypothesis involving the interplay of hereditary and environmental factors. *Quart. J. Stud. Alcohol,* 7:567, 1946/47.
60. WOLF, DELIA: Zur Frage der Beziehungen zwischen dyskrinem und schizophrenem Krankheitsgeschehen. Ueberprüfung der bisherigen Untersuchungen an grösserem Untersuchungsgut. *Arch. Klaus-Stiftg.* Zürich, 21:149, 1946.
61. ZUEBLIN, W.: Untersuchungen aus dem Grenzgebiet zwischen Psychopathologie und Endokrinologie. Untersuchung eines akromegaloiden Psychopathen und seiner Familie. *Arch. Psych.,* 180:H.3/4, 284, 1948.
62. ZURGILGEN, B. A.: Untersuchungen über die konstitutionelle Verwandtschaft von Tuberkulose und Schizophrenie. *Diss.* Zürich, 1949.

A COMPARATIVE STUDY OF THE CONSTITUTIONS OF SWISS AND AMERICAN ALCOHOLIC PATIENTS

MANFRED BLEULER, M.D.

In the summer of 1950, after having finished the examination of 50 American alcoholics of a high social level, a study of alcoholics of the University of Zürich Psychiatric Clinic Burghölzli was started from the same points of view and with the same technique. This new material should, first, increase the number of patients and increase the reliability of the conclusions drawn from the American material; second, it was collected for the purpose of comparing the constitutional background of alcoholics of quite different social and cultural standards. Such a comparison will throw a light on the question as to whether the findings in regard to the constitution of alcoholics are only true in a definite social group or are characteristic for alcoholism in different social and cultural groups.

It is planned to study a much larger group than 50 alcoholics in Zürich and to work for several years on them. The findings on all the alcoholics studied in Zürich will be published later in detail. As an addendum to this study on 50 American alcoholics, however, there will be given a preliminary brief survey of the first 50 Swiss alcoholics, whose constitutional backgrounds have been studied. It is also desirable to compare roughly the findings on the Swiss and on the American alcoholics.

Among the 50 cases from Zürich were 38 males and 12 females (34:16 in the American material). At the time of examination 24 were married,* nine divorced, one separated, two widowed and 14 single. (The corresponding numbers in the American material are very similar.) The age distribution at the time of examination is as follows:

---

* Three of these had previously been divorced, one widowed.

30–40 years	12 patients
40–50 years	19 patients
50–60 years	10 patients
60–70 years	6 patients
over 70 years	3 patients

(The Zürich patients are on the average six years and two months older than the American patients.)

Burghölzli, being a Clinic run by the State of Zürich, admits patients from the entire population; the Burghölzli patients are not a selection of people of a high social and intellectual background as were the patients of the Payne Whitney Clinic and the Westchester Division of The New York Hospital. Among the males were: one commercial clerk, 22 artisans, two gardeners, one farmer, one landlord and cheesemaker, four laborers, three railway-workmen, three occasional workers, one farmhand. The professions of the female patients before their marriages were as follows: six housewives (one of them was at the same time a saleswoman), one commercial clerk, one waitress, one cook, one dancing partner, one barmaid, one laundry maid, one housemaid. The professions of the husbands of the married female patients were: one newspaper director, one businessman, one accountant, one commercial traveller, one university graduate without occupation, three artisans, two laborers, one chef, one waiter.

All of the Zürich alcoholics are white; 48 are of Swiss origin, one is an Italian and one a German. Of the 48 Swiss, 36 came from German-speaking communities, one from French- and two from Italian-speaking communities. None of them was of English or American descent.

The alcoholism of the 50 Zürich patients had started at the following ages:

15–20 years	8 cases
20–30 years	24 cases
30–40 years	11 cases
40–50 years	3 cases
not exactly known	4 cases

(On the average the alcoholism of the Zürich patients started slightly earlier than the alcoholism of the American patients.)

The duration of the alcoholism at the time of examination was:

1–5 years	1 case
5–10 years	6 cases
10–20 years	17 cases
over 20 years	22 cases
not exactly known	4 cases

(The duration of alcoholism was, therefore, much longer in the Zürich group than in the American group.)

In nearly all of the Zürich alcoholics there was evidence of mild physical damage due to chronic alcoholism, in five cases there was a marked liver cirrhosis present and in two cases an alcoholic epilepsy. Eleven patients had suffered from delirium tremens, five from alcoholic hallucinosis and nine from Korsakow's psychosis. All patients developed a personality deterioration of an alcoholic nature. The degree of this deterioration varied on a wide scale. As a whole, the Zürich group showed more numerous and more severe physical and psychiatric complications of alcoholism than the American group.

In short, the 50 alcoholics from Zürich are mostly of Swiss descent and socially on a much inferior level than the American alcoholics. The Zürich alcoholics are, on the average, older than the American alcoholics, their alcoholism started earlier, lasted longer, and was of a more severe degree.

The following table summarizes the *findings on the relatives of the alcoholics from Zürich*:

TABLE X
SURVEY OF CLOSE RELATIVES OF FIFTY ALCOHOLICS FROM ZÜRICH

	Total	Schizophrenia	Probable Schizophrenia	Manic-depressive Psychoses	Involutional Depressions	Other Depressions	Senile and Arterio-sclerotic Psychoses	Epilepsy	Other Organic Psychoses	Psychoses with Unknown Diagnosis	Alcoholism	Probable Alcoholism	Alcoholic Psychoses	Feeble-mindedness	Neurotic & Psycho-pathic Personality Alterations	Suicide
Parents	98	—	—	—	—	—	2	—	—	1	17	3	—	1	9	1
Siblings	173	3	—	—	—	1	—	2	—	—	7	1	—	10	13	1
Half-siblings	33	—	—	—	—	1	—	—	—	—	—	—	—	—	3	—
Children	62	—	—	—	—	—	1	—	—	—	—	—	—	1	7	—
Wives & Husbands	45	—	—	—	2	—	—	—	—	—	3	—	—	—	5	—
All Relatives	411	3	—	—	—	3	3	3	—	1	27	4	—	12	37	2

The corrected percentage for schizophrenia among the siblings of the Zürich alcoholics is 2.25%, while there are no schizophrenics among the parents, half-siblings and children. Among all those close relatives the corrected percentage for the incidence of schizophrenia is 1%, exactly the same number as in the general population. The conclusion drawn from the families of American alcoholics holds true, therefore, in the case of the alcoholics from Zürich: There is no increased incidence of schizophrenia among the relatives of alcoholics compared with the general population.

The rather high incidence of manic-depressive psychoses among the American alcoholics was supposed to be due to their high social level. The finding of no manic-depressive patients among the 411 relatives of the Zürich alcoholics (who had a much lower social background) argues for this assumption.

Epilepsy and feeble-mindedness occur in the Zürich alcoholics more frequently than in the American alcoholics; this is to be expected, because there exists a negative correlation between the occurrence of epilepsy and feeble-mindedness and the social and intellectual level of a group. It seems that epilepsy and feeble-mindedness in the relatives of the Zürich alcoholics is even somewhat higher than in the average population (but the difference is not statistically reliable). This could easily be explained by the fact that the general social and intellectual level of the Zürich alcoholics is even lower than the level of the average population.

The incidence of alcoholism in the relatives of the Zürich alcoholics runs as shown in Table XI.

These figures show clearly that the incidence of alcoholism among the relatives of the Zürich alcoholics is much higher than in the average population, just as it was true for the incidence of alcoholism among the relatives of the American alcoholics of high social and intellectual level. The incidence of alcoholism is particularly high among the fathers and mothers of the Zürich alcoholics and relatively low among their siblings. It is not clear how this difference in the two generations is to be explained.

The percentage of *psychopathic personality developments* among the relatives more than 10 years old are: for the parents 9.2, for the siblings 7.5 and for the children 11.3. These figures are not quite as high as the percentages of psychopathic developments among the

TABLE XI

FREQUENCY OF ALCOHOLICS IN THE FAMILIES OF FIFTY ALCOHOLICS OF ZÜRICH

	Number of Relatives Above 10 Years	and Number of Alcoholics Among Them	Percentage of Alcoholics Among the Relatives Above 10 Years	Number of Male Relatives Above 10 Years	and Number of Alcoholics Among Them	Percentage of Male Alcoholics Among the Relatives Above 10 Years	Number of Female Relatives Above 10 Years	and Number of Alcoholics Among Them	Percentage of Alcoholics Among the Female Relatives Above 10 Years	Number of Relatives Above 40 Years	and Number of Alcoholics Among Them	Percentage of Alcoholics Among the Relatives Above 40 Years	Number of Male Relatives Above 40	and Number of Alcoholics Among Them	Percentage of Alcoholics Among the Male Relatives Above 40 Years	Number of Female Relatives Above 40	and Number of Alcoholics Among Them	Percentage of Alcoholics Among the Female Relatives Above 40 Years
Parents.......	98	20	20.4	49	16	32.6	49	4	8.2	90	19	21.1	45	16	35.5	45	3	6.6
Siblings	162	8	4.9	77	6	7.8	85	2	2.3	110	8	7.3	49	6	12.2	61	2	3.3
Half-siblings..	32	—	—	15	—	—	17	—	—	21	—	—	11	—	—	10	—	—
Children......	47	—	—	22	—	—	25	—	—	7	—	—	2	—	—	5	—	—
Husbands and Wives......	45	3	6.6	13	2	15.4	32	1	3.1	33	3	9.1	9	2	22.2	24	1	4.2

relatives of the American alcoholics nor as high as the percentages among the relatives of Swiss schizophrenics of the same social level as the Zürich alcoholics. They are, however, much higher than the percentages of psychopathic developments in an average Swiss population. It seems therefore that the high incidence of psychopathic personality developments holds true for the relatives of alcoholics of different social and cultural backgrounds; it is, however, more marked in the relatives of alcoholics of a high social level. The reason for this difference in degree is perhaps due to the fact that a psychopathic personality development might be recognized more easily in an individual in a responsible and outstanding position than in an individual in an humble position like a farmhand.

The number of husbands and wives is too small to permit a comparison between those of the Zürich and American alcoholics. The differences are statistically not significant. If we add the numbers of the husbands and wives of the Zürich and the American alcoholics, however, we arrive at a number large enough to allow the following statement: The husbands and wives of alcoholics are more frequently alcoholic or psychopathic than the average population.

The findings in the families of the Zürich alcoholics are much the same as those in the families of alcoholics from Basle of a similar social level, who were studied by Brugger.

In regard to the *physical constitution* of the 50 alcoholics from Zürich, the *endocrine condition* is of particular interest. Fourteen of the 50 alcoholics have a history of distinct endocrine derangements. This is exactly the same proportion of endocrine derangements among alcoholics as found in the American material. (Of the 38 male alcoholics there were 10 with endocrine derangements, of the 12 female alcoholics, four.) The nature of the endocrine derangement can be summarized as follows:

Three cases (two males, one female) of distinct hyperthyroidism as shown by clinical records;

One case (female) with a large struma (which made strumectomy necessary) and with a nervous condition before the operation, with regard to which it is not certain whether it was of a hyperthyroid nature;

Two cases (male) of marked acromegaloid constitution;

Three cases (two males, one female) of infantilism (in the male cases pathologically late puberty and infantile voice, in the female case dwarfism, infantile body proportions, and late puberty);

One case (male) of severe one-sided testicular atrophy and very infantile penis;

One case (female) of masculine physical features and an amenorrhea of seven year's duration in the 20's;

One case (male) of female hair distribution, physical infantilism and gynecomasty;

Two cases (male) of acquired testicular atrophy and loss of male hair distribution.

The question whether there exists a causal relationship between alcoholism and endocrine pathology was studied individually in every case. This study demonstrated: In two cases a causal relationship could be excluded (in one case the Basedow had been completely cured by strumectomy 12 years before the onset of alcoholism; in one case the unilateral testicular atrophy and underdevelopment of the penis did not interfere with the sexual functions and was—as far as could be elicited by the psychological analysis—not felt to be a psychological stress).

In three cases of testicular atrophy and loss of hair (in one further complicated by gynecomasty) the endocrine derangements were clearly the sequelae of the alcoholism.

In nine cases, however a marked causal influence of the endocrine derangement on the origin and course of alcoholism could be demonstrated: Four times there were infantile personality traits connected with the infantile physical make-up, three times the hyperthyroidism was connected with a tense and anxious mood and twice the acromegaloid condition was connected with the well-known personality derangement frequent in cases of this physical stigmatisation (apathetic mood interrupted by sudden mood swings or sudden uncontrolled impulses). All these emotional conditions were closely related to the psychodynamics of the alcoholism.

Besides the 14 cases of distinct endocrine derangements there were 13 more cases of very mild or suspicious endocrine derangements among the Zürich alcoholics (while there had been four among the American alcoholics). The nature of these mild endocrine derangements or of the signs suspicious of such was: five cases of mild male infantilism (late puberty, infantile voice, or infantile hair distribution in one case complicated by episady), one precocious male puberty, two very marked pre-menstrual tension, one very severe climacteric complaint, one case of nodular struma without signs of hyperfunction, one case of partial Cushing's syndrome, one case of gynecomasty during a period of undernourishment, and one case of very slight acromegaloid condition. In six of these cases a causal relation between alcoholism and suspicious endocrine derangement could not be demonstrated; the gynecomasty was the sequel of undernourishment during longstanding alcoholism; twice the alcoholism had much to do with the emotional infantilism connected with the physical signs of infantilism, three times the alcoholism was impaired by premenstrual or climacteric tension states and the case of mild acromegaloid condition was connected with the emotional disorder often connected with such.

The *personalities* of the Zürich alcoholics were much more difficult to determine than the personalities of the American alcoholics. Since the Zürich alcoholics are older and have been suffering for a longer time than the American patients, the pre-alcoholic period is on the average much more distant from the time of the examination. There is, therefore, less reliable information available. Furthermore, educated informants are much more able to give a reliable description of the personality than uneducated informants and most of the American informants had higher education than those in the Zürich group. For this reason it is impossible to compare the personalities of the two groups in detail. In particular, the sexual and erotic life of the Zürich alcoholics will not be discussed, the information being too scanty and unreliable.

Two of the Zürich alcoholics were psychotic (one had chronic schizophrenia, the other epilepsy with deterioration), three were slightly and one severely feeble-minded. (Among the American cases, one was manic-depressive and none feeble-minded.) Seventeen of the remaining cases displayed a marked psychopathic development even before the onset of their alcoholism as compared with 18 among the American alcoholics. Eight (20 in the American material) were borderline cases, and 20 (10 in the American material) were seemingly within normal limits of their personality development before the onset of alcoholism. The statement that pre-alcoholic personality disorders are frequent among alcoholics, but are not to be demonstrated in all alcoholics holds true therefore for the Zürich group.

As to the *quality of the morbid personality developments*, the material allows the following statements: In the Zürich group there are no cycloid psychopathic personalities and no marked obsessive and compulsive traits. This has to be explained by the well known fact, that cycloid personalities as well as compulsive and obsessive personalities are more frequent in persons with a high social and intellectual background than in uneducated and primitive persons. The most common morbid traits in the pre-alcoholic personalities of the Zürich alcoholics are infantilism, insecurity, inability to mix with other people, hyperirritability and sensitivity, and social irresponsibility.

The *environment during childhood and adolescence* of the Zürich alcoholics was evaluated in the same way as for the American alcoholics. In spite of the very different cultural and social background of the Zürich alcoholics, they had suffered from broken homes with the same frequency as the American alcoholics. The parents' home was broken in 25 of the 50 Zürich cases (and in 22 of the 50 American cases). The ages of the patients at the time of the breaking up of the home and the reasons for it are the following ones:

TABLE XII

BROKEN HOMES IN THE LIFE HISTORIES OF FIFTY ALCOHOLICS FROM ZÜRICH

Home broken by	Age of Patient When Home was Broken				
	0–5 Years	5–10 Years	10–15 Years	15–17 Years	17–20 Years
Separation of parents..............	—	—	—	—	—
Divorce of parents................	1	1	—	—	—
Death of one parent..............	6	5	6	3	1
Patient taken away from family.....	1	—	1	—	—
Total.........................	8	6	7	3	1

The age of the patients when their parents' home was broken up, is quite similar in the Zürich and in the American group; the reasons for the broken home, on the other hand, are somewhat different: In the Zürich group the home was less frequently broken on account of separation and divorce and more frequently on account of the death of one parent than in the American group.

When the home conditions of the Zürich alcoholics were judged as "favorable," "fair," and "poor" in the same way as for the American alcoholics, the figures of Table XIII were gathered:

TABLE XIII

QUALITY OF EARLY ENVIRONMENT OF FIFTY ALCOHOLICS FROM ZÜRICH

	Home Environment			
	Favorable	Fair	Poor	Total
With both parents.....................	10	9	6	25
In broken homes				
With father alone....................	1	1	—	2
With mother alone....................	1	3	3	7
With father and step-mother..........	1	—	3	4
With mother and step-father..........	—	—	3	3
With two step-parents...............	3	1	3	7
With step-father alone...............	—	—	—	—
With step-mother alone..............	—	—	—	—
In a home.........................	—	1	—	1
Early independence.................	—	—	1	1
Total...........................	16	15	19	50

It is again striking to discover how similar the distribution of favorable and unfavorable home conditions during childhood and early adolescence is for the Zürich and American alcoholics—in spite of their very different social level. In both groups only 10 of 50 patients had grown up with both parents in seemingly favorable conditions

TABLE XIV

ATTITUDE OF FIFTY ALCOHOLICS FROM ZÜRICH IN REGARD TO THEIR PARENTS

FATHER PICTURE

Favorable and normal — 15 (14 males, 1 female)

Unfavorable	Borderline cases	Abnormal
Rejected		
As too strong & domineering	3 (males)	7 (5 males, 2 females)
As too weak & effeminate	—	2 (males)
As too vague & distant	4 (3 males, 1 female)	11 (7 males, 4 females)
Overaccepted		
Admired	1 (female)	—
Highly ambitendent		
Loved and feared	—	2 (males)
Loved and held in contempt	3 (1 male, 2 females)	2 (1 male, 1 female)
Total	11 (7 males, 4 females)	24 (17 males, 7 females)

MOTHER PICTURE

Favorable and normal — 29 (24 males, 5 females)

Unfavorable	Borderline cases	Abnormal
Rejected		
As too strong & masculine	1 (female)	3 (males)
As too weak & helpless	—	—
As too vague & distant	6 (3 males, 3 females)	7 (6 males, 1 female)
Overaccepted		
Loved & pitied	—	—
Highly ambitendent		
Loved & feared	—	2 (1 male, 1 female)
Loved & held in contempt	—	2 (1 male, 1 female)
Total	7 (3 males, 4 females)	14 (11 males, 3 females)

TO BOTH PARENTS

Favorable and normal — 13 (12 males, 1 female)

Unfavorable	Borderline cases	Abnormal
To father, normal; to mother, disturbed	1 (male)	1 (male)
To father, disturbed; to mother, normal	8 (6 males, 2 females)	8 (6 males, 2 females)
To both parents, disturbed	1 (female)	18 (12 males, 6 females)
Total	10 (7 males, 3 females)	27 (19 males, 8 females)

and in both groups 19 of the 50 patients had suffered from deplorable conditions at home. Thirty-one of the 50 Zürich alcoholics (and 30 out of the 50 American alcoholics) were brought up either in broken homes or under appalling circumstances by both parents.

The main characteristics of the attitudes of the Zürich alcoholics towards their parents were determined just as it was done for the American alcoholics. The result is less certain in the case of the Zürich alcoholics; they were less intelligent and more deteriorated by their alcoholism and, therefore, very vague and unreliable in regard to the description of their emotional attitudes towards the parents as shown in Table XIV.

These figures in regard to the parent-picture of the Zürich alcoholics demonstrate a high number of disturbed parent-child relationships; the attitude of the Zürich alcoholics towards their mothers, however, seems to be more favorable as was found true for the American alcoholics. Two reasons may account for this difference: The mother of a poor family, who has to work hard in her household, might more easily be accepted and loved by the child than a mother, who can afford domestic help and has no urgent duties in her household; or the uneducated and more deteriorated Zürich alcoholics might simply not be able to speak about their disturbed emotional attitude in the same clear way as the American alcoholics.

What was said about the *close linkage between constitution and environment* in regard to the American alcoholics also holds true for the Zürich alcoholics: Constitutional and environmental factors could by no means be separated. An unfavorable personality constitution in a close relative of a patient impaired the environment; on the other side, an explanation of an abnormal personality development could be found in environmental stress situations.

SUMMARY AND CONCLUSIONS

1. The findings in regard to the constitution of 50 alcoholics from Zürich are summarized and compared with the findings on American alcoholics.* The Zürich alcoholics are on the average less intelligent and from a lower social level than the American alcoholics, their alco-

---

* During the last few months, the group of alcoholics in Zürich has been increased to 90. The findings from these 40 additional patients are mainly identical with those of the 50 alcoholics presented in this paper.

holism started earlier in life, had lasted longer at the time of the examination and had caused more severe somatic and psychiatric damage.

2. The conclusion drawn from the study of the American alcoholics in regard to the family picture of alcoholics holds true when checked in the Zürich group: Schizophrenia, manic-depressive psychoses, epilepsy and feeble-mindedness occur with the same frequency in the relatives of alcoholics as in groups of the average population of the same social level. On the other hand, alcoholism and psychopathic personality developments occur much more frequently among the relatives of alcoholics than in the average population. Not only the blood relatives of alcoholics, but also their husbands and wives are more frequently alcoholic or suffering from morbid personality developments than the average population.

3. Endocrine derangements are as frequent among the Zürich alcoholics as among the American alcoholics. In both groups there can be frequently demonstrated a causal interrelationship between alcoholism and endocrinopathology. The majority of the alcoholics, however, do not show clinical evidence of endocrinopathology.

4. Morbid personality developments before the onset of alcoholism can be almost as frequently demonstrated in the Zürich group as in the American group of alcoholics.

As to the quality of the unfavorable personality developments there do exist some differences between two socially and intellectually different groups of alcoholics.

5. The Zürich alcoholics suffered from broken homes and other poor early home conditions with the same high frequency as the American alcoholics; in both groups the emotional attitude towards the parents is frequently severely disturbed; the abnormal rejection of the mother picture, however, could be demonstrated less frequently among the Zürich alcoholics.

6. Environmental and constitutional influences are just as much linked together in the Zürich as in the American material.

ALCOHOLISM IN THE CANTONESE OF NEW YORK CITY: AN ANTHROPOLOGICAL STUDY

MILTON L. BARNETT,* PH.D.

INTRODUCTION

Chinese drink and become intoxicated, yet for the most part drinking to intoxication is not habitual, dependence on alcohol is uncommon and alcoholism is a rarity. These are central tendencies of the range of drinking behavior manifested by individuals comprising Chinatown's society. At the extremes of this range are the behavioral syndromes typified by total abstinence on the one hand, and chronic drinking on the other. These findings are at variance with the common claim that excessive drinking does not occur among the Chinese.

Reflecting the interest in the relationship of cultural factors to alcohol consumption and chronic alcoholism, a study was undertaken in 1947 to determine the frequency of alcoholism in the Chinese community of New York. Dr. Richard P. Wang, a psychiatrist trained in Shanghai and at the Johns Hopkins Medical School, studied individual Chinese drinkers and analyzed records of such patients who had been admitted to city, private and state hospitals. This survey revealed a low incidence of alcoholism. It was difficult to find a sufficient number of Chinese patients for an adequate psychiatric analysis. From this exploration by Dr. Wang, it became obvious that the study of Chinese alcoholism required understanding of sociological factors, and that there was a need to examine the problem in its broader cultural context.

The goal of a new research design, which was put into effect in

---

* The Department of Sociology and Anthropology of Cornell University cooperated in this study.

January 1949, was to study the social environment of which the individual drinker is a participant. The writer was selected as a member of the interdisciplinary team in part on the basis of linguistic proficiency in Chinese. Miss Ivy Ch'en, a graduate student in social work in New York, also joined the research venture. A division of labor was planned, consistent with the disciplines represented by the team members. In conformity with the plan of the alcoholic studies conducted in the Department of Psychiatry, it was accepted that: "Research into the etiological factors of alcoholism, a goal to which our efforts are directed, must include the study of the individual in his immediate environment as well as in the culture in which he lives."[2] The field work on which this study is based was done by the writer in New York's Chinatown, from February to September 1949.

The vast majority of Chinatown's population emigrated from or is descended from four contiguous counties (*hsien*) in one province, Kwangtung, and generally known as the "Cantonese." The group therefore has a certain degree of homogeneity insofar as dialect, historic tradition, and local culture are concerned. It can be argued that interpretations derived from research data have a validity in terms of reference to that special Kwangtung sub-culture which could not be obtained were the population more representative of China as a whole. At any rate, regional and linguistic differentials disappear as variables, facilitating the problem of control.

An analysis of drinking behavior and its effects, based upon precise quantitative data, is not being presented here. But this has not been our goal. At best we can provide broad generalizations derived from information gathered by techniques normally employed in a reconnaissance study. As with most anthropological studies, our concern has been with similarities rather than differences. Emphasis has been on the society and its traditions, on what appear to be predominant, shared behavioral patterns, in contradistinction to the individual variations of behavior. Typicality has not been assumed for this Cantonese society as a whole. One becomes too aware of contradiction and variation to neglect them. The division of labor of the research team was such that analysis of the individual psychology of the deviates from drinking norms was made by the clinician. The function of the social scientist was to concentrate on the internal consistencies which exist in the culture and have their roots in the common experiences which all members of the society share throughout their individual life spaces. The aim here has been not to make an analysis of Chinese alcoholics, but rather to present a picture of the social milieu in which they live. Our immediate task was not to describe those who depart radically from the norms which are implicit or stated in the culture, but rather to characterize the norms themselves and the social controls which operate to insure adherence or prevent violation.

METHODS AND PROCEDURES

A review of the literature pertaining to the community made it apparent that it would be necessary to obtain a fairly comprehensive understanding of the community and its culture, both the dynamics of the internal structure and the relations of Chinatown to the rest of New York City. In order to obtain this data, the techniques and methods of cultural anthropology were employed: observation, examination of records, press and other published materials, formal and informal interviews, and projective tests. There are limitations on the establishment of rigorous, objective measures employable in observing and recording drinking behavior. The gross techniques used include a variety of subjective "hunches." Such impressionistic reactions should be reported inasmuch as they are in a large part based on non-articulate, minimally perceived cues.

It was possible to obtain certain limited types of data during the first stages of field work despite the general hostility which existed toward most outsiders. Eventually, warm relations were developed with a number of persons and this made it possible to obtain entry into homes, associations and other phases of social life in the community. Informal headquarters, *ch'ut yap*, were established by the writer in a small shop, a tong headquarters, the offices of several clubs and associations. However, interviews took place for the most part in homes or places of work. To insure uniformity of procedures, psychological testing was done in private, either at the Payne Whitney Clinic or in a room in the community. Identification with the hospital and an explicit interest in Chinese customs aided in dispelling any manifestly negative reactions; only one person refused to take the Rorschach test.

In addition to field activity in Chinatown, periodic meetings were held with representatives of hospitals and social service agencies to discuss problems arising from their contacts with Chinese clients and patients. Concrete issues based on cultural differences were introduced and discussed by persons attached to ten different institutions. These sessions were rewarding to the team as a source of information; reciprocation occurred through the opportunity to exchange data and some direct assistance rendered by the Payne Whitney group.

In some respects it may be said that informants were not representative of the community as a whole. Known users of opiates, for instance, were avoided lest suspicion of one's motives be incurred. It was difficult to establish relations with transient seamen. Lastly, it was felt that too few contacts were maintained with elderly China-born persons, male and female. While they were often observed in the company of others and some interaction between them and the writer occurred, information concerning old-age status is fragmentary and primarily drawn from secondary sources, that is, from interviews with younger people.

THE SETTING OF CHINATOWN

Chinatown is situated in the lower East Side section of Manhattan. Wedged in between the expansive City Hall district and the depressed areas of the Bowery and Chatham Square are the homes of perhaps one-fourth of metropolitan New York's Chinese population. The heart of the neighborhood consists of a cluster of eight city blocks, cut into various shapes by winding, narrow streets. The northern boundary is Canal Street, a wide thoroughfare running east and west. Connecting three major traffic routes—the Manhattan Bridge, the West Side Highway, and the Holland Tunnel—Canal Street becomes a boundary line marked by a steady flow of cars, busses, and trucks. During the morning and late afternoon and evenings, the stream slows down to a virtual standstill—a mass of vehicles inching their way to or from Brooklyn.

The western edge of Chinatown is marked by Baxter Street, decked with cluttered fire escapes, washlines and crowded doorfronts. Many Chinese families reside in the one block running south of Canal, but an Italian population prevails as the majority group.

Baxter terminates abruptly at Columbus Park, two square blocks of playground and benches.

Worth Street, running through the Civic Center into Park Row and the New Bowery, forms the southern border of the community. At this latter juncture, going north, is the Bowery, a cobblestoned street cut off from the sky by an elevated train structure. The Bowery is lined with cheap restaurants and lodging houses. Large numbers of unemployed, declassed men roam its sidewalks, bartering and selling various objects, ranging from gold watches and rings to secondhand shoes and spectacles. During winter nights men huddle in doorways, seeking shelter from the cold by covering themselves with old newspapers. During the warmer months, they sprawl on the sidewalks, lying in sleep or drunken stupor. The constant rumble of trains overhead completes the oppressive atmosphere of this eastern boundary of Chinatown.

Actually, the population of the Chinese-American community has spread beyond the traditionally defined "Chinatown." Clusters of families have moved into the run-down apartment houses of Little Italy north of Canal Street. Chinese names on mail-boxes in the tenements of the Jewish neighborhood are no longer uncommon, and a Chinese grocery store on Henry Street bases its trade on the local colonization. The Chinese children who may be seen playing on the sidewalks of Forsyth or Broome Streets, and Chinese social clubs occupying store and loft space on East Broadway serve as additional indices of the fact that Chinatown's population is no longer confined within that small, overcrowded area. However, Chinatown is still the focus of the Chinese population; and the group solidarity that was manifestated by the foundation of a ghetto-neighborhood was, at least in great measure, a product of social necessity. The Chinese had been widely dispersed throughout the western sections of the country. In an atmosphere where legal recourse was virtually impossible, the Chinese suffered indignities and humiliation, physical assaults, murder and robbery. Concentration of numbers within a compact residential area provided a modicum of protection from molestation. Chinatown* offered a semblance of security in which in-group feelings of solidarity were crystalized and reinforced. Involuntary choice

---

* The Cantonese refer to the community as *Wa Fau,* China Port or Market.

as well as "voluntary segregation,"[12] a need for mutual aid in the face of severe external pressures underlies the foundation of the Chinese section of New York City during the 1880's in the wake of anti-Chinese agitation on the Pacific Coast.

The census of 1940 reports 12,753 Chinese in New York City, 10,967 males and 1,786 females.[15] Of the total, 4,745 were native-born American citizens, with the remaining five-eights, 8,008, for-eign-born. The ratio of males to females is approximately 6:1 or, more precisely, 614.1 males per 100 females. The predominance of male immigrants prior to the Chinese Exclusion Act is also reflected in the fact that whereas only 32.3 per cent of the males are reported as native-born, 67.1 per cent of the females were reported as having been born in the United States. China-born brides brought to this country by their American-veteran husbands since the end of World War II may stabilize to some degree the unbalanced sex ratio.

Most estimates suggest that between 4,000 and 5,000 Chinese live in the locality of Chinatown.[3] The figures of the 1940 Census Bureau reports for New York City (12,753) and the large metropolitan area (18,000) are probably too low. Census takers were assiduously avoided by those who feared exposure of their illegal entry into the United States. Further difficulties and resultant inaccuracy stem from the dual residences maintained by those who work elsewhere in the city environs. Language barriers, illegally procured birth certificates and citizenship papers, as well as a reluctance to reveal information to strangers, are characteristic of many people in the community. These factors have very likely added to the understatement of New York's Chinese population.

Chinatown serves as the community center for those Chinese who live in other parts of New York City, in Long Island, Westchester County and Northern New Jersey. Various association headquarters, friends, families, and service agencies attract the outsiders in large numbers on week ends. Thus, a semi-transient population also plays an active role in Chinatown's community life, and in many respects must be considered as part of its membership. Of those who have few ties or no identification with Chinatown, four major groups pre-vail in New York: (1) the colony of personnel attached to the United Nations and Chinese government delegations; (2) students from China, most of whom reside in uptown Manhattan in the vicinity of Columbia University; (3) a small community of Shanghai people living in the West Thirties; and (4) the relatively small number of individuals from East, Central, and North China who dwell throughout the city. Barring an occasional dinner downtown or periodic treks to shop for Chinese groceries, these groups tend to avoid contact with Chinatown.

As in other Chinese-American communities, the majority of the residents come from Kwangtung Province. In New York, practically all of the China-born are from one of the Four Districts, the *Sz-yap*,* four contiguous counties lying to the southwest of Canton: T'oi Shan, Hoi P'ing, Sun Wei, and En P'ing.† Of these, T'oi Shan immigrants are most numerous.‡ Hok Shan, Canton City, Chung Shan, and other Kwangtung districts are also represented among Chinatown's inhabitants, but in considerably smaller numbers. Hok Shan lies adjacent to the *Sz-yap* and its inhabitants tend to identify themselves with that region.

A closely-knit group of Hakka§ people comprise a small, but extremely influential section of the local population. Although most of them come from Kwangtung, they do not regard themselves as Cantonese. Buttressed in number by transient seamen, the Hakka have gradually been accepted as part of the communty. Few of China's other provinces are represented in Chinatown, their emigrants being insignificant in number.

Differences in district background reflect themselves in language. The *Sz-yap* varieties of Cantonese are the most widely used in the neighborhood, their mutual intelligibility making for relatively

---

* There is no official or widely accepted romanization for Cantonese. The orthography used here and in the following pages is based on E. J. Eitel, *A Chinese Dictionary in the Cantonese Dialect* (London, 1877).

† Listed as T'ai-Shan, K'ai-p'ing, Hsin-hui and En-p'ing in A. Hermann, *Historical and Commercial Atlas of China* (Cambridge: Harvard Univ. Press, 1935.)

‡ Their numerical strength is seen in the influence of the T'oi Shan district association, Ning Young, in local politics. The need to counter T'oi Shanese power resulted in the formation of the Lin Sen society in which are banded all other Kwangtung persons. This predominance can also be observed in directories of Chinese-Americans.* That this distribution is of no recent development is reflected in a listing of 83 prominent Chinese in New York City. Of the 76 reported as coming from Kwangtung, T'oi Shan is represented by 43 persons.[16]

§ Primarily bilinguals who speak Hakka and Cantonese, a large number of these Chinatown residents come from fishing and farming settlements north of Canton.

smooth communication. The standard vernacular, however, is the Canton City dialect, which has considerable prestige value in the community. Used on formal occasions and taught to the children of Chinatown in the Chinese Language School, Canton City dialect may be said to occupy the same status in relation to the local colloquial variations that Pekingese has to other Mandarin dialects.

PATTERNS OF DRINKING

A Buddhist precept states: *Pat yam shue tsau,* "Drink not wine." The people in the Four Districts of the province of Kwangtung did not take this admonishment too seriously. Drinking was very much a part of the daily routine. Various informants stated that at an early age, the male child had contact with wine and was encourged to drink it. A man from Hoi P'ing recalled being drunk at the age of six. Others reported similar experiences. A young boy was told by his *tai kung,* paternal grandfather, that as an adult he would probably drink much. He had the responsibility, therefore, of learning to control himself. Such strictures at this age would seem to be relatively rare. More frequently, the offering of wine to children was casual, though their reactions to it were observed with interest and amusement. Children were not punished for drinking and at best scolded if they drank too much. Predictions about a youngster's tolerance for alcohol, *tsau leung,* were made. The individual who didn't react to drink by having a flushed face, *tsau wan,* was more likely to contain himself.

Not only was the child offered wine during meals; but in some villages, there was direct access to a wine jar located in the village temple. Here was stored wine donated by those families whose sons had reached social adulthood. Young boys as well as youths and men were free to imbibe when they wished. Learning to drink, therefore, came at an early age and as a result of participation. The children drank and watched others drink at social gatherings, at religious ceremonies, in the market place, and in their own households.

The children drank, and they soon learned a set of attitudes that attended the practice. While drinking was socially sanctioned, becoming drunk was not. The individual who lost control of himself under the influence of liquor was ridiculed and, if he persisted in his defection, ostracized. His continued lack of moderation was regarded not only as a personal shortcoming, but as a deficiency of the family as a whole. As we know, in Kwangtung this very often meant the entire village.

The social organization of Chinatown does not permit the same type of socialization with respect to drinking. Nevertheless, although parents are more careful and less permissive about children drinking, the latter are allowed tastes of distilled liquor if they request it and do drink wine in various forms on a variety of occasions. Second-generation parents and those more acculturated to American values tend to be considerably more restrictive. Despite this trend, drinking plays an important part in many social contacts and there is no condemnation of drinking as such.

Types of Alcoholic Beverages. Four package stores operated by Chinese are located in the community. It is estimated that at least 50 per cent of their customers are Chinese. One, located directly in the center of Chinatown, probably sells 80 to 90 per cent of its stock to Chinese. The largest sales are of Scotch whiskey; cognac and Canadian whiskies are also popular. Bourbon and rye whiskies, rum, and gin are seldom purchased. The sale of wine to Cantonese is almost entirely limited to sherry, which is often used in cooking and perhaps approximates Cantonese *pak tsau* or *pak kon*. The other types of wine are sold in much smaller quantities. They are kept in stock, of course, but primarily to supply the needs of the local Italian population as well as the wants of the transient Bowery personnel.

Some Chinese wines are available in the community. The imported varieties are relatively expensive, although by no means prohibitive. One can buy a quart for a few dollars. *Ng ka p'ei* is perhaps the most popular. It is a fiery, reddish brandy which is often used for ceremonial purposes and at special functions. *Sam shiu* is a general term for the more potent types of distillations. *Mai tsau*, rice wine, is obtainable in a number of forms. Occasionally, one hears of North Chinese wines made of wheat or *kaoling,* but these are rare.

Domestic varieties are limited in number. Some of these may be purchased commercially. Others are brewed for private consumption and, to be sure, some are brewed for public sale without benefit of appropriate federal license. Occasionally, an individual runs afoul of the law for possessing an unregistered still.

Despite the availability of Chinese liquors, there appears to be no extensive use of them. One hears of medicated wines being used for their tonic qualities, but apart from this reason, *wai sz k'ei* (whiskey) and sherry seem to have become acceptable substitutes.

The Home. Drinking with meals, or at least with some food, is a basic usage. The Chinatown businessman usually drinks when he dines at home. It is the prerogative of the father; occasionally, older sons may be invited to join him. With such a routine, one seldom finds a large quantity being consumed. The diner will have, in all, about three ounces of whiskey per meal. This practice is accepted by the family members; the child, setting the table, anticipates her father's arrival by having a glass or jigger ready for him. If the China-born father has grown daughters, it is very likely that they will want to indulge once in a while. Father may frown and mother protest, but cajolery permitted of the girls usually prevails. Households such as these have rum and cola or ginger ale available for this kind of family spree, and even a normally abstentious mother will sip sherry or a diluted rum drink. If the home is not attached to the place of business, it is likely that the father will have lunch away. At his place of work, wine may be served on occasion with the meals. Beer is finding wide acceptance in Chinatown and it becomes a less expensive substitute for whiskey.

Most of the time the Chinese drinks his whiskey straight. Water is sometimes added, but in small quantities. The drink is not consumed until one is seated at the dinner table. It is not downed in one or two gulps, but sipped while the meal is in progress.

After a busy week end, or perhaps because all of one's family are gathered together, a festive attitude might encourage even larger quantities of liquor being consumed than one is wont to have daily. Getting tipsy under such conditions is not abjured, so long as one keeps a sense of proportion in his behavior.

Drinking Games. At the wedding banquet sponsored by the groom's family, the meal is initiated with a ceremonial toast. Thenceforth, until the very end of the dinner, the usual banquet pattern prevails. People eat and people drink. They drink singly, as each desires, and they quaff the wine or whiskey in accordance with the number of familiar drinking games which enliven the affair and which, like *ch'ai mui*, guessing fingers, serve as tests of *tsau leung*, liquor capacity.

In the "Flower Game," for example, A quotes a line of verse or traditional Chinese prose which contains the word flower, one of its synonyms, or the name of a flower. If the word is *nth* in the phrase, A counts around the table in clockwise order, beginning with himself. The *nth* person must then drink a cupful of wine. At this point it is the latter whose privilege it is to offer an appropriate quotation, and the game continues. Failure to have a ready line also requires paying forfeit by drinking.

Participating in the game necessitates more than passing acquaintance with literary allusions and accordingly provides intellectual challenge and stimulation for the contestants. Alertness and a reservoir of timely phrases result in recognition of talents and, if a player is so inclined, permit a concerted attack on a given individual, forcing the latter to drink heavily. The outcome is often decided not by literary knowledge but rather by drinking capacity, by skill in withstanding the befuddling effects of liquor. This is only one example of the many games which are popular among the Chinese in which the loser must pay the penalty by drinking.

In the occidental play for drinks, the winner in a cast of dice or matching of coins earns the free drink. The Chinese system works in reverse of this. For each game that a player loses, *he* must drink. Thus, in a three out of five match, the loser will have "gained" one drink more than the winner. Again from the viewpoint of the Chinese, this is a loss. The basic motive of the game is consistent with the motive in intensive, social drinking. The Chinese doesn't drink to get drunk. He drinks so that the other man will get drunk.

As a Chinese banquet progresses the diners urge each other to drink more. One is solicitous in filling the glass of another. When games become too slow a drinking procedure, more direct methods are sought. The matching of drinks is undoubtedly the most common form used in Chinatown. One simply proffers the whiskey bottle to his neighbor or chosen drinking companion. The latter, accepting it, pours into both his and the donor's glasses the same amount. In this way the challenged individual determines the quantity to be consumed. He may defer making the decision, yielding to the initiator of action who then proceeds to pour equal amounts. They drink in unison and swallow the contents of the glasses in one or more consecutive gulps. This is done with dispatch for the match is not considered terminated until both have finished the set amount. Upon completion of the round, either drinker is liable to challenge by someone else, and the same procedure ensues. The game seems to be played first at each table and after a while, table rivalries develop. Thus, for a time at least, several matches may be engaged in concurrently. With the movement of drinkers from one group to another, the attention of the entire party seems to focus on this activity. With shouts of encouragement, suggestions as to who shall compete, and calls of *kan pui* ("dry cup") the other diners participate in spectator fashion, applauding, eating and drinking as they look on the scene. Each of them, however, may be called upon to take the center of the stage.

As the bouts gain momentum and particularly as activities switch to inter-table competition, conversation becomes raucous. The challenger often approaches his opponent with exaggerated steps and exaggerated posturing. The whiskey bottle is offered for acceptance with a sharp thrust, the gesture seemingly maintained until observed by others, or it may be slammed on the table apparently to create noise and thereby the desired attention. The earlier solicitous attitude and casual friendliness is no longer existent. In its place may be a direct challenge. Now there is no polite invitation, but a dare. A selective process develops retiring many from this type of interplay and leaving it to a smaller number who seem not to rest between drinks but are impelled to further bouts. With the challenge now may be an imprecation or personal disparagement. Tones are louder and sharper. Couched in the broader context of laughter and play, rivalries emerge which are settled only by the victory of one over the other—either by refusal to drink and thus default, by obvious difficulty in downing a drink, or by behavior designating one as the poorer drinker.

If the dinner is held in a restaurant, it is unlikely that the small Chinese wine cups will be available. In their place are water tumblers or tea cups. It is more than probable, too, that occidental whiskey will be the main or sole drink rather than wine—Chinese or otherwise. The intensity of alcoholic consumption can be seen, it seems to the writer, in the materials at hand. With a large drinking vessel rather than the small Chinese container of perhaps an ounce, it is possible to consume more in a shorter time. This is precisely what occurs. As the men become more inebriated and as the spirit of the affair, let alone of the drinking, takes hold, individual drinks increase in quantity. The writer has seen, (and had to cope with) a water tumbler filled to the brim with whiskey. Since this is the amount poured by one of the contestants, one does not demur, let alone decline. To do so would be to "lose face." The good drinker learns to hide his dismay or distaste, and rise to the occasion as best he can.

Individual Controls. How shall the man challenged by another respond? He may pour an amount which he deems sufficient, and with no outward concern merely go ahead with the drinking. On the other hand, he may feel compelled to react to the challenge by pouring an amount which might correspond to "raising the ante." The intent is made obvious by facial movement such as an arched eyebrow or a fixed stare at the opponent. Indeed, he may ask *"Kaushaima?"* ("Enough?") as though to suggest that if this is not the case, he is prepared to pour more. If the challenger accedes, he stops—or perhaps adds more anyway.

Some people have the fortitude to resist becoming embroiled in a drinking match. To the advances of a would-be challenger, indication of unwillingness to drink is made by upturning one's glass. Those who are known to be unwell are excused. Others may have to face blandishments and jibes, but the refusal will be honored. Failure to respond to an invitation is not necessarily interpreted as a denial of fellowship. Divorced from specific personal relations underlying a given situation, refusal is not defined as an antagonistic asocial act.

Facing a *kon pui* ("bottoms up") situation which may be repugnant for physiological or emotional reasons, it is possible to withdraw and not meet a challenge. Dr. Merrill Moore has suggested that:

> If one does not wish to accept this challenge to *kan pei* he may say "Sue bien." . . . which means, *"As I please* and *not* as you insist."[9]

As drinking progresses and as inhibitory feelings against becoming drunk set in, individual efforts at deceit may be employed. Sticking a thumb in one's own cup while liquor is being poured decreases the volume. Diners with "wet thumbs" are many and the ruse is easily discovered. Awareness of limits of one's capacity generates a set of feelings which motivate against drinking. A conflicting incentive impels a recalcitrant person to demonstrate his *tsau leung* as at least equal to that of the next man.

The "wet thumb" technique is a model for other efforts of reducing one's own intake at the expense of the adversary. Unequal pouring of drinks, "accidental" tipping of one's cup as it is raised to the lips, and other devices are employed to forestall further intoxication. Some drinkers become desperate, surreptitiously pouring drinks into soon-to-be-saturated napkins. One even observes a drinker artfully holding a ricebowl between his knees under the table, using it as a receptacle for whatever he can manage to dispose of without detection.

When a drinking party reaches this stage, moods are generally elated. A social situation that permits each man to watch others cheat and at the same time, to delude himself into thinking that his own actions remain undiscerned, is pleasant indeed.

Most of the bouting appears to be among generation peers. The writer has observed younger men approach elders, but this seemed to be done as a gesture of politeness or friendship—with no great amount consumed unless the older man took the initiative.

Women who participated were highly acculturated and played public roles in the community—as proprietors, interpreters, etc. In these cases, too, the amounts were moderate—perhaps a two ounce drink at best. Often wine is made available to the women present. A traditional wine and honey mixture may be found at wedding feasts.

Children are not given full glasses of wine. While many boys in their early teens participated in the toasting, there were several who did so consuming water rather than whiskey. Without exception these were children of second-generation mothers, the latter directing their sons to abstain.

Drinking behavior with regard to generation status tends to be more flexible among the second generation, permitting a somewhat greater degree of informal relations irrespective of age. Thus, at one dinner, Shorty, a man in his fifties who plays a prominent role in both China- and native-born circles, received a good deal of drinking attention. A leader in Chinatown politics, influential in community affairs, *toi piu* ("delegate") of the most powerful tong in Chinatown* whose task it is to handle public relations, he seemed to be the constant object of those who would drink with him. Genial in his response to each drinking invitation, he maintained an aplomb and poise despite his alcoholic intake. Those who initiated the

---

* His tong position is all the more unusual in view of his American birth.

matches were for the most part younger and more frequently, second generation. He greeted each challenger with humor, quipping in either English or Cantonese, to the delight of those seated nearest him. He consistently deferred determination of the quantity to the other man. "Everybody likes to have a drink with good old Shorty," he told an outsider. "I don't understand it." While the younger people approached Shorty, it was the latter who made affable overtures to his contemporaries and polite toasts to his elders.

When the occasion for the banquet is the celebration of a wedding, the groom accompanied by his father and brothers, salutes his guests. This ceremonial takes place when the last course is served. The toasting group makes the rounds of the tables at which the diners are seated. The groom bows or nods his head, thanks his guests for having come, and urges them to participate in the festivities. The welcome is made at each table, and with each stop, the groom sips twice from his cup. This gesture of respect is welcomed by the guests who treat it not so much with an air of deference but one of pleasure. After all, if there are many guests and the groom must greet these, is it not likely that he will have to drink a great deal? And if this is so, might he not become drunk? The guests will attempt to encourage heavy drinking by the groom, in an effort to get him drunk. Indeed, as he is called upon to drink up, there may be jesting of an erotic nature with regard to the bridal pair and the groom's role. Even before the formal pledging of the guests, individuals will join the groom at his table and offer a toast to him and his father. With each proffer of congratulations the groom must drink; common courtesy and the spirit of the affair demand this of him.

Any young man occupying the status of groom recognizes the intent of the guests. Even with this forewarning, he may become entrapped by the jollity of the evening and indiscretely drink beyond his normal capacity. Or, motivated by more subjective factors, perhaps insecurity at being in the limelight, or feeling he must justify his newly acquired status by proving he is a voluminous, but contained drinker —the groom participates with each drinking group he meets on his rounds. Each drink he downs will be greeted with applause. Often, flushed with such concerted admiration, he may take a second drink before moving on.

On the other hand, the young man may be wary and determined

not to become a foil of the group in this particular custom. One young
man was steadfast in his determination. Responding to the admonish-
ments of his father, he drank with the latter and his three brothers
at the first two tables visited. After this, however, he held an empty
cup, raising his arm in toast with the others and going through the
steps of drinking. Such simulation was met with laughter, urging,
but no strong protestation.

It is necessary that the foregoing focus on patterns of drinking and
behavior at banquets should be seen against a broader canvas. The
banquet is a social occasion, reunion of family and friends, taking
place within the community and marking a special event. If the
drinking is intense, no less so is the eating. Indeed, the latter can more
readily be said to be the major interest of the evening, in pursuit of
which all apply themselves with vigor.

Behavioral restraints are relaxed in an intimate atmosphere which
is permissive. While there are suggestions of individual aggressions,
the latter are cushioned by the general festiveness and friendship
which are thematic of the event. Should pugnacity develop, it will
be restrained. Expressions of eroticism will be applauded, yet should
they become too suggestive, the speaker will be hushed. Evaluations
of individuals are articulated by some with astonishing frankness,
then tempered with expressions of familial affection or platitudes
of friendship. In all of this, drinking aids as a "solvent of inhibitions"
helping to create an atmosphere of freer emotionality, volubility,
and social interplay not found in the daily routine of the people.

Ceremonial Use. Rites connected with life crises involve the
ceremonial use of wine, although no sacred value appears to be placed
upon the wine itself. The unavailability of Chinese wines during
World War II has had considerable effect upon the usage of liquor
during ceremonials. Utilized as substitutes during the shortage,
Western alcoholic drinks appear to have been retained beyond the
period of temporary need. Selection of liquor today depends more
upon price and availability than on the source of manufacture.

Soon after the birth of the first-born son, there may be placed
beside the child some small bowls, containing rice, sugar, salt cabbage
and wine. Fielde reports that in the Swatow area the size of the bowls
signifies that their user will not be a glutton, but rather, like the
nature of the food itself, will be robust. "A picture of the sun, the

symbol of a bright intelligence, is cut from an almanac, dipped in the wine, and used to wash the child's mouth . . . "[4] In the current study, such detail was not available. Informants knew of some of the elements of the usage, but none spoke of any awareness of its practice in Chinatown. However, at the celebration of the baby's first haircut, given some four weeks after birth, irrespective of age order or of sex, the child is toasted by the assemblage with wine. The suggestion of wine as purifier or sanctifier in the first instance is, of course, not apparent in the second.

After a male has reached adulthood, when his 21st, 31st, and other birthdays in that series are celebrated, wine plays a role in the act of the toast, as it does in other festive occasions. Toasting is interactive, guests drinking to the individual being honored and as in the case of a wedding feast, the groom and his father taking the lead in pledging their guests.

While traditional wedding ceremonials are rapidly being discarded among acculturated and Christianized families, the former still occur in obviously modified forms. Of pertinence to this discussion, however, is the fact that the first day of celebration still includes the sharing of wine by the young couple. Two cups are involved, with a little wine poured into each. The groom sips from his, then it is taken by an attendant woman who holds it to the lips of the bride. (The bride is expected to be too embarrassed to hold it herself.) Some wine is poured from the bridegroom's cup into that of the bride, and a little is poured into his from her cup. They then drink some of the mingled wine, consumating the act of alliance. The act of *t'uen uen*, completing the perfect circle, signifies harmonious union of the pair. Herein is the essence of the marriage ceremonial which, when carried out in detail, lasts for a period of several days.

Alcoholic beverages are also used in the rites for the dead. These require no special delineation here. Periodic offerings of wine, fruit, vegetables and other dishes are presented to the deceased. Frequency of these, along with other rites, are clearly defined by traditional usage on the basis of kinship. Despite the tendency to deviate from the rigors of mourning obligation, there is still adherence to fundamental practices.

As in China, there is much variation depending upon economic means, although strenuous efforts are made to maintain a minimum core of commonly accepted practices. Guests arriving to commiserate with the family of the deceased may not be welcomed with wine if this is well beyond financial power of the group. But tea will be its substitute and its presence will neither derogate the mourners nor malign the sincerity of their grief. Wine does become a part of the offerings to the spirit of the deceased in the daily ritual called for in the period directly following the death of an adult. The three cups of wine will have their place on the table along with dishes of food and burning incense. On the first day of the 10th month, when symbolic gifts are prepared to ensure the deceased's having a comfortable winter, wine will be among the offerings.

At the time of Ch'ing Ming, when the annual visits to the graveyards take place, wine or whiskey will be taken along with a whole boiled chicken and other items to be used in the rites of respect to the deceased. The dishes are set out on the grave and among them are three cups of wine. After obeisances are completed, the liquor is poured around the periphery of the grave. Lack of knowledge of such behavior on the part of Chinese-Americans often gives rise to strife. Two young men, attending the first memorial service for their father, drank the libations after they finished kowtowing. This resulted in a bitter argument, with the China-born men who were present excoriating the sons, berating them as worthless *chuk sing*.* The incident also hastened the severance of betrothal of their sister. Her fiance asserted that such ignorance of ritual would spell disaster to his own family, should the girl eventually be entrusted with the training of their children.

While the use of alcohol is found at all functions denoting life crises, a significant difference may be noted in its application. In the ceremonials surrounding the occasion of death, its use is perfunctory, symbolic, and stripped of any recognition of effect upon the living user. The other extreme is found in its use in celebrations centered upon the living. Here wine adds to and in part makes for the hilarity which reigns on such occasions. In the broader social functions and in the more formalized ceremony, such as that of bride and groom

---

* The soft pith of bamboo—without substance and without useful qualities. This is a general term of derogation levelled at second-generation Cantonese, suggesting an absence of the body of traditions in custom and behavior brought by China-born parents to the United States.

co-mingling their wine, drinking emphasizes interpersonal ties and confirms the solidarity created by new alliances. As Granet would say, those present "share in the communion" by drinking together.

Health and Medicine. Leong Gor Yun, speaking of *ginseng,* observes that "Many a Chinese . . . will save money on necessary food until he is near collapse in order to buy some of this quick and powerful tonic. Besides, taking a tonic now and then is a sign of wealth which the Chinese are proud to show."[8] The high value attached to *ginseng,* the price of which reached an astonishing figure during the war years, reflects a concern about physical well-being strikingly observable in Chinatown. Within the home there is nearly a continual effort to either maintain good health or alleviate signs of ill health. The lively sales of American patent medicines currently attest to curative interests. A mother, concerned about the condition of a child after some tension-producing situation, will attempt to prevent a headache rather than wait to cope with the reality of one. Heating fresh ginger over the gas flame of a stove, the mother slices it into thin pieces and sticks these on the forehead and temples of the child. The technique, said to cure violent headaches, apparently is preventive as well.

The dual efforts of prevention and cure place a special significance upon the role of alcoholic beverages. Liquors are used in the preparation of medicinal brews, often are altered by the addition of some beneficial item of *materia medica,* or are in their own direct use seen as advantageous to good health.

As constituent parts of herbalist prescriptions or home remedies, their tonic, blood purifying and curative qualities are believed to be highly efficacious. Serving *po,* mending soup, containing *ng ka pei* or some other liquor, to expectant mothers in the periods prior to and following childbirth, is typical. Partaking of the dish means "adding to your blood," *po heut.* It is said to be particularly beneficial to older persons, keeping their bodies warm, helping body temperature. Of similar contribution is a soup, *yeuk ts'oi po yeung,* with a base of herbs, mutton, and wine. It is served to the entire family for its strengthening effects, prepared by the mother on no regular occasions but whenever she deems it necessary. Nearly all Chinese-American informants spoke with displeasure of this dish, primarily protesting its olfactory characteristics.

Wine used as a medicine should be heated; all of the medicated foods are prepared thusly. Accordingly, whenever possible, medicated wines such as *kop kaai* (a wine containing fragments of dried Gechonidae, red spotted lizards) and *fu kwat tsau* (wine in which tiger bone has been dissolved) are heated before serving. To do otherwise would be wasteful, a loss of pharmaceutical effects. Most medicated wines are imported from China. The fact that their containers, bearing the label "Chinese Medicine" pass through customs with a lowered duty, thus enabling some varieties to retail in the United States at prices lower than that of Chinese table wines, may serve as additional inducement for their use. Their distinctive medicinal flavors, quite unlike those of rice or other wines, apparently does not detract from their occasional use at dinner. The ready availability of some of these in restaurants and shops also enhances their widespread use. Less expensive *yeuk tsau* (the general term for medicated spirits) are often used externally, serving the function of a linament.

Potency of alcoholic beverage rather than palatability is a determinant of healthfulness. The stronger the brew, the more it is valued in a pharmaceutical sense. This, however, is provisional. To have a drink warms the body. To drink excessively is seen as burning out the system. The undesirability of the latter offsets any positive qualities a drink may have and serves to reinforce the norm of moderation. It is of interest to note that although beer is drunk, it is not viewed in a positive light from the health standpoint. Beer is seen as *saan heut,* dissipating the strength of the blood, due to its coolness.

Second Generation. The Chinatown second generation is not so far removed from the community's value system as to permit an abrupt break with the above-described drinking behavior.

The boy's initial contacts with drinking are casual. He observes his father and other elders drink at the dinner table and is himself offered an occasional sip. At festival times his parents are even more permissive. Unlike the general practice in Kwangtung, he is not encouraged to drink freely. On the other hand, he is not rebuked for drinking when he makes a move to do so. Imbibing wine is more frequent than the drinking of whiskey. Potency of the drink enters as a variable influencing preference. It is conceivable that in some families price differentials also act on parental attitudes deterring a youngster's use of whiskey.

Exceptions are to be found in Christian homes, where there may be total abstention for the entire household. Research findings are too meager here and do not permit many meaningful generalizations. Both drinking and the practice of abstention appear to cut across sectarian lines. Prohibitory attitudes were fairly strong among the members of one evangelical group, but the representativeness of this viewpoint was not ascertained. It is not unlikely that church affiliation might have some effect on parental attitudes toward drinking by children, if not sharply changing adult practices. Where Christianized second-generation persons were parents, this tendency of restraint was even more apparent.

A possible exception is to be found in one group of late teenagers who seemed to manifest a "zoot-suit" syndrome of extreme, ostentatious clothing, excursions into petty crime, truancy from school and similar delinquent behavior. Boasting of their poor reputation, members speak blithely of their rating as a "bad gang." Among this group's leaders and leadership aspirants, drinking at a Chinatown bar has a special place. This was seen by other second-generation young men as an exhibitionistic act of bravado and as an attempt at playing "tough." A rank-and-file member of the group said:

> Very few of the fellows drink. If it isn't training season,* we have a drink at the meetings of the team. Schenley's or White Horse. But most of the guys don't drink much, except A . . . and B . . . and C. . . . R likes to sit at the bar and chew the fat and drink. The biggest phoney in town. Thinks he's hot stuff. Gives orders—a lot of talk, but he's yellow.

Members of the group seemed intrigued with their own toughness and continually attempted to convince others as well as themselves of this fact. Having a drink at meetings served as ritualistic support of this desired self-image, patterned in large measure after Hollywood gangster heroes. The act of sitting at a bar, rather than inbibing *per se*, is additional token of the role being played by these adolescents. The marginal character of the gang is held in check to some degree by community controls—family and peers—and an awareness of being Chinese and thus, "different" in the eyes of white Americans. This latter influence tends to inhibit any marked acculturation in the

---

* The clique has a baseball team in an amateur league.

direction of drinking patterns which permit freer behavior in more varied circumstances. Local sanctions are still effective in minimizing clean-cut deviation from community norms. Chinese self-consciousness in the presence of whites in a non-Chinese community further brakes the process.

In the presence of family members or close friends, the occasional indulgence in wine by the unmarried girl is condoned, but drinking outside of an intimate household is abjured. Even here, consumption will be limited to small amounts and accompanied by cautious permission on the part of any elders present. Such drinking will be treated as "a joke," but one does not carry the joke too far. *Tsau wai shik chi mui*, "Intemperance leads to immorality." Drinking is seen as an unmaidenly act, precursor to the lowering of the behavioral guards and thus, as a threat to chastity. The unmarried girl who drinks on more than highly infrequent occasions—perhaps in a toast at some formal event—may be considered loose in moral conduct and unfit for consideration as a desirable wife. Indulgence is seen as indicative of a syndrome of characteristics inconsistent with the ideal role definition of a marriageable girl. Those mothers who concede to American custom by permitting their daughters to go on unchaperoned dates will admonish them to refrain from drinking.

Indoctrinated by parents, trained by previous behavior and imbued with a fear of dire consequences, most girls heed these maternal warnings. Total abstention is by no means uncommon, and this is attended by a number of concommitant attitudes toward those who do drink. A young woman of 23, who claimed to be "more Chinese than most Chinatown girls" asserted that she regarded an invitation to drink while on a date as highly insulting. "It means he has no respect for you. If you take a drink, he'll try to do other things. Once I went to a football game and the fellow took out a flask. He said it'd warm me. I never went out with him again and my mother told his aunt about it, too." Several girls iterated this same point in somewhat less obdurate manner, namely, that when an escort persisted in suggesting drinking after an initial declination, severance of relations was desirable. The foregoing should not be construed to mean that Chinese-American girls as a group are totally abstemious. However, the intrusion of western standards on traditional Chinese norms and exposure to dual value systems seem to have resulted in no great breakdown of reserve in drinking behavior. While drinking in public for some may be symbolic of liberation from traditional, confining custom, other outlets for self-expression with less unpleasant connotations are preferred. A group of young women having dinner together may experiment with cocktails or highballs. Such trials, bearing the quality of adventure, are limited in scope and incidence, and eventuate, at best, in a periodic nonchalant ordering of a drink. Many girls drink only when a brother or close relative is present in the party (and usually, with permission of the latter); others reject liquor all the more when in the company of close kin. When the dating process becomes transformed into courtship, less rigorous attitudes may develop, but there will still be caution and decided moderation. One goes through the ritual of the dating-dining pattern and has a cocktail before dinner. The drink is ordered as a thing to be done rather than as a thing to be desired.

Some young Chinese-American couples not infrequently order drinks when on a dinner date prior to attending the theater. Strolling through Central Park on a summer afternoon, they will stop at the Tavern-on-the-Green or some other café and have a long drink, sitting self-consciously and watching the activity of others. These excursions are often marked by stilted conversation; there is no free chatter or casualness. The near unconventionality of the date, sensitivity to being recognizable as Orientals and thus subject to unfeigned stares, and the playing of a drinking role not accepted in the sub-culture, are factors active in influencing this restrained behavior. Drinking in public is at best a token of acculturation, a conspicuous sign of "belonging" to a more cosmopolitan world. It is accomplished by many only with a great deal of conscious effort.

Liquor plays an insignificant role in the formal and informal social gatherings held by Chinese-Americans. Unless a non-Chinese is present, drinks usually are not served other than with the customary midnight supper. Here finances may dictate selection of the type of alcoholic drink served. In the homes of workmen, beer may be offered with the meal in place of more expensive drinks, especially during the summer months. While there is a distinct preference for whiskey, there is no stigma attached to the use of beer in these households. Embarrassment is not evident and apologies are not forthcoming.*

In the homes of some younger married couples, entertainment of

---

* The wife of a young, moderately successful businessman was profuse in her regrets about serving her guests domestic sherry.

guests may include the serving of highballs or long rum or gin drinks. Sherry may be available as an alternative for the women. Serving drinks becomes a social "must" for those who attempt to act within a non-Chinese frame of reference. Despite this attitude, neither heavy drinking nor drinking as a major activity of the evening is prevalent. There are no "wild parties" in the American, urban middle-class sense of the term.

Those who strive for mobility, reaching out toward the ways of the broader society, often use a geographic mechanism to acquire prestige. Affairs more congruent to occidental patterns are planned and held outside of Chinatown. A necessary prerequisite for the feeling of security is provided by familiar surroundings. Moved out of an habitual environment, Chinese-Americans find themselves unable to function with ease.

It has been suggested that drinking among Chinese-Americans is of no consequence when they are outside the community. Within the neighborhood and in contact with generation elders, the restraints are several, following previously described cultural patterns of drinking and age-status behavior. Even when the Chinese-American is not in his own milieu, when his actions are not open to judgment as untoward from a Chinese viewpoint, and when departure from ceremony will not be interpreted as characteristic of *chuk sing*, there is still no breaking away into that behavior which the group would regard as intemperate. The following incident may illustrate this point.

At a late supper there was heavy drinking. A younger man, employed as cashier in a well-known restaurant, became quite intoxicated and fell asleep. One of the party dashed out of the hall and returned with a camera and flash equipment. He took a photograph of the recumbent figure. The following day, on the bulletin board used by this group there was posted a print of the offender. The upper part of his body was slouched over the table. The face had been cut out so that identification was difficult. Underneath was a hand-printed caption stating that here was the picture of a man who drank too much and didn't know how to control himself. If he persisted in disgracing his friends the same print would appear—with the face included. Recalling the incident, men who were involved treated it with laughter. This had been a real joke on L..., said one person.

Another agreed, but said it really wasn't funny. L... didn't know how to drink and he might get into trouble. What they had done was amusing, but they were serious, too. They would have gone ahead with the threat but this was unnecessary. On the next drinking occasion, L... very carefully had no more than two beers. Several weeks later L... and the writer were seated at the same table during a banquet. Tea was available, and whiskey was the only other beverage served. L... self-consciously contained himself, sipping tea and avoiding the drinking duels that guarantee immoderation. The last was no difficult task for he was challenged but once, his drinking partner pouring only small quantities of liquor.

The application of social sanctions against intemperate drinking is quite clear in this instance. Ridicule and subsequent loss of face are threats which are often effective. In a community where gossip is rife and family prestige is cherished, indiscreet behavior easily upsets a delicate balance of interpersonal relations. But it is not only the family name that is important in Chinatown. Associational affiliation is also regarded by many as sufficiently meaningful to assure protection of the group's reputation. In the foregoing case, the friends who acted shared in common membership in a local organization whose personnel is jealous of its prestige and sensitive to any criticism leveled against it. What amounted to a threat of public castigation was seen as a necessary defensive measure. The act of denunciation before the community is more in keeping with Chinese custom than with American. Seen in its particular context the incident reflects a basic Chinese-American attitude toward public drunkenness as well as illuminating social controls drawn by the second generation from their Chinese cultural frame of reference.

ALCOHOLISM

In the preceding descriptions and the cases cited, references have been made frequently to attitudinal sets in the drinking patterns. Insofar as drinking itself is concerned, permissiveness is predominant. One infers the primary function of drinking to be that of social catalyst. The act is often as important as its ultimate effects. The family may sit down to a Sunday dinner, the meal begun by the father ceremoniously downing a drink. Perceptive informants formulate it in this manner: "It was like a ritual . . . he'd swallow his

drink and wipe his mouth and smile at all of us. He likes this togeth-
erness." One drink suffices; an unstated toast to the family is implicit.

When a group is involved in drinking, as at a banquet or evening
meal, the fundamentally social motives in drinking activity are apparent and are expressly defined as such. The initial results range
from geniality to hilarious merrymaking. These are essential components of the social solidarity being celebrated, whether friendship
group or family association.

Behavior. Inebriety, however, while generating good humor, also
releases aggressions. That the latter is evoked by drinking is clearly
evident and it is at this point that an ambivalence in attitudes toward
intoxication may be discerned. Insofar as drinking functions to
cement social relations, there is permissiveness with regard to inebriety. When a drunken state results in aggressive behavior which is
perceived as a threat to group harmony, it is deplored and disapproved.

The most common form of aggression displayed is on a verbal
level. Even here it is essentially repressed, or when expressly stated,
countered by further comment designed to ameliorate the situation.
If appeasement is not forthcoming from the aggressor, someone else
in the group will take the necessary step, often employing humor as
an emollient. "Joking" serves a dual purpose as verbal insult and
social lenitive. The net result is that verbal conflict is not permitted to
flourish. An offender will be quieted by someone in superordinate
status or be drawn away from the group by a solicitous friend. The
chastized individual usually submits without quarrel.

The writer has "sensed" a satisfaction or pleasure that attends the
solicitation of the squiring friend who protects a drunken companion
from further embroiling himself in a network of acrimony or hostility. The observer "feels" apprehensive about the sincerity of the
concern displayed over the unwise drinking of another. The drinker
"passes out" or becomes ill and is assisted in leaving the table or
room. The anxious mien of his guide seems sanctimonious. The latter
explains to questioners that So-and-so isn't feeling well and needs
some help. This listener, at least, often has received the impression
that an additional message is being conveyed: So-an-so's *tsau leung,*
capacity for wine, is low indeed. Does this not mean, too, that the

speaker can be characterized as *tsau tak,* having a high tolerance for liquor yet maintaining himself as morally excellent, as virtuous? Or So-and-so has committed a grave *faux pas* being blatantly critical of another in no complimentary fashion? The report of his drunken blunder races from table to table with overtones of shock, dismay, and disapproval. *Tsau hau shat i,* pronounces someone explaining the unseemly defection. "The effect of drinking is loss of decorum." Having said this, he invites his neighbor to join him in a drink. Are there no undertones of malicious pleasure in this procedure? Admittedly the preceding questions are highly impressionistic. Any validity they may have rests in their reality as cues perceived by the observer, as intimations of manifold covert motivations.

In narrating the drinking games, the notion was advanced that a Chinese "doesn't drink to get drunk. He drinks so that the other man will get drunk." The contention is affirmed by these observations, if the latter have any reliability. Taking into account hostility manifested by the drinker, we must also acknowledge the possibility of aggression on the part of drinking companions.

While verbal conflict and covert hostility exhibited by encouraging others to get drunk are fairly common features of the Chinese drinking pattern, physical assault is rare. Jane Snow Wong, relating the celebration of a child's first haircut at *mi ut,* four weeks after its birth, describes a scene of what might be construed as mild violence, or rather an aborted attempt at it.

> Those who drank were offered Chinese spirits, and those who did not, like the women, had sparkling apple cider, which was an imitation champagne always served at Chinatown's celebrations or feast occasions . . . The dramatic highlight of the evening was unexpectedly provided by Third Uncle on Mother's side, who drank too much rice wine and became violent. He started to become quarrelsome, broke some dishes, and finally let fly some wild punches. At that point, Daddy and one of his cousins took some rope and tied his hands behind him, led him downstairs, and left him on the floor to sober up. Then they returned and the fun went on. No one seemed to be bothered by Third Uncle's behavior. They commented that he often became violent after drinking.[17]

Specific persons may be known to behave characteristically in this manner, but frequency of aggression on an individual scale has no correlation with the pattern of behavior of the group. When anger aroused while drinking is overtly manifested, its release is generally accomplished by verbalization or displacement.

Inhibition of physical violence involving other persons may be released by redirecting it against inanimate objects. Slamming one's fist on the table or deliberately breaking something is typical of this sort of behavior. For example, a man in his late twenties, venting anger during an argument while drinking, rose from the table at which he was seated, walked unevenly to a window, and rammed his fist through one of the panes of glass. If the generalization that violence is rare but that displacement does occur on occasion, this latter constriction of aggression might possibly be seen as inverted hostility leading to self-mutilation.

On the basis of data derived from interviews and direct observation, simple assault during drinking bouts appears to be rare in New York's Chinatown. Further support of the generalization about infrequent incidence may be found in the records of the police. Examination of these at the local precinct located at the easterly edge of Chinatown reveals a total of 17,515 arrests of Chinese during a 16-year period extending from January 1, 1933 to June 30, 1949.* The charges of arrest state specific offenses involving gambling, prostitution and the use of narcotics. There were, for example, 18 violations of the Alcoholic Beverage Control Law and these dealt with illegal sale of liquor. Of the 17,515 arrests none were made for assault or disorderly conduct wherein drunkenness was specifically charged. That arrested men may have been under the influence of liquor is by no means precluded by the data. No comments were made on the "blotter" concerning intoxication of the arrested persons. A number of unsurmountable methodological problems presented themselves in the record examination which prevent conclusive statements about the data. Nevertheless, we are safe in assuming that the factor of violence while under the influence of liquor, at any rate, is negligible.

The captain of uniformed policemen at the precinct, discussing law and order in the community, scouted alcoholism as a problem. Some of his comments are pertinent at this point:

---

* The writer is indebted to Messrs. Alfred Wong and Joseph Sherfey for their examination and analysis of the records. From their compilation, only a small segment is represented here.

We have lots of trouble in the Bowery, of course. The down-and-outers who use the flop-houses or the hallways. No trouble with Chinese. Don't remember having any. None of my men ever have. You know, that's funny. Once in a while you see a Chinese (they don't like to be called Chinaman) and he's pretty well tanked up. If he's alone, he'll walk quietly close to the walls and the stores. When they're drunk they're helpless. (Question by M. L. B.) What I mean is they don't act up. You don't have any difficulty with them. Just take them home. There's no acting up, the way some of the others do. Did you know that in my time here (five years, M. L. B.) there hasn't been a single case of a Chinese arrested for assault? Even when they're drunk, they're quiet.

Police contacts with those under 16 years of age indicate no liquor problems. Of the approximate 17,000 cases handled by the juvenile aid bureau of the city's police department, only 12 involved Chinese.* With the exception of one case involving pregnancy of a minor, the charges (in the eyes of the police) were minor ones. Marking the walls with chalk was a typical act which the police were called to handle. It should be pointed out that the 12 cases go beyond China-town and represent the total for the five boroughs.

Apart from their intrinsic value as social data concerning legal violations, the significance of the arrest figures is somewhat lessened when it is recalled that Chinese seldom initiate litigation in the courts when other Chinese are involved. It can be expected that strenuous efforts would be made to protect an assailant from the police. The latter are well aware of this and judiciously leave sanctions in the hands of the community whenever possible. It is by no means incon-ceivable that, particularly in cases of violence, steps to cover misdeeds from the broader public might be taken. Nevertheless, it is with reasonable assurance that one states that aggressive responses of in-tensity, sequent to drinking and ranging from simple assault to homi-cide, are scarcely known in Chinatown.

A somewhat less passive portrait of Chinese under alcoholic in-fluence is seen in another context. In attempting to secure further insight into the effect of liquor on behavior sequent to drinking, hos-pital records may be of some avail. Unfortunately, these tend to be uneven in compilation of vital data, diagnostic terminology, and level

---

* These figures are entirely unofficial. The policy of the Police Department's Juvenile Aid Bureau is not to make ethnic distinctions in their own published reports.

of observation. Dr. Richard P. Wang, embarking on a study of case records of all Chinese patients with diagnoses of "alcoholism" and "drug addiction" who were admitted to Bellevue Hospital, found one period of several years in which the records were satisfactory. These were examined by a psychiatric social worker of the Payne Whitney Psychiatric Clinic, under the direction of Dr. Wang. The four-year span from 1940 through 1943 provides us with pertinent information. During this period, 28 admissions of Chinese were recorded. Three patients entered twice. Thus a total of 25 individuals, diagnosed as being in an alcoholic state, are being considered here. All of the patients were male. Of the group, 21 were born in China, one reported Hawaii as his birthplace, and two claimed birth in the United States. There was no entry of birthplace on one record.

The degree of inebriation is not clear. No definition of criteria for the use of terms such as "acute alcoholism," "chronic alcoholism," or merely "alcoholism" is forthcoming. While patients were diagnosed in one of these categories, there were secondary requirements for medical or surgical treatment. Tentative evaluation of various aspects of the data was made by Wang[16] and these are not relevant here. Our present interest in examining the records is to see whether some consistent measures of behavior after drinking can be derived.

Three different temporal descriptions may be found in the case records, although not necessarily in sequence for any single patient. Often there is a report on the condition of the patient prior to being taken to the hospital. Secondly, there is a report on his behavior during the medical examination. Occasionally, there is mention of his behavior after treatment. That behavioral set which is most salient became the basis for sorting, with degree of aggression as the variable. In general, there would appear to be a three-point scale of behavior.

1. The first of these indicates an absence of overt aggression. The patient is described as:

"Quiet, coöperative, pleasant, listless, agreeable, etc."

These adjectives recur, often in combination, and may have additional comments. For example, a patient described as "quiet and coöperative" is also "too weak to talk." Another who is "quiet and seclusive" tends to be "preoccupied and listless." We include in this category all those records indicating that which appears to be passivity during examination and treatment.

2. The second general cluster is one in which there is evidence of considerable emotionality. Lack of coöperation is found as well as verbal aggression. Descriptions include the following: "raving and screaming . . . overactive and agitated"; "abusive and uncoöperative en route to hospital"; "noisy and resistant"; "boisterous."

3. Finally, in a third group the behavior characteristics were related to "violence": " . . . very violent—fighting with police officers." "Found unconscious . . . by police. After working on him for an hour, he became violent . . . Brought in in restraints." (When a government interpreter arrived, the patient became quiet and coöperative.) " . . . has stab wound as a result of a drunken brawl . . . (with) common-law-wife." (Wife is non-Chinese.) "Patient violent . . . Brought to ward in restraints on stretcher." "Became violent after a drinking bout . . . Quiet during the night—but after imbibing Chinese wine re-enacted last night's scene. Brought in by brother."

A number of problems emerge in establishing this last grouping. In the last case mentioned in the above list, the examining doctor offered the impression that alcoholic psychosis was present, and indeed, the same might be ventured for others in the previous categories. We are not concerned here with clinical diagnoses, but only in establishing a simple breakdown of degrees of aggression manifested in overt behavior as reflected in the case reports. Further, it is impossible to establish the degree of inebriation for possible correlation with the aggression displayed. Lastly, it is not in our province to differentiate between drinking which is a basic component of psychosis and drinking which is a secondary manifestation or symptom.

In a different vein, distinction possibly ought to be drawn between the incidents reporting hostile reaction to the police and the remaining cases. Frequent reference has been made to feelings of apprehension about becoming involved with white officialdom. Presence of policemen elicits anxiety in an individual whose equilibrium already is disturbed by excessive alcoholic intake. Imputation that provoked violence might not necessarily have occurred, however, is unjustifiable. Divorcing it from social context, "violence" has been used as the major criterion for the grouping purely as an index of behavior accompanying or resultant to drinking. Of the 28 case records examined, we now have the following division:

1. Passive or coöperative behavior   16
2. Emotional lability accompanied by verbal aggression   5
3. Violent behavior   5
                                                                  ——
                                                            26 total

(Two cases are as yet uncategorized and perhaps merit special mention. These deal with the same patient, with a five-month interval separating them.)

The numerical differentials have no statistical significance. The value of the hospital case records lies in the broadening of our conception of the effects of drinking on behavior.

It is of more than passing interest that several of the cases were transfers from other of Manhattan's hospitals. These are equipped to handle emergency cases, but send on to Bellevue those individuals who are intractable or those who require extended treatment or hospitalization. Thus, Bellevue records provide more than a local picture in that aspects of a city-wide representation are present. This fact is helpful and fortunate, for there exists a danger of accepting the local police records and statements as final and conclusive. The attitudes of the latter toward the Chinese are manifestly favorable, tending to be patronizing as well as congenial. This is not surprising because it is undoubtedly true that in many respects the Chinatown "beat" is a pleasant one. The incidence of crime is low and the tight social organization provides outlets for handling cases without resort to courts. The police estimates of the occurrence of drunkenness and alcohol problems cannot be considered accurate because of the tendency of the Chinese to keep their problems to themselves.

Social Controls. In a number of instances on the preceding pages, reference has been made to community sanctions employed against those who drink to excess, that is, those who permit their insobriety to result in behavioral characteristics antithetic to group values. The practical joke of photographing a drunken individual was representative of a complex of pressures. The disapproval of the group was voiced, yet "face" was temporarily saved. The threat of public exposure was reinforced by calling upon the moral obligation of the drinker to protect his family name as well as that of his association.

In a society where individuals are identified as the sons of their fathers and where the prescriptions of filial piety are internalized to a high degree, these pressures can be relied upon as effective instruments of censure.

The problem was handled by the group and kept within the group. The incident was not bruited about the neighborhood despite its humorous aspects. It was a private affair. Protection of a friend from neighborhood gossip becomes a social duty. This obligation is further intensified when the community is defined to include whites and their public officials. The police captain who was quoted earlier to the effect that Chinese do not become violent when drunk, let alone sober, had a further comment with respect to the paucity of arrests of Chinese inebriates:

> I guess another reason we don't pick them up is because you very seldom see a fellow who's drunk alone on the street. There's always somebody to take care of him, friend or relative or somebody. That's why this precinct is a pleasant assignment. There's no bickering. The people handle their own situations. We have narcotic addiction, of course, and we pull them in for gambling, some larceny maybe, but that's about it.

G. Y. Leong's flat statement that " . . . habitual or public drunkenness is unknown in Chinatown," cannot be accepted.* The data we have already presented indicate otherwise. While public drunkenness is not unknown, it can be said to be a comparatively rare sight on the neighborhood streets. It is sharply discouraged. Thus there is all the more reason for solicitous care being given to suppress the conviviality of a friend after he leaves the shelter of a "company flat" or dining place.

The writer knows of two incidents in which physical punishment appears. In one of these, the married son of a prosperous merchant had walked into the family establishment drunk and boisterous. In full sight of the staff employed there, the father forcefully slapped his son's face and turned away from him. Shortly after the incident, it was common knowledge in the community. Second generation and China-born alike were condemning the son's behavior which was seen as unseemly not only because he appeared in an intoxicated con-

---

* G. Y. Leong, *op. cit.*, p. 232.

dition before his father, but primarily because of the embarrassment he had caused the latter.

Habitual drinking in excessive quantities by women is rare and treated with severity. The writer on one occasion was visiting with some friends at their place of business when a Chinese-American woman walked into the shop. Married and in her late thirties, she lived in the community. No customers or other outsiders were present. It became obvious in a very short time that she was highly intoxicated, barely in control of motor abilities. Her voice was louder than usual. After several minutes of chatter, the host abruptly ordered her to return home and when she demurred, threatened to strike her. He upbraided her as a disgrace to her husband and likened her behavior to that of a prostitute. She responded with an erotic witticism, managed a goodnight to his wife and the others present, and sauntered out of the room. As soon as she had departed, one of the group was sent to follow her closely and make sure that she returned home. There was no attempt at face-saving. The rebuke had the force of public condemnation.

In the brief discussion which ensued, the chastiser stated his objections to her behavior. He felt no compunctions about his actions. He had no misgivings, he said, about women drinking if they were judicious and in the protective company of their husbands. Then the latter could assume the necessary responsibility. But for her to walk about the neighborhood streets *kwat tsui,* helplessly drunk, was intolerable to everyone. What would *lo fan* (foreigners) think seeing a Chinese woman in such a drunken state? The speaker's wife demurred, saying that Mrs. G. had many problems. Her husband answered, *T'o sang mo no.* "Native born have no brains."

On what basis did the host reprimand Mrs. G? Clearly it was not because of his role as a male. The others present included one man slightly older than he, who took no initiative in the matter until he was sent as Mrs. G's escort. The reprover and Mr. G. are officials in the same "benevolent organization," with the former in the superordinate status. Authority in this association is hierarchical with many arbitrary powers vested in the leadership. Just as Mr. G. was subordinate to the host and regarded by the latter as his "man," so Mrs. G. was also considered to be under his control and subject to his correction. Mrs. G. flaunted sexuality as a sign of rebelliousness but this independence was momentary. She adhered to the incredibly rigid discipline of the association. Her husband was subsequently censured for her behavior and admonished to take steps necessary to curb her drinking *in public.* (It was conceded that her drinking habits were chronic.)

Sanctions vary with attitudes about a given situation. Not all cases are cause for concern or criticism or action. It is conceded that when one is down and out, he is more prone to be *shi yam,* given to drink. For example, a man whose wife had contracted tuberculosis lost his job. Shortly after this, his son was run over by a car and was subsequently in very poor physical shape for six months. The man took to drinking excessively on frequent occasions. His drunkenness evoked sympathy rather than criticism. Withdrawal into intoxicating stupor was a socially acceptable act.

Another case concerns a cook in a Chinatown restaurant who was prone to get drunk very frequently. His employer never remonstrated with the cook even though he had to endure irregularity in work hours if not in performance. The periodic binges resulted in occasional short-term absenteeism. During one of these spells, when the cook's absence was creating many inconveniences in the routine of the restaurant, the manager was asked why he tolerated such behavior. "He is my cousin," the manager explained, "and we were boys together in the same village. He just misses his wife and children. I feel sorry for him. *Tsau m kaai chan shau*—drink can dispel genuine grief." Behavior resulting in periodic drunkenness elicited compassion rather than condemnation. Commiserating with the motives underlying the drinking, the manager of the restaurant made the major adjustments and suffered the occasional difficulties and nuisances of this arrangement.

Fellow-feeling about concern over family can be predicted in the community. The family is a common source of status relationships and of security for the individual. When insecurity emerges as a result of an intra-familial situation, it frequently appears as the stated reason for drinking to excess. A young man of 36 years was rescued by firemen from a fire escape on the 15th floor of a lower mid-town hotel. He was in an excited, alcoholic condition at the time. He stated later that he had been worried about his family in China, having had no news of them for six months. When he learned they were safe, he drank and "went crazy." Such an incident receives coverage in the language press and is bound to become an item for discussion over the eating tables, in the shops, or during a rest interval in the workday. The act as a demonstration of devotion to family will be far more salient than as one of unseemly behavior. Condoning excessive drinking by adult males may be expected if the situation warrants their imbibing.

Except for reasons of conviviality or ritual, then, drinking to be a socially acceptable act requires justifications rooted in the broader system of sentiments. Drinking for drinking's sake is frowned upon as strongly as the indecorous behavior that sometimes accompanies inebriety. When it occurs and is recognized as such, it will be deplored privately by most people and publicly by those serving as disciplinarians. The result of this negative attitude is self-consciousness on the part of those vulnerable to criticism. It is seen in the furtive behavior that characterizes drinking at bars by those who frequent the one bar where Chinese may sometimes be found. Some fortify themselves by numbers. Others may use the defense of self-disparagement.

Johnny, an American-born man about 40 years of age, is just such a person. A professional gambler, he invariably carries a half-pint bottle of liquor on his person and occasionally takes a nip. He prefers gin and drinks with every meal. One evening, while eating with a number of friends, he brought out his bottle of gin and, turning to the non-Chinese present, asked "Do you mind?" He seemed quite concerned about the other's reaction and even though reassured, felt compelled to discuss his drinking. Addressing himself to the group, he attributed his habit to his father, who apparently drank a good deal and introduced him to liquor at the age of fifteen. In pursuing his point, he went on to denounce himself as a person, placing blame on his drinking. "That's why I'm not respected. There isn't a girl in town who'd marry me."

His complaint of attitudes of non-respect had foundation. Not only was there not "a girl in town who'd marry" Johnny, but there wasn't a father who'd permit his marriageable daughter to become involved. The asocial act of habitual drinking, forcefully made apparent by the ever-present half-pint, discounted his rating as a prospective son-in-law. That he drank gin made things worse. If gin must be used, it should be done in cooking. As a drink, it is worthy of consumption only by *lo fan*. Johnny's reputation as a drunkard came not from being highly intoxicated (none interviewed recalled ever seeing him in that state), but from drinking at times other than those socially condoned, namely without meals. Awareness of his problem classified him as a *tsau kw'an,* one captured by liquor though conscious of its harm. The negative sanctions were effective in occasioning a desire to stop drinking, but not of sufficient force to negate his compulsion to drink.

Social controls can be applied only to those who are detectable as violators of norms. In the case of drinking other than at mealtimes, the use of medicated wines obscures the situation. How shall one determine whether the use of such liquors is generated by a need for whatever curative powers the drink purportedly possesses or by a desire for alcohol and its effects? From the viewpoint of the investigator, habitual use of such medicines demands scrutiny. From the viewpoint of the Chinese, there is no relation between intensive use of medicated wines and *tsau peng,* dipsomania. It has been indicated elsewhere that considerable anxiety exists about health in the community. Taking medicine, then, is surely desirable. The difficulties of discerning this type of drinking for purposes of research are obvious. That the practice is not too widespread is due primarily to the fact that Chinese wines are expensive when compared to domestic varieties. One facet of the problem is revealed in an interview by Dr. Richard P. Wang:

> Dr. Fey said one of the difficulties in knowing the exact number of alcoholics among the Chinese was that many of his patients took alcohol as a medicine, with or without Chinese herbs. . . . They regard alcohol (as) a tonic and did not consider drinking itself a form of "sickness." Alcohol would come to his notice only through some of the symptoms he considered the results of drinking. . . . "*

The excessive drinker is not seen as an ill person because of his drinking. He drinks because he is ill, attempting cure or alleviation of his difficulties.

It is suggested that the consumption of medicated wines facilitates excessive drinking with detection and disapprobation by others.

---

* *Op. cit.,* p. 4.

Further, it engenders solitary drinking, an act foreign to the Chinese pattern. This tendency may be seen developing within one social segment in Chinatown, the aged, where general data, unfortunately, are most lacking.

The traditional Chinese pattern of veneration of the aged requires some continuity in age statuses. The situation in Chinatown is one in which a considerable number of elderly men are resident without immediate family ties in the community. With prospects of returning to China remote, their lives are shorn of realizing those aspirations which motivated their emigration from Kwangtung. There is an absence of filiality, with themselves as objects of respect. Status, to have meaning, requires reciprocation. A lack of advantages accruing to the aged prevails here. Moreover, with the absence of a younger generation to pay homage and learn from one's own behavior, there is a consequent lack of incentive to behave in a manner justifying the status of "venerable elder." Of what use is proper demeanor when there is no one to appreciate it? These "single" men live in *fong,* company rooms, and earn their livelihood either through part-time work or by acting as caretakers for the quarters. Many are assailed by the ailments that come with age and, requiring medication, consume herbal liquors. Drinking for these men becomes a refuge from the reality of their social isolation. Except in a minority of cases where there are close ties with the *kung so,* family associations, there is no provision in the community structure for their support. Where there is no positive effort at solution from within the structure, the controls of the society cannot be effective.

General consensus among physicians, social workers, nurses and others having fairly intimate contact with the community is that alcoholism is not a widespread social psychiatric problem. From various kinds of data and personal contacts, members of the research group were able to learn only of a relative handful of individuals who might be classified as chronic alcoholics.* Most Chinese may be hearty drinkers, but they can scarcely be characterized as hardened drinkers. From acquaintance with the chronic group and a somewhat larger

---

* Chronic alcoholism is defined as a state in which the extent of drinking interferes with the functioning of the individual in his society, impairing successful attainment of the totality of his levels of aspiration, and in which awareness of the situation does not result in altering of drinking behavior.

number of compulsive drinkers, a few gross impressions may be offered.

It is very striking that this group of deviates from the patterns of drinking share in common a high degree of marginality to the culture in other respects. Some have been those who were unable to achieve acceptance by the broader community despite their high level of acculturation and training, and were forced to fall back with reluctance on the resources of the Chinese culture. Others manifest a professional air as interpreters of the culture to outsiders, becoming self-appointed spokesmen for the local population. Still others persist in frantic efforts to be identified as "American" in their ways. Among this group, place of birth appears to be a negligible factor. The major problem of a social nature seems to be that of failure of adjustment in group identification and membership. They stand out in contrast with the larger number of the community's population, first or second generation, who also can be considered marginal, straddling affiliation in two cultures, coping with problems stemming from this situation. Since the sociological factors influencing both groups appear to be genotypic, the existence of divergency in reaction warrants intensive study of their immediate environments.

For the majority of Chinese-Americans, the social structure and its system of controls which range from ideological concepts to friendship patterns to negative sanctions, provides a breadth of drinking behavior which is permissive and not overly repressive. The close interlocking of social groupings and the intimate, overlapping nature of the local economic structure have made these controls all the more effective.

Thus far these controls have prevailed successfully, maintaining in the community a correspondence to the generally accepted picture of drinking in China as a non-pervasive social problem. How long this tendency will last is questionable, depending upon the nature of the changing culture of Chinatown which will assuredly take form as the second and third generations mature.

CONFLICTS AND COMPATIBILITIES

A variety of ecological, social, and economic factors have influenced family and generation relations in Chinatown so that traditional solidarity has been weakened. Attitudes concerned with individual rights, evaluation of merit based upon behavior rather than ascription of status, and similar values derived from American culture have been instrumental in evolving a more equalitarian pattern of kinship relations. The current emergent configuration is more loosely constructed than the traditional Chinese structure with its tight pattern of hierarchical obligations grounded in generation and sex. This contemporary pattern is composite, the product of resolution of compatibilities and disharmonies of two cultural sets in contact. As a synthesis, it reflects its inner contradictions which are the cause of much ambivalence and confusion in behavior.

The development of this less rigid, changing network of interpersonal relationships has not resulted in any significant shift in effective group controls. The community is one in which the majority are natives of China; their offspring are products of a socialization process in which Chinese values and practices have predominated. Further, the former are by far the more influential in the social organization of the community, in its political and economic life. And as we have seen, the tendency to live a quasi-ghetto existence has served to perpetuate and reinforce immigrant behavioral modes.

While some modifications of the Chinese patterns have developed and adjustments have been made to life in the American culture, it can be said that on the whole the same fundamental expectations and obligations of interpersonal behavior found in the Kwangtung culture persist in Chinatown. That these have continued as a major influence in the behavior of the neighborhood's residents, despite the conflicts existent in the mesh of intercultural patterns, perhaps is explainable by the fact that the stresses we have described are of recent gestation. The covert aspects of culture tenaciously persist although conspicuous acculturation is manifested in recent changes.

It is within the context of the interplay of dual social forces that the pattern of drinking behavior in Chinatown is to be seen. Despite the incompatibilities occasioned by varying definitions and possibilities of cultural alternatives, and notwithstanding the aggressions and anxieties emanating from this generalized tension-producing situation, the relative unimportance of alcoholism as a social problem among the Chinese prevails.

Weston LaBarre's observations on drinking in China, apparently drawn from the region in Kunming when it was a center for those who had withdrawn from the coastal and other enemy-occupied areas during the war, are of particular interest since they largely parallel the Chinatown findings:

> As for drinking, the Chinese indulge in it on all occasions of eating, and without the slightest discernible ambivalence, lacking the really very intricate attitudes that have been built up toward it in the West. But the Chinese are not so violently addicted to excessive use of alcohol as have been some North European peoples. They seem not to seek either the frenzy or the escape of intoxication, though they will drink to a point of overflowing benevolence in social contexts. But the solitary Chinese drinker is unthinkable and the problem alcoholic an evident rarity. This is true despite the fact that at parties the Chinese will merrily, even half-maliciously, urge drinking upon their guests with an obligatory *gam bei* or "down the hatch," as well as the more lenient *sui bien,* or "as much as you like." The fact seems to be that in spite of ample and even copious consumptions of alcohol on defined occasions, its use appears never to become an emotional problem.[6]

We have seen that Chinatown attitudes toward drinking are essentially permissive. Within the home and in larger gatherings, drinking has a social function. The guest on a visit who refuses a drink tendered at dinner may be regarded as somewhat peculiar if not ungracious. The male adult who regularly has a drink of whiskey before his evening meal is no more regarded as a tippler than are those in other of our American sub-cultures who have a martini in the late afternoon. However, the Chinese who after work would like to indulge in a relaxing and social drink prior to or at the onset of his meal does so at home, and not in a bar en route home.

While drinking with the evening meal is common, consumption is limited to no more than an initial drink or so. On the other hand, at banquets and festive dinners drinking prevails throughout most of the meal. On these celebrative occasions a certain amount of alcoholic levity in the privacy of the home or similar intimate surroundings is usual. Alcohol acts as a catalyst above a certain point wherein inhibition or suppression is removed and converted into elation. Confidence abounds. Drinkers become expansive in demeanor and vivacious in speech and action. Whereas conviviality is a desired end, it creates its own social antithesis—internalized norms and external social forces acting in concert to inhibit once again. For most Chinese drinkers, intake of alcohol leading to insobriety typically results in quieting, soporific psychological effects. Emotional outbursts tend to be curbed; violence is not the norm nor is it approved. Public drunkenness is an unusual sight on Chinatown streets and is strongly discouraged.

Wine or stronger beverages have a function in ritual, particularly those dealing with major life crises. Use of alcohol, however, appears to be functional, served in accompaniment of food. It has no intrinsic sacred character. When used in this manner, its consumption is limited in quantity, its use not designed for change of mood. Thus, while alcohol may be served at receptions held by the family in the period following death of a member, its use is token, employed in tacit toast to the departed and to the mourning group. The ceremonial offering of food and drink at memorial rites is terminated by the living partaking of the "remainder" not consumed by the spirit of the deceased. Motives underlying ancestral piety at such times are sometimes challenged, the derisive suggestion being made that worship is used as an excuse for lavish eating. Any foundation the charge may have with respect to food apparently has no relation to drink. Consumption is minimal, and withdrawal or escape are clearly not the objective of imbibing.

Jesting about the use of food in memorial services is rare. Jokes about drinking are numerous. The host is the potential butt of ridicule or sport with regard to the quality and quantity of liquor that he serves. Witticisms about the thimble-size wine cups being served half-full are legion. Stories about the guest suffocating to death after having mistakenly swallowed the tiny cup used by his host are told with several variations. The major recurrent theme of drinking stories is the parsimonious offering of liquor.

The negative sanction inherent in such tales is countered by the popularity of more expensive forms of alcohol. There is a strong tendency to prefer Scotch whiskey and cognac to the exclusion of other liquors. This preference is accompanied by the use of medium and high-priced brands. In this respect, the quality of a drink is secondary. A good Scotch will not be used if the brand is not well known. Since profuse drinking is tied up with drinking under special circumstances such as a meal in a restaurant rather than at home, it is the nature of the event that is a partial determinant. Such indulgences provide variation from the routine and monotony of the work-week. A Chinese waitress observed, "When they go out they like to spend a lot of money, so they buy the best." The "best" in liquor is a highly advertised drink, one well known beyond the boundaries of the neighborhood. Wholesale liquor salesmen characterize Scotch whiskey as a "prestige drink," and account for its popularity in Chinatown because of this. One man whose sales territory includes Chinatown said, "Chinese are great imitators. If the boss drinks Scotch, I want to drink Scotch. If the boss drinks a good Scotch, I want a good Scotch." The comment is not without insight. Those in key positions in the neighborhood appear to influence drinking fads as well as other phases of community life. When a certain leader switched from one brand to another, several followed his preference.

The tendency to suppress individuality within the group does not preclude the need to acquire and maintain standing within it. One acts in ways which will achieve approval. In commercially-oriented Chinatown, efforts to establish one's self in the eyes of the group are facilitated by a display of economic well-being. Being a lavish host is indicative of this success.

The "dutch treat" is frowned on and derided as a measure of pettiness.* Sharing is more or less expected, but on the basis of taking turns. There is a "host" on such occasions, and in a peer group that has some stability, what amounts to rotation in paying the full bill occurs. Each member eventually has the opportunity to pay for the others. Vying for payment of the bill often takes unusual forms of maneuvering. While a subtle holding back by those less able to pay sometimes seems observable, verbal insistence, indignant protest and expostulation prevail.

Playing the host is all the more marked when Chinese and non-Chinese are dining together in a local restaurant. In this situation, the picture of each diner anteing his share of the bill would be regarded as humiliating to the Chinese present. This feeling is derived largely from the felt observation of Chinese lookers-on, other dinner guests or restaurant workers. The Chinese in such circumstance is nearly

---

* In some respects, the second generation cling to this pattern more closely than the China-born. A member of one group was harrassed with ridicule when he suggested that some young men, going for a trip in his car, "chip in" on expenses. Jibes were being thrust at him a year after his unfortunate blunder.

coerced into paying for the group. Even if the non-Chinese should insist upon paying their share, the waiter generally will give the bill to the Chinese, thus facilitating the latter's carrying out of the host-role.

The etiquette of the host-guest relationship in Chinese society is well defined by a proliferation of prescribed behavior. Elaboration of ritual in the act of hospitality is indicative of its place in Chinese culture. Superimposed upon this pattern is the fact that in the United States social mobility is limited, for the most part, to the confines of the Chinese community. Gratification of personality needs is achieved primarily in Chinatown. With a curbing of other outlets for individual expression, ostentation for many becomes a mechanism for eliciting recognition from others. The use of Scotch is thus more readily appreciated than a blend of whiskies. Ample servings become a "must." Urgings to drink take on new motivation. Alcohol has yet another function, serving as a measure of an individual's status within the group. Here again it is the situation in which drinking is involved which is significant. The concomitants of status-striving and status justification are far more important than drinking. The consumption of alcohol is high, but alcoholism does not emerge as an issue for public concern.

Women experience similar circumscription of participation in the prevailing culture patterns of the broader community. It may be argued that the shock of rebuff is less intense for them in that expectations drawn from the syndrome of status obligations and prerogatives are fewer and more constricted. On the other hand, they have contact with the relatively freer behavior permitted American women. Second-generation young women have been reared in a cultural milieu which has a wide set of values stressing individuality and freedom. Protest against restriction, no matter from which cultural source, has no expression in excessive drinking. The higher degree of social mobility for the Chinese female in the United States, the strategic position because of the uneven sex ratio and consequent minimizing of social dependence, and opportunities for narcissistic indulgence in dress and appearance condoned and encouraged by American communication media, are additive "assets" alleviating hostility.

Wu Ching-chao, in his pioneer study of Chinatowns, quoted a statement by a Chinese-Hawaiian concerning drinking by young women which is pertinent here:

It is obvious that many young Chinese are following the bad examples set by some of our friends of other races. How do I know? I have seen such cases, besides having heard about them. Some years ago it was a rare thing for a Chinese girl to be seen drunk. Is it a rare sight today? I am afraid it is not. About this drinking problem, let me say something: Some girls of my race seem to think that they can and should do everything that the Haole girls do. As a result, they pet, drink, smoke, etc. I was very much surprised the first time I saw a Chinese girl drunk, but I am used to the sight now. I know several girls who come from well-to-do and well-known families in the city who indulge in drinking. Every time they go to a party, they ask for drinks. Smoking is nothing to them . . . I have actually seen girls who were foolish enough to drink until they were drunk and had to be taken home. How their parents feel about this, I do not know.[13]

While the values and attitudes of the person cited are perhaps of greater objective worth than the reporting of drinking practices, it is instructive to note the direct contrast with the data of the current study. The disorientation described is not applicable to the second-generation girls in New York's Cantonese community.

The subordinate social status of the latter is reflected in the sharply differentiated sex division with respect to drinking. While boys and men drink freely and often copiously, unmarried women and girls are seldom permitted to imbibe. Only after marriage and on special occasions is drinking by women sanctioned. It is by no means rare for women to be served a liqueur or brandy while visiting among themselves. Consumption of alcohol at parties attended exclusively by women is not excessive. Insofar as ceremonial drinking is concerned, they are excluded from it to the same extent that they are from major participation in rituals. On the whole, community attitudes toward drinking by women are unfavorable. A drunken woman is treated with more severity than a drunken man. The few women who are known tipplers are criticized strongly and, while not ostracized, are not warmly accepted by the more stable elements of the community.

While behavior has shifted from traditional modes, the cultural locus of the Chinese-Americans, both male and female, is closer to that of their parents than that of the metropolis. The existence of conflicts in role behavior has made for both interpersonal and individual stress but no discernible social disorientation. Even those who are marginal and who have made intensive efforts to pursue

American alternatives have tended to fall back on the resources of Chinese culture when they were unable to achieve acceptance by the broader community. Feelings of independence derived from the non-community culture are subsumed under the subservient role played as Chinese family member.

We have accepted the conclusions of various writers* that while alcoholic drinks are known in China and often consumed in generous quantities, alcoholism does not emerge as an issue for public concern. This set of observations has been supported by our own research in one overseas Chinese community. Here we have seen the transposition of a cultural pattern with minimal modification. In Chinatown as in China, drunkenness is by no means unknown, but it is not prevalent. Sanctions to discourage its recurrence, as well as other forms of norm violation, are employed within the family and its extensions, the associations, and closely-knit economic enterprises.

The absence of alcoholism at first sight might appear unexpected. Conditions surrounding the life of the Cantonese community are conducive to the generation of considerable emotional stress and anxiety. The dominantly economic motives which sent people from their Chinese households have not been completely satisfied. Expected transiency in the United States was based upon a boasted high availability of wealth. For most, however, stay has been prolonged; some have preferred to remain here, others have married and reoriented life plans, most have been unable to find fortunes readily made.

Unique cultural and historical factors have resulted in restriction of socio-economic life for the group. Economic activity has been limited because of the prevalence of prejudicial attitudes on the part of the majority group. Vocations pursued of necessity have been those low on the prestige scale of local values. Meniality of work is accompanied by long hours and difficult working conditions. While occupations have become more diversified in recent years, the focus has been on *Chinese* characteristics of the wares or services rendered. The narrowness of economic activity has been matched by narrowness of social life. Various forms of discrimination have been instrumental in the development of a compressed population living in close quarters within a small district. The extremely disparate sex

---

* WESTON LA BARRE, *op. cit.* See also, (7, 5, 1).

ratio has prevented the development of stable or normal sex relations in the community. Compensation for the unequal sex ratio by inter-marriage with members of other ethnic groups has been prevented, in the main, by the bias both within and without the sub-culture. Thus, most sex relations have been in the shade of illegality, that is, prostitution, with its attendant absence of emotionality. The complex of satisfactions derived from Chinese familism are not available for most of Chinatown's male membership.

Stereotyped categorization of Chinese in the United States has led to a constriction of participation by them in the various cultural alternatives offered most persons. The social distance manifested by white Americans has resulted in a persistence of Chinese ethno-centrism and in a general keeping apart from white society. The community, fearing unfavorable comments or actions from other Americans, is self-conscious of the behavior of its members. Thus external pressures make for even greater communal stability. The pace of acculturation is braked by these interaction processes, influencing native-born and China-born alike. The presence of an integrated sub-culture with its concentration of population, dominated by an attitude of self-protection, deters the development of drinking patterns more consistent with the broader culture. Whereas the second generation has demonstrated adaptability to the prevailing out-group culture patterns, the impress of community discipline has been of sufficient strength to hold relatively constant the traditional attitudes and behavioral aspects of drinking.

SUMMARY

Drinking of alcoholic beverages is widespread in New York's Chinatown. Drunkenness is, however, not prevalent because the attitude of the family as well as of the community discourages its occurrence. The incidence of chronic alcoholism is low and alcoholism as a social problem is relatively unimportant.*

---

* A very recent study by the Department of Neurology and Psychiatry of National Taiwan University Hospital has come to our attention since this article went to press. While it is impossible to comment extensively on his paper, it is pertinent to note that Dr. T. Y. Lin, reporting on studies in three Formosan villages, confirms the findings of the Cantonese-American research. (Lin Tsung-yi: A Study of the Incidence of Mental Disorder in Chinese and Other Cultures. *Psychiatry, 16:*313–336 (1953.)

The role of alcohol can be understood from a study of the social environment. On the whole the fundamental expectations and obligations of Kwangtung culture persist in Chinatown. Within the home, and at social gatherings, drinking represents an important social function. At meals and banquets heavy eating is accompanied by considerable alcohol consumption. When intoxicated the Chinese drinker is usually quiet, and public drunkenness is uncommon and strongly disapproved. There may be a release of aggression which is rarely manifested in violence, but usually in expansive behavior and speech.

In the cultural setting of Chinatown, drinking by women is restricted, and an intoxicated woman is treated more severely than a man. There is a permissive attitude to drinking by boys and they soon learn a set of attitudes which sanctions drinking socially but disapproves of intoxication.

The second generation exhibits considerable acculturation and there is a general loosening of the traditional controls in the Chinese family. In this setting one might expect the younger Chinese to show a trend toward heavy drinking—especially in view of the psychological strains of their position between American and Chinese ways of life. Thus far, however, the social controls seem to have proven more effective than the forces of disorganization and the younger generation show few cases of alcoholism.

BIBLIOGRAPHY

1. CONDIT, I. M.: *The Chinaman As We See Him.* New York, Revell, 1900, p. 59.
2. DIETHELM, O.: Research project on the etiology of alcoholism. *Quart. J. Stud. Alcohol.,* 9:72, (June) 1948.
3. FEDERAL WRITER'S PROJECT: *New York Panorama.* New York, Random, 1939, p. 84, *et al.*
4. FIELDE, A. M.: *A Corner of Cathay.* New York, Macmillan, 1894, p. 73.
5. KULP, D. H.: *Country Life in South China.* New York Teachers College, Columbia University, 1925, p. 326.
6. LA BARRE, W.: Some observations on character structure in the Orient, II. The Chinese, Part Two. *Psychiatry,* 9:376, (Nov.) 1946.
7. LATOURETTE, K. S.: *The Chinese, Their History and Culture.* New York, Macmillan, 1946, pp. 697–698.
8. LEONG, G. Y.: *Chinatown Inside Out.* New York, Barrows, 1936, pp. 23–24.
9. LEW, LING: *The Chinese in North America.* Los Angeles, East-West Culture Publishing Association, 1949, pp. 192–265.
10. LINDESMITH, A. R.: *Opiate Addiction.* Bloomington, Principia Press, 1947, pp. 45–56.

11. MYERSON, A.: Alcohol: a study in social ambivalence. *Psychiatry, 1:*13–20, (June) 1940.
12. ROSE, A. and ROSE, C.: *America Divided.* New York, Knopf, 1942, p. 41.
13. Survey H Document 42, quoted in WU, C. C.: *Chinatown: A Study of Symbiosis and Assimilation.* Ph.D. dissertation, University of Chicago, 1929, p. 272.
14. U. S. BUREAU OF THE CENSUS: *Sixteenth Census of the United States:* 1940. Characteristics of the Population.
15. VAN NORDEN, W. M.: *Who's Who of the Chinese in New York.* New York, Van Norden, 1918.
16. WANG, R. P.: *Alcoholism in Chinatown, New York: Its incidence.* Unpublished manuscript, 1948.
17. WONG, J. S.: *Fifth Chinese Daughter,* New York, Harper, 1950, pp. 26–27.

INDEX